Defence Innovation and the 4th Industrial Revolution

This book examines the implications of disruptive technologies of the Fourth Industrial Revolution (4IR) on military innovation and the use of force. It provides an in-depth understanding of how both large and small militaries are seeking to leverage 4IR emerging technologies and the effects such technologies may have on future conflicts.

The 4th Industrial Revolution (4IR), the confluence of disruptive changes brought by emerging technologies such as artificial intelligence, robotics, nanotechnologies, and autonomous systems, has a profound impact on the direction and character of military innovation and use of force. The core themes in this edited volume reflect on the position of emerging technologies in the context of previous Revolutions in Military Affairs; compare how large resource-rich states (US, China, Russia) and small resource-limited states (Israel, Sweden, Norway) are adopting and integrating novel technologies and explore the difference between various innovation and adaptation models. The book also examines the operational implications of emerging technologies in potential flashpoints such as the South China Sea and the Baltic Sea.

Written by a group of international scholars, this book uncovers the varying 4IR defence innovation trajectories, enablers, and constraints in pursuing military-technological advantages that will shape the character of future conflicts.

The chapters in this book were originally published as a special issue of the *Journal of Strategic Studies*.

Michael Raska is Assistant Professor and Coordinator of the Military Transformations Programme at the S. Rajaratnam School of International Studies, Nanyang Technological University in Singapore. His research and teaching focus on theoretical and policy-oriented aspects of military innovation, emerging technologies, and East Asian security and defence.

Katarzyna Zysk is Professor of International Relations and Contemporary History at the Norwegian Institute for Defence Studies in Oslo, which is a part of the Norwegian Defence University College in Oslo, Norway. Her research focuses on security, defence, and strategic studies, including Russia's military strategy and warfare, maritime security and geopolitics in the Arctic, military change, and defence innovation.

Ian Bowers is Associate Professor at the Centre for Joint Operations at the Royal Danish Defence College in Copenhagen. His research focuses on the implications of multi-domain operations for small states, the application of seapower, deterrence, and East Asian security.

Defence Innovation and the 4th Industrial Revolution

Security Challenges, Emerging Technologies, and Military Implications

Edited by
Michael Raska, Katarzyna Zysk and Ian Bowers

LONDON AND NEW YORK

First published 2022
by Routledge
4 Park Square, Milton Park, Abingdon, Oxon OX14 4RN

and by Routledge
605 Third Avenue, New York, NY 10158

Routledge is an imprint of the Taylor & Francis Group, an informa business

Introduction, Chapters 1–3 and 5–7 © 2022 Taylor & Francis
Chapter 4 © 2020 Katarzyna Zysk. Originally published as Open Access.

With the exception of Chapter 4, no part of this book may be reprinted or reproduced or utilised in any form or by any electronic, mechanical, or other means, now known or hereafter invented, including photocopying and recording, or in any information storage or retrieval system, without permission in writing from the publishers. For details on the rights for Chapter 4, please see the chapter's Open Access footnote.

Trademark notice: Product or corporate names may be trademarks or registered trademarks, and are used only for identification and explanation without intent to infringe.

British Library Cataloguing in Publication Data
A catalogue record for this book is available from the British Library

ISBN: 978-1-032-21398-9 (hbk)
ISBN: 978-1-032-21399-6 (pbk)
ISBN: 978-1-003-26821-5 (ebk)

DOI: 10.4324/9781003268215

Typeset in Myriad Pro
by Newgen Publishing UK

Publisher's Note
The publisher accepts responsibility for any inconsistencies that may have arisen during the conversion of this book from journal articles to book chapters, namely the inclusion of journal terminology.

Disclaimer
Every effort has been made to contact copyright holders for their permission to reprint material in this book. The publishers would be grateful to hear from any copyright holder who is not here acknowledged and will undertake to rectify any errors or omissions in future editions of this book.

Contents

Citation Information vi
Notes on Contributors viii

Introduction 1
Michael Raska, Katarzyna Zysk, Ian Bowers and Richard A. Bitzinger

1 The sixth RMA wave: Disruption in Military Affairs? 6
 Michael Raska

2 From closed to open systems: How the US military services pursue innovation 30
 Zoe Stanley-Lockman

3 Artificial intelligence in China's revolution in military affairs 65
 Elsa B. Kania

4 Defence innovation and the 4th industrial revolution in Russia 93
 Katarzyna Zysk

5 4IR technologies in the Israel Defence Forces: blurring traditional boundaries 122
 Yoram Evron

6 Small states and autonomous systems: the Scandinavian case 144
 Magnus Petersson

7 Not so disruptive after all: The 4IR, navies and the search for sea control 163
 Ian Bowers and Sarah Kirchberger

Index 187

Citation Information

The chapters in this book were originally published in the *Journal of Strategic Studies*, volume 44, issue 4 (2021). When citing this material, please use the original page numbering for each article, as follows:

Introduction
　Introduction
　Michael Raska, Katarzyna Zysk, Ian Bowers and Richard A. Bitzinger
　Journal of Strategic Studies, volume 44, issue 4 (2021), pp. 451–455

Chapter 1
　The sixth RMA wave: Disruption in Military Affairs?
　Michael Raska
　Journal of Strategic Studies, volume 44, issue 4 (2021), pp. 456–479

Chapter 2
　From closed to open systems: How the US military services pursue innovation
　Zoe Stanley-Lockman
　Journal of Strategic Studies, volume 44, issue 4 (2021), pp. 480–514

Chapter 3
　Artificial intelligence in China's revolution in military affairs
　Elsa B. Kania
　Journal of Strategic Studies, volume 44, issue 4 (2021), pp. 515–542

Chapter 4
　Defence innovation and the 4th industrial revolution in Russia
　Katarzyna Zysk
　Journal of Strategic Studies, volume 44, issue 4 (2021), pp. 543–571

Chapter 5
　4IR technologies in the Israel Defence Forces: blurring traditional boundaries
　Yoram Evron

Journal of Strategic Studies, volume 44, issue 4 (2021), pp. 572–593

Chapter 6
Small states and autonomous systems - the Scandinavian case
Magnus Petersson
Journal of Strategic Studies, volume 44, issue 4 (2021), pp. 594–612

Chapter 7
Not so disruptive after all: The 4IR, navies and the search for sea control
Ian Bowers and Sarah Kirchberger
Journal of Strategic Studies, volume 44, issue 4 (2021), pp. 613–636

For any permission-related enquiries please visit:
www.tandfonline.com/page/help/permissions

Notes on Contributors

Richard A. Bitzinger is Senior Visiting Fellow with the Military Transformations Programme at the S. Rajaratnam School of International Studies (RSIS), Nanyang Technological University, where his work focuses on security and defence issues relating to the Asia-Pacific region, including military modernisation and force transformation, regional defence industries and local armaments production, and weapons proliferation. Formerly with the RAND Corp. and the Defence Budget Project, he has been writing on Asian aerospace and defence issues for more than 20 years. His articles have appeared in such journals as *International Security, Orbis, China Quarterly*, and *Survival*. He is the author of *Arming Asia: Technonationalism and Its Impact on Local Defence Industries* (2017), and *Towards a Brave New Arms Industry?* (2003).

Ian Bowers is Associate Professor at the Centre for Joint Operations, Royal Danish Defence College, Copenhagen. His research focuses on seapower, the future operating environment, Asian security and deterrence. His research has been published in the *Journal of Strategic Studies*, the *Naval War College Review* and the *Korean Journal of Defence Analysis*. His latest volume is *Grey and White Hulls: An International Analysis of the Navy-Coastguard Nexus*, co-edited with Collin Koh.

Yoram Evron is Senior Lecturer in the Department of Asian Studies at the University of Haifa, Israel. His current research focuses on civil-military relations, military procurement, and China's military procurement, as well as China-Middle East relations and East-West Asia relations. Dr. Evron is the author of *China's Military Procurement in the Reform Era: The Setting of New Directions* (2016). His recent articles include 'China-Japan Interaction in the Middle East: A Battleground of Japan's Remilitarization' (*The Pacific Review*), and 'The Enduring US-led Arms Embargo on China: An Objectives– Implementation Analysis' (*Journal of Contemporary China*).

Elsa B. Kania is PhD candidate in Harvard University's Department of Government, and she is also Adjunct Senior Fellow with the Technology and National Security Program at the Center for a New American Security (CNAS).

Sarah Kirchberger is Head of Asia-Pacific Strategy and Security at the Institute for Security Policy at Kiel University (ISPK) and Vice President of the German Maritime Institute (DMI). She was previously Assistant Professor of Sinology at the University of Hamburg and a naval analyst with shipbuilder TKMS. Her research focuses on China's space and naval development, China's defence economy, Russian-Chinese-Ukrainian arms-industrial cooperation, and the South China Sea issue. Her latest monograph is *Assessing China's Naval Power: Technological Innovation, Economic Constraints, and Strategic Implications*.

Magnus Petersson is Professor of International Relations, and Head of Department of Economic History and International Relations, at Stockholm University. Previously he worked as Lecturer, Researcher, and Head of Research and Development at the Swedish Defence University (1998–2008), Professor of Modern History at the Norwegian Institute for Defence Studies (2008–2020), and Analyst at the Swedish Defence Research Agency (2020–2021). He has published widely on Nordic and Transatlantic security and defence issues.

Michael Raska is Assistant Professor and Coordinator of the Military Transformations Programme at the S. Rajaratnam School of International Studies (RSIS), Nanyang Technological University in Singapore. His research interests focus on the evolution of military technologies and defence innovation, wars and conflicts in East Asia, and cyber warfare. He is the author of *Military Innovation and Small States: Creating Reverse Asymmetry* (2016) and co-editor of *Security, Strategy, and Military Change in the 21st Century: Cross-regional Perspectives* (2015).

Zoe Stanley-Lockman is Associate Research Fellow in the Military Transformations Programme at the Institute of Defence and Strategic Studies at the S. Rajaratnam School of International Studies in Singapore. Her research interests are in the areas of defence innovation, security-related emerging technologies, defence industries, and military capability development. Previously she worked as a defence analyst at the European Union Institute for Security Studies in Paris and Brussels. She holds a Master's degree from Sciences Po Paris and a Bachelor's degree from Johns Hopkins University.

Katarzyna Zysk is Professor of International Relations and Contemporary History at the Norwegian Institute for Defence Studies (IFS), which is part of the Norwegian Defence University College (NDUC) in Oslo. At the IFS, she also served as Deputy Director, Head of Centre for Security Policy, and Director of Research, and she was Acting Dean of the NDUC. She was visiting scholar at Center for International and Security Studies at Stanford University; The Changing Character of War Centre at the University of Oxford; Center for Naval Warfare Studies at the US Naval War College. Currently, she also serves as Visiting Professor at Sciences Po (CERI) in Paris and Nonresident Senior Fellow at the Atlantic Council. Her research has focused on security, defence, and strategic studies, including Russia's military strategy and warfare, nuclear deterrence, maritime security and geopolitics in the Arctic, and military change and defence innovation.

Introduction

Michael Raska ⓘ, Katarzyna Zysk, Ian Bowers ⓘ and Richard A. Bitzinger

ABSTRACT
This special collection of essays explores how militaries are integrating, adapting and leveraging 4th Industrial Revolution (4IR) technologies and examines the varying strategic and operational implications. Its core themes reflect on the position of the 4IR in the context of previous Revolutions in Military Affairs; a comparison between how large resource-rich states and small resource-limited states are adopting and integrating 4IR technologies; the difference between various 4IR innovation and adaptation models; and the operational implications of such technologies in terms of manpower, operational domains force structure and the application of force.

Technology is widely regarded to be a crucial element of military effectiveness and advantage. As Keith Krause once put it, 'the possession of modern weapons is a key element in determining the international hierarchy of power.'[1] In theory (and often in practice), the possession of cutting-edge military-relevant technologies equals more effective weapons systems, which shapes military power that in turn translates into greater geopolitical power. Simultaneously, the transnational diffusion of military-related technologies is an essential factor affecting the distribution of power in international politics. Consequently, the global dissemination of advanced, militarily relevant technologies should be as great a security concern as the spread of weapons systems themselves.

Moreover, we live in a time when 'militarily relevant technologies' are becoming harder and harder to identify and classify. Advanced technologies – many of which are embedded in commercial rather than military-industrial sectors – offer new and potentially significant opportunities for defence applications and, in turn, for increasing one's military edge over potential rivals. Unlike during the Cold War, spending on military R&D in the West is now dwarfed by its commercial equivalent. Technological advances, especially in the area of military systems, are

---

[1]Keith Krause, *Arms and the state: Patterns of Military Production and Trade* (Cambridge: Cambridge University Press, 1992), 19.

a continuous, dynamic process; breakthroughs are constantly occurring, and their impact on military effectiveness and comparative advantage could be both significant and hard to predict at their nascent stages. Consequently, the military is no longer the primary driver of technological innovation. Instead, militaries are looking to turn technologies primarily developed in the commercial sector, although with dual-use potential, such as artificial intelligence (AI), autonomous systems, and advanced supercomputing into the next generation of combat systems.

However, such technologies and resulting capabilities rarely spread themselves evenly across geopolitical lines. The diffusion of new and potentially powerful militarily relevant technologies – as well as the ability of militaries to exploit their potential – varies widely across the globe. This unequal distribution in turn, will naturally affect how these technologies and capabilities impact regional security and stability. Therefore, it is critical to assess the relative abilities of militaries to access and leverage new and emerging critical technologies, their likely progress in doing so, and the impediments they may face, ultimately with an eye toward how it will affect relative gains and losses in regional military capabilities.

How these new technologies will integrate with current operational constructs and force structures is a matter of much debate in militaries across the world. The level of human involvement in the future of warfare, the need to alter doctrines, force structures and recruitment patterns are all matters that are being challenged by new technologies.

Further, on a strategic level, new technologies will continue to create new dynamics. Alliances are becoming more closely interconnected, strategic concepts such as deterrence and strategic stability are being tested. New technologies are both challenging and empowering large and small states alike and may encourage new phases of arms competitions across the world.

In short, the so-called 4th Industrial Revolution (4IR) promises to create a new set of challenges when it comes to identifying new and significant military technologies and understanding how these capabilities will create military advantage and, therefore, political leverage in the decades to come. In particular, the 4IR is creating a new set of conditions for the development and application of new military technologies. These conditions will have profound implications for a) how militaries adopt new technologies; b) how on an operational level, militaries adapt to and apply new technologies and c) our understandings of both the operational and strategic battlespace and d) strategic stability and instability.

This special issue uses a thematic and case study-based approach. In the opening paper, Michael Raska directly links the 4IR with the next wave in the modern Revolution in Military Affairs debate. In contrast to previous IT-RMA waves, which have failed to achieve their intended strategic outcomes, the emerging AI-RMA wave differs: it is global, embedded in a contest for military-technological superiority between major powers; diffused by a convergence of civil-military sources of innovation; and the resulting shift toward autonomous and AI-enabled weapons systems in warfare.

Next, Zoe Stanley-Lockman and Elsa Kania in two essays examine how the US and China respectively are adapting to the 4IR. The contrasts are striking. The US uses a diverse number of innovation models to leverage the 4IR. This diversity can be seen in the different approaches the service branches are taking, which Stanley-Lockman argues is resulting in varying levels of success across the US military. China, on the other hand, is using a top-down strategy of military-civil fusion, which aims to create and leverage synergies between defence-commercial developments and supply chains.

Katarzyna Zysk examines Russia's approach to the 4IR. She reveals that despite grand ambitions and a number of new initiatives, Russia struggles and will continue to struggle to leverage the 4IR. It is constrained by a range of structural and circumstantial problems and lacks the resources and capabilities of its near-peer competitors, the US and China. Nevertheless, Russia has also shown the ability to experiment with and exploit 4IR technologies to amplify traditional symmetric responses and enable asymmetric capabilities, including hypersonic weapons and the application of AI in grey zone operations.

Yoram Evron and Magnus Petersson look at smaller states. Evron's paper explores Israel's highly successful approach to the 4IR. He argues that Israel is uniquely placed to take advantage of the 4IR given its historical emphasis on technology to offset its geostrategic limitations and the close relationship between the Israeli private technology sector and the Israeli military. In contrast, Petersson in examining the case of three Scandinavian countries – Sweden, Denmark and Norway – demonstrates that these states are investing significant sums in the military applications of the 4IR. Yet, there is little public doctrinal or strategic thinking about their utility. Instead, the discourse focuses more on the legal and ethical implications of such technologies than their near-term integration in Scandinavian armed forces.

Finally, Ian Bowers and Sarah Kirchberger place 4IR in an operational context. In examining the disruptive power of the 4IR on the application of seapower, they find that such technologies may change the inputs of seapower, particularly in the use of networked warfighting capabilities. However, using two case studies, the South China Sea and the Baltic Sea, they find that in the key operational output of attaining sea control, these technologies will not disrupt naval warfare. They argue that the 4IR will intensify the competition between the operational attributes of detection, stealth, range and lethality, but will ultimately sustain existing understandings of seapower and its strategic effects.

Taken together, these essays may only scratch the surface of the 4IR debate: what the 4IR entails, how it impacts military effectiveness and advantage, and what are the wider, long-term implications of such military developments. However, by shedding more light on the likely effect of the fourth industrial revolution when it comes to defence innovation, we hope to advance what is bound to be a broad, long-term dialogue.

Acknowledgements

This special issue has evolved from international research collaboration and subsequent workshop (2019) co-organised by the S. Rajaratnam School of International Studies, the Norwegian Institute for Defence Studies, and the Institute of Security and Defence Policy at Kiel University. The editorial team would like to express a sincere gratitude to all participants who helped in the project, anonymous reviewers, and editors of the *Journal of Strategic Studies*.

Disclosure statement

No potential conflict of interest was reported by the author(s).

ORCID

Michael Raska ⓘ http://orcid.org/0000-0002-8283-2438
Ian Bowers ⓘ http://orcid.org/0000-0003-4628-6764

Bibliography

Krause, Keith *Arms and the State: Patterns of Military Production and Trade* (Cambridge University Press: Cambridge 1992), 19.

The sixth RMA wave: Disruption in Military Affairs?

Michael Raska

ABSTRACT
The Revolution in Military Affairs, its concepts, processes, and debates, have evolved in five 'IT-RMA waves' since the 1980s. None of them, however, have fully achieved their intended outcomes as their ambitious premises have exceeded available technologies, budgetary resources, and operational capabilities of a given era. This paper argues that a new 'artificial intelligence-driven RMA' wave differs in the political, strategic, technological, and operational diffusion paths and patterns. While the AI-RMA may affect select countries and regions disproportionately, its technological advances coupled with an ongoing strategic competition is sufficiently broad to stipulate significant military changes across geopolitical lines.

Introduction

After nearly three decades of debating the Revolution in Military Affairs (RMA), security studies is once again reflecting narratives of a 'disruptive' or significant military change brought by the convergence of emerging 'next-frontier' technologies, novel operational concepts and organisational force structures.[1] In particular, the application of advanced machine-learning algorithms in select areas of warfare promises to enable unprecedented capabilities concerning the speed of information and data processing, automation for weapons platforms and surveillance systems, and ultimately, decision-making.[2] For example, advanced sensor technologies such as hyperspectral imagery, computational photography, and compact sensor design, promise

---

[1] Andrew James, 'Emerging Technologies and Military Capability', in Richard Bitzinger (ed.), *Emerging Critical Technologies and Security in the Asia-Pacific* (London: Palgrave Macmillan 2016), 6–21.
[2] Zachary Davis, 'Artificial Intelligence on the Battlefield', *PRISM* 8/2 (2019), 114–131; M. L. Cummings, "Artificial Intelligence and the Future of Warfare', *Chatham House Research Paper*, 26 January 2017; Paul Scharre and Michael C. Horowitz, 'An Introduction to Autonomy in Weapon Systems', Center for a New American Security, 13 February 2015; Michael Horowitz, 'The Promise and Peril of Military Applications of Artificial Intelligence', *Bulletin of the Atomic Scientists*, 23 April 2018; Greg Allen and Taniel Chan, 'Artificial Intelligence and National Security', *Belfer Center for Science and International Affairs*, 6 July 2017.

to significantly improve target detection, recognition, and tracking capabilities and overcome traditional line-of-sight interference.[3] State-of-the-art materials, including composites, ceramics, and nanomaterials with adaptive properties, promise to make military equipment lighter but more resistant to the environment.[4] Emerging photonics technologies, including high-power lasers and optoelectronic devices, may provide new levels of secure communications based on quantum computing and quantum cryptography.[5] Moreover, the convergence of these technologies with artificial intelligence (AI) systems, robotics, additive manufacturing (or 3D printing), quantum computing, directed energy, unmanned systems and other 'disruptive' technologies of the 4th Industrial Revolution (4IR), are increasingly synonymous with sources of strategic and operational advantages in future warfare.[6]

While the strategic context differs, the diffusion of these technologies has prompted theoretical and policy-prescriptive questions similar to those posed in security studies since the early 1990s: Does the diffusion of emerging technologies signify a 'disruptive' shift in warfare or is it a mere evolutionary change? If emerging technologies stipulate a disruptive shift in warfare, what are defence resource allocation imperatives, including force structure and weapons procurement requirements? How can military organisations exploit emerging technologies to their advantage? Furthermore, how effective are emerging technologies to counter security threats and challenges of the 21st century, characterised by volatility, uncertainty, complexity, and ambiguity?

In this context, this paper positions its argument along two main lines: First, RMA conceptions and debates on the impending major change in warfare have progressively evolved over the past three decades. In 2006, Colin Gray briefly mentioned five stages or 'RMA waves' that have guided both theoretical and policy-oriented debates in strategic studies: (1) the intellectual discovery in the Soviet strategic thought in the 1980s, (2) the conceptual adoption and adaptation in the United States military in the early 1990s, (3) the culminating point of the RMA debate in mid-to-late 1990s, (4) the shift toward 'defence transformation' in the early 2000s, and (5) critical reversal questioning the RMA thesis from 2005 onwards.[7] This paper argues that since the mid-2010s, with the accelerating research and development of

---

[3]Sara Freitas, Hugo Silva, José Almeida & Eduardo Silva, 'Hyperspectral Imaging for Real-Time Unmanned Aerial Vehicle Maritime Target Detection', *Journal of Intelligent and Robotic Systems* 90 (2018), 551–570.
[4]Mark Burnett, et. al., 'Advanced Materials and Manufacturing – Implications for Defence to 2040 , *Defence Science and Technology Group Report*, Australia Department of Defence (2018), https://www.dst.defence.gov.au/sites/default/files/publications/documents/DST-Group-GD-1022.pdf.
[5]International Institute for Strategic Studies, 'Quantum Computing and Defence', in IISS, *The Military Balance 2019* (London: Routledge 2019), 18–20.
[6]DARPA, 'Strategic Technology Office Outlines Vision for Mosaic Warfare', *DARPA News*, 4 August 2017, https://www.darpa.mil/news-events/2017-08-04.
[7]Colin Gray, *Strategy and History: Essays on Theory and Practice* (London: Routledge 2006), 113; Michael Raska, *Military Innovation and Small States: Creating a Reverse Asymmetry* (London: Routledge 2016), 30.

novel technologies such as artificial intelligence and autonomous systems, a new AI-driven RMA wave has already emerged (See Figure 1).

Second, notwithstanding significant advances in military technologies and the use of force in the initial five RMA waves, these trends have not been fully implemented relative to their envisioned conceptions. Their varying and often ambitious premises have generally exceeded available technological capabilities, financial resources, and operational requirements of a given era. Moreover, Gray's 'Five RMA' waves have actually been subsets of one comprehensive 'information technologies RMA,' or IT-RMA, which focused on integrating digital technologies into existing conventional weapons platforms and systems. The new AI-enabled RMA wave, however, differs from the past IT-RMA waves in several ways. Firstly, for the first time in decades, the US faces a strategic peer-competitor, China, capable of pursuing and implementing its own AI-RMA that can potentially negate strategic and operational advantages of the US military across geopolitical lines, particularly in East Asia. Secondly, advanced military-industrial sectors are no longer the primary drivers of technological innovation; instead, advanced technologies with a dual-use potential are being developed in the commercial sectors, including those of small states and middle powers, and then being 'spun on' to military applications. Finally, the diffusion of autonomous and AI-enabled weapons systems, coupled with novel operational constructs and force structures, challenge the direction and character of human involvement in future warfare.

Accordingly, the main question is not whether the AI-RMA wave is 'the one' that will bring about a fundamental discontinuity in warfare, and if so, how and why? Instead, it is whether the US AI-RMA can be nullified – or at least weakened – by a corresponding *Chinese* AI-RMA? Consequently, how will the global diffusion of emerging technologies affect strategic stability, alliance relationships, arms control, ethics and governance, and nearly all aspects of international security? These questions will arguably shape the next decade of debates in security studies with diverse theoretical and policy-oriented viewpoints, interpretations, and arguments. To advance these debates, however, it is essential to reflect on the intellectual history of the five IT-RMA waves, critically pointing out their failures to fully achieve their intended conceptual visions, while highlighting the differences in the strategic contours of the AI-RMA wave. As this paper shows, the IT-RMA waves trace their conceptual roots to Russian strategic thought, followed by varying experimentation and implementation paths in the US military, while the AI-RMA wave is a global phenomenon. It is embedded in the growing US-China systemic rivalry and their varying 'techno-nationalist' visions and approaches to dominate in areas of disruptive technologies of the 4IR.[8] At the same time, its diffusion paths and patterns are shaped by defence

---

[8] Paul Evans, 'Techno-Nationalism in China-US Relations: Implications for Universities', *EAI Background Brief*, 30 April 1527, 2020.

	1980's	1990-95	1995-2000	2000-2005	2005-2010	2010-present
Wave	Intellectual Discovery	Early Adaptation in the West	IT-RMA Technophilia	Shift to Defence Transformation	Second & Third Thoughts	AI-Enabled RMA
Type			IT-RMA			4IR
Term	Military-Technical Revolution	Military Revolutions vs RMAs	Revolution in Military Affairs	Defence Transformation	Modernisation 'Plus'	Disruptive Defence Innovation
Country	Soviet Union	US	US	US	US / NATO	US China Russia Israel / Others
Warfare	Electronic Warfare	Information Warfare		Digitised Warfare	Hybrid Warfare	Automated Warfare
Operational Concepts (Examples)	Reconnaissance-Strike Complexes Operational Manoeuvre Groups	Dominant Battlespace Knowledge	Network-Centric Warfare	Effects-Based Operations Network-Centric Warfare	COIN Dynamics Network-Centric Warfare	Multi-Domain Operations PLA Intelligentised Warfare
Impetus	Technology/ Military Innovation	Technology/ Military Innovation	Technology/ Military Innovation	Technology / Defence Innovation / Low-Intensity Conflicts	Technology / Defence Innovation/ Low-Intensity Conflicts	Strategic Competition/ Emerging Technologies/ Civil-Military Convergence
Strategic Competition	Yes	No	No	No	No	Yes
Implementation	No	Limited	Limited	Partial	Partial	Ongoing

Figure 1. Overview of the six RMA waves. **Source**: Author; Adapted from Raska (2016).

innovation trajectories of select advanced small states and middle powers such as Australia, France, Israel, Singapore, South Korea, United Kingdom, and others. These states seek to leverage advanced technologies such as AI systems not only to alleviate their traditional defence constraints but also to advance their power and influence in the international arena.[9]

First RMA wave: Electronic warfare & military-technical revolution (MTR)

In the early 1980s, Soviet strategic forecasters debated the first-generation of RMA theories under the conceptual umbrella of the Military-Technical Revolution (MTR).[10] As Dima Adamsky noted, the Soviet MTR debate focused on two aspects: (1) the implications of scientific progress on the direction and character of future military operations; and (2) responding to Western doctrinal and technological innovations, notably the 1982 US AirLand Battle (ALB) and NATO's Follow-on Forces Attack (FOFA).[11] Indeed, following the Yom Kippur War in 1973, Russian analysts interpreted US advances in precision-guided munitions, advanced C3I systems, electronic warfare, and computer simulation as strategically detrimental to their baseline principles, methods, and forms of waging wars.[12] Lessons learned in the wars between Israel and Soviet-backed Arab neighbours showed that radar detection and precision firepower combined with new electronic warfare systems produced high attrition rates.[13] The ALB doctrine – attacking deep in the rear through a combination of stand-off precision fire, interdiction, and ground offensive operations - threatened Soviet operational-tactical and operational-strategic art based on large strategic formations and concepts of echelonment.[14]

In 1984, Gorbachev's call for 'new thinking' in defence and national security affairs opened a dialogue between Russian military-technical analysts and civilian social scientists on the challenges imposed by the MTR.[15] Leading military theorists such as General of the Army Makhmut Akhmetovich Gareev, then Deputy Chief of the Soviet General Staff and Chief of the Directorate for

---

[9] Itai Barsade and Michael Horowitz, 'Artificial Intelligence Beyond the Superpowers,' *Bulletin of the Atomic Scientists*, 16 August 2018.

[10] Raska, *Military Innovation and Small States: Creating a Reverse Asymmetry*, 30.

[11] Dima Adamsky, 'Through the Looking Glass: The Soviet Military-Technical Revolution and the American Revolution in Military Affairs', *Journal of Strategic Studies* 31/2 (2008), 257–94.

[12] Jacob Kipp, 'The Russian Military and the Revolution in Military Affairs: A Case of the Oracle of Delphi or Cassandra?', *US Foreign Military Studies Office Paper* (1995), 3; Williamson Murray and MacGregor Knox, 'Thinking about Revolutions in Warfare', in MacGregor Knox and Williamson Murray (eds.), *The Dynamics of Military Revolution, 1300–2050* (Cambridge: Cambridge University Press 2001), 3.

[13] Keith Shimko, *The Iraq Wars and America's Military Revolution* (Cambridge: Cambridge University Press 2010), 6.

[14] Murray and Knox, 'Thinking about Revolutions in Warfare', 3; Philip Petersen, 'The Soviet Conceptual Framework for the Application of Military Power', *Naval War College Review* 34/3 (1981), 21; Department of the Army HQ, *The Soviet Army: Operations and Tactics – Field Manual 100-2-1* (Washington DC: Department of Defence 1984), 1–12.

[15] Kipp, 'The Russian Military and the Revolution in Military Affairs: A Case of the Oracle of Delphi or Cassandra?', 6.

Military Science, and Marshal Nikolai V. Ogarkov, chief of the Soviet general staff from 1977 to 1984, conceptualised the MTR through the evolutionary lens of Marxist-Leninist dialectics in the continuity and change of military art. For example, Gareev argued that varying political, geostrategic, and economic limitations, such as the cost of modern military technologies, impose limitations to the MTR, while novel technological innovations such as information processing bring revolutionary aspects in new types of weapons.[16]

Similarly, following his ousting from the general staff in 1984, Ogarkov published in professional periodicals and monographs, examining the impact of emerging technologies on Soviet ways and means of warfare. He cautioned that the diffusion of precision-guided munitions coupled with enhanced sensors would result in qualitatively new and incomparably more destructive forms of warfare than ever before.[17] In future warfare, he argued, the integration of unmanned systems, space-based systems, and automated detection systems in a 'network of networks' would enable a near-simultaneous engagement of an entire array of targets at greater distances, precision, lethality, and speed. As such, Soviet conceptions of military effectiveness based on quantity as a source of military advantage, would be outweighed by quality.[18]

In this context, Soviet military thought at that time focused on the development of two interrelated operational concepts: (1) Reconnaissance-Strike Complexes (RSC) and (2) Operational Manoeuvre Groups (OMG).[19] Both concepts reflected Soviet adaptations of 'deep battle' by mobile groups using novel forms of weapons technologies, capable of engaging 'an array of targets at extended ranges with a high degree of accuracy and lethality'.[20] However, as the political and socio-economic conditions in the Soviet Union started to deteriorate from the early 1980s, while the Red Army was both entrenched and overextended in a protracted war of attrition in Afghanistan – the military lacked the technological means, financial resources, and organisational flexibility to implement these concepts. Intellectually, however, Russian conceptions on the MTR during this period provided greater analytical and critical depth than comparable writings in the West. Thus, the intellectual discovery and initial analysis of the MTR is credited to Russian strategic and military discourse.[21]

---

[16] *Ibid.*, 20.
[17] Philip Petersen, 'The Modernization of Soviet Armed Forces', *NATO's 16 Nations* 31/4 (1984), 34.
[18] Nikolai Ogarkov, *Istoriya Uchit Bditelnosti* (*History Teaches Vigilance*) (Moscow: Voenizdat 1985); Dusko Doder, 'Ousted Soviet Chief of Staff Returns to Scene as Author', *The Washington Post*, 10 June 1985.
[19] *Ibid.*
[20] Andrew Krepinevich, *The Military-Technical Revolution: A Preliminary Assessment* (Washington DC: Office of Net Assessment 1992), 6.; Barry, Watts, 'What is the Revolution in Military Affairs?', *Northrop Grumman Analysis Center*351 (1995), 2.
[21] Dima Adamsky, *The Culture of Military Innovation: The Impact of Cultural Factors on the Revolution in Military Affairs in Russia, the US, and Israel* (Palo Alto, CA: Stanford University Press 2010); Shimon Naveh, *In Pursuit of Military Excellence: The Evolution of Operational Theory* (London: Frank Cass 1996), 236.

Second RMA wave: Conceptual adaptation in the US military

Throughout the 1980s, US intelligence monitored changes in Russian military thinking.[22] The CIA, for example, published National Intelligence Estimates (NIE) that identified trends and developments in Soviet weaponry coupled with the emergence of RSC and OMG operational concepts.[23] However, these assessments underestimated the strategic significance of the MTR, and characterised it in terms of incremental military modernisation efforts, conditioned by Soviet technological, manpower, and resource limitations.[24] Some also argued that the MTR was only 'propagandistic hyperbole'.[25] In the early 1990s, however, the Office of Net Assessment (ONA) in the Office of the US Secretary of Defence (OSD) began investigating Soviet writings about the MTR as part of its mission of assessing military balances, which stipulated understanding Soviet conceptions of modern warfare. Headed by Andrew Marshall, the ONA began to expand its focus to explore the hypothesis that an MTR was underway. In 1990, for example, the ONA conducted a major review of the Soviet MTR literature to determine its validity and resulting policy imperatives, resulting in the 1992 publication: *Military-Technical Revolution: A Preliminary Assessment*. The report viewed the MTR as a fundamental discontinuity in warfare – not only in the technical aspects of the speed in which change takes place, but rather in the *magnitude* of the change itself, which 'at some point ... will invalidate former conceptual frameworks by bringing about a fundamental change in the nature of warfare and, thus, in our definitions and measurement of military effectiveness'.[26]

However, the ONA report argued that Soviet MTR conceptions were confined to the technological dimension while mitigating the significance of organisational, operational, and human drivers of change. With this assumption, the term MTR evolved into the Revolution in Military Affairs (RMA) concept and its widely quoted definition – 'the application of new technologies into military systems combined with innovative operational concepts and organisational adaptation that alters the character and conduct of military operations'.[27] In doing so, RMA combined four key drivers of a major military change: (1) technological change; (2) military systems development; (3) operational innovation; and (4) organisational innovation. 'When (and only when) these elements are combined', the report argued,

---

[22]Raska, *Military Innovation and Small States: Creating a Reverse Asymmetry*, 33.
[23]Adamsky, 'Through the Looking Glass: The Soviet Military-Technical Revolution and the American Revolution in Military Affairs', 257–94.
[24]Office of Soviet Analysis, 'Trends and Developments in Warsaw Pact Theater Forces 1985–2000, *National Intelligence Estimate* No. 11–14 (1985).
[25]James Blaker, *Understanding the Revolution in Military Affairs: A Guide to America's 21st Century Defence* (Washington DC: Progressive Policy Institute 1997), 5.
[26]Krepinevich, *The Military-Technical Revolution: A Preliminary Assessment*, 3.
[27]*Ibid.*, 3.

'dramatic improvement in military effectiveness and combat potential would take place'.[28]

During this period, the strategic studies literature focused on the lessons from the first Gulf War (1991), pointing to the emergence of novel military technologies, particularly precision-guided munitions, as a proof of the US military superiority embracing the RMA in the post-Cold War era.[29] Specifically, RMA studies reflected four key themes: (1) historical assessments of technology as a contributor of military effectiveness in war; (2) the sources and nature of military innovation; (3) the interpretations of processes of change brought by the Information Revolution; and (4) policy implications linked with short-and-long-term consequences of the RMA for military organisations.[30] In the varying debates, two terms began to appear (often interchangeably): *Military Revolutions (MR)* and *Revolutions in Military Affairs (RMA)*.[31] The MR implied a broader *socio-political and military* paradigm shift in the ways and means society, the state, and military organisations prepare and conduct war.[32] In other words, MRs would signify a grand-strategic dimension of a major military change beyond the battlefield and military organisations. In contrast, within or alongside the major MRs would be varying RMAs, characterised by Murray and Knox as 'periods of innovation in which armed forces develop novel concepts involving changes in doctrine, tactics, procedures, and technology ... RMAs [also] take place almost exclusively at the operational level of war. They rarely affect the strategic level, except in so far as operational success can determine the large strategic equation. RMAs always occur within the context of politics and strategy– and that context is everything'.[33]

The conceptual adaptation phase focusing on the origins and character of MRs *vis-à-vis* RMAs began to shape defence policy planning, particularly in the US military. As Jeffrey Cooper noted, the RMA debate in the early 1990s divided US policymakers into two contending camps: (1) those who focused on the external perspective of the RMA as a means of attaining strategic objectives in the post-Cold War era; and (2) those viewing the RMA through internal processes as an organising principle or a tool to shape and determine future policy, acquisition programs, resource allocation, and bureaucratic relationships.[34] In retrospect, the early adaptation of the RMA in Western

---

[28]*Ibid.*, 3.
[29]George and Meredith Friedman, *The Future of War: Power, Technology, and American Dominance in the 21st Century* (New York: Crown 1996); Max Boot, *War Made New Technology: Warfare and the Course of History, 1500 to Today* (New York: Gotham Books 2006).
[30]Raska, *Military Innovation and Small States: Creating a Reverse Asymmetry*, 35.
[31]Geoffrey Parker, 'Military Revolution 1560–1660–A Myth?' *Journal of Modern History* 48/2 (1976), 196–214.
[32]Murray and Knox, 'Thinking about Revolutions in Warfare', 7.
[33]*Ibid.*, 12.
[34]Jeffrey Cooper, 'Another View of the Revolution in Military Affairs,' in John Arquilla and David Ronfeldt (eds.), *Athena's Camp: Preparing for Conflict in the Information Age* (Santa Monica, CA: RAND 1994), 99.

strategic thought during 1990–94 showed both streams of the debate – a broader search for a new strategic paradigm that would reflect the underlying geopolitical shift of the world order into a post-Cold-War era, while recognising the potential of emerging information technologies on the future of warfare. However, the output of US and European RMA studies at that time was not comprehensive and as a result 'offered only limited or broad policy choices'.[35]

Third RMA wave: Information warfare and IT-RMA technophilia

Starting in the mid-1990s, the RMA became the 'acronym of choice'[36] in the US defence planning and strategic studies community, 'arousing tremendous excitement among American defence planners'.[37] Historical analyses of MRs and RMAs were superseded by a plethora of studies focusing on the varying policy aspects, i.e. how to increase military effectiveness with new technologies at a reduced cost.[38] For example, key questions included how does the RMA impact defence planning and management, what are the critical changes needed to implement the RMA in organisations, and perhaps most importantly, how to implement the RMA at the operational level. In 1996, for example, Admiral William Owens, then Vice Chairman of the Joint Chiefs of Staff, conceptualised the *System-of-Systems* approach as the overarching operational vision for the RMA.[39] This concept focused on linking existing (and in some ways overlapping) inter-service platforms and systems – particularly, command, control, computers, communications, and information (C4I) systems coupled with intelligence, surveillance, and reconnaissance (ISR) systems into one interoperable network. By networking the varying C4I architectures and ISR information systems, the military would attain novel situational awareness capabilities – defined as 'Dominant Battlespace Knowledge' (DBK), across a large area of operations (200-by-200-mile boxes). DBK, in theory, would enable speeding up of decision-making processes, and allow directing 'precision force in action and results'.[40] In this context, Owens argued that the US military should accelerate the pursuit of RMA by embracing substantial technological, organisational, structural, and doctrinal changes.

It should be noted that before Owens' appointment as the Vice Chairman of the Joint Chiefs of Staff in 1994, the US military services did not widely perceive the RMA as a major military change, but rather as an evolving continuation of existing military-technological development. In other words, a phenomenon

---

[35]Steven Metz and James Kievit, *Strategy and the Revolution in Military Affairs: From Theory to Policy* (Carlisle: Strategic Studies Institute 1995), 1.
[36]Williamson Murray, 'Thinking About Revolutions in Military Affairs', *Joint Forces Quarterly* 16 (Summer 1997), 69.
[37]Metz and Kievit, *Strategy and the Revolution in Military Affairs: From Theory to Policy*, 1.
[38]Raska, *Military Innovation and Small States: Creating a Reverse Asymmetry*, 39.
[39]William Owens, 'The Emerging US System-of-Systems', *Strategic Forum* 63. (1996), 1–6.
[40]*Ibid.*, 1.

more of modernisation than a revolution.[41] Owens' System-of-Systems vision, however, challenged these perspectives by projecting a future of unprecedented technological and operational inter-service compatibility. At the same time, it defined a set of new procurement priorities toward select military technologies that would enable better connectivity, interoperability, and jointness coupled with precision firepower. As a result, the US military accelerated the institutional adoption and adaptation of the RMA, as seen in the official publications such as the 1996 *Joint Vision 2010* and the 1997 *Quadrennial Strategy Review*. In particular, the *Joint Vision 2010* published by the Office of the Joint Chiefs of Staff, provided a template for translating Owens' system-of-systems concept into a joint operational framework.[42] However, its critics argued that despite two decades of military-technological advances and operationally focused thinking in the US military, the JV2010 would still represent a linear extension of the previous strategic context, existing technologies, and operational doctrines such as the AirLand Battle.[43] Therefore, in order to represent a paradigm shift that would account for information revolution in the new strategic context of the post-Cold War era, a radically different approach would be required. This idea is evident, for example, in the 1997 publication of the National Defence Panel's (NDP) report titled *Transforming Defence: National Security in the 21st century*. The report argued that the security environment of the 21st century will be 'quantitatively and qualitatively different from those of the Cold War and will require a fundamental change to US national security institutions, military strategy and defence posture'.[44]

Fourth RMA wave: Digitised warfare & defence transformation

While military-technological aspects remained an essential driver in the RMA debate in the early 2000s, the varying narratives increasingly reflected also changes in the global and regional security environment such as the rise of non-state actors, terrorism, and asymmetric warfare threats and challenges.[45] With the changing strategic impetus, the RMA debate in the US shifted toward the concept of defence transformation, which further extended the scope of envisioned military change.[46] Following the 9/11 terrorist attacks,

---

[41] *Ibid.*, 7.
[42] Office of the Joint Chiefs of Staff, 'Joint Vision 2010, US Department of Defence, July 1996.
[43] Paul Mitchell, *Network Centric Warfare and Coalition Operations: The New Military Operating System* (London: Routledge 2009), 34.
[44] National Defence Panel, *Transforming Defence: National Security in the 21st Century* (Washington DC: US Department of Defence 1997), 3.
[45] Ronald O'Rourke, 'Defence Transformation: Background and Oversight Issues for Congress', *CRS Report for Congress* 322,238 (2007).
[46] Steven Metz, 'America's Defence Transformation: A Conceptual and Political History', *Defence Studies* 6/1 (2006), 1–25.; Thomas Adams, *The Army After Next: The First Postindustrial Army* (Westport, CT: Praeger 2006); Thomas Mahnken and James Fitzsimonds, 'Tread-Heads or Technophiles Army Officer Attitudes Toward Transformation', *Parameters* 34/2 (2004), 57–72.

defence transformation became an 'all-encompassing umbrella for multifaceted initiatives'.[47] These would embrace strategic and operational imperatives to fundamentally restructure US forces and that of its allies by radically transforming defence planning, organisational force structures, and operational conduct.[48] In the words of Richard Bitzinger, 'the transformation of the US armed forces was initially promoted as nothing less than a fundamental shift in the way wars would be fought in the future. Nothing was sacred: every piece of defence dogma was on the table for debate and discussion – force structure, organisation, equipment, budgets, doctrine, and strategy'.[49]

In October 2001, Donald Rumsfeld, then the Secretary of Defence, established the Office of Force Transformation (OFT), led by Vice Admiral Arthur K. Cebrowski, tasked with coordinating the implementation of various transformation visions, plans, and programmes across the US military services. These included a plethora of transformation-related documents and roadmaps.[50] For example, the 2003 *Transformation Planning Guidance* (TPG) defined defence transformation as a 'process that shapes the changing nature of military competition and cooperation through new combinations of concepts, capabilities, people and organisations that exploit our nation's advantages and protect against our asymmetric vulnerabilities to sustain our strategic position, which helps underpin peace and stability in the world'.[51] Other notable policy documents included *Elements of Defence Transformation* (2004), *National Defence Strategy* (2005), and the *Quadrennial Defence Review* (2006). At the same time, US military services published their select transformation plans and visions. For example, under the *Navy Sea Power 21* strategy (2004), the US Navy (USN) would transform by conducting more flexible and expeditionary deployments in littoral (i.e. near-shore) waters, relying on new platforms such as multi-mission destroyers and cruisers, new types of modular mission-ships with smaller crews.[52] Similarly, the *Air Force Transformation Flight Plan* (2003), envisioned more expeditionary character for future missions of the US Air Force (USAF), which would be transformed into a 'global reconnaissance and strike force' dominating air, space, and cyberspace.

---

[47] Raska, *Military Innovation and Small States: Creating a Reverse Asymmetry*, 42.
[48] Peter Dombrowski and Andrew Ross, 'The Revolution in Military Affairs: Transformation and the Defence Industry', *Security Challenges* 4/4 (2008), 13.
[49] Richard Bitzinger, *Transforming the US Military: Implications for the Asia-Pacific* (Barton: Australian Strategic Policy Institute 2006), 6.
[50] Office of the Joint Chiefs of Staff, '*Joint Vision 2020: America's Military – Preparing for Tomorrow*', US Department of Defence, June 2000.
[51] Office of the Secretary of Defence, 'Transformation Planning Guidance', US Department of Defence, April 2003, 3.
[52] Office of the Secretary of Navy, 'Sea Power 21: Projecting Decisive Joint Capabilities', US Department of the Navy, October 2002.

Meanwhile, the US Army would be reorganised into modular, brigade-sized forces called Units of Action, and deployed in more distant areas and adaptable to the needs of specific contingencies.[53] 'Digitised warfare' became the buzzword in the Army's Force XXI effort, and the 'Millennium Challenge' exercise.[54] The idea was that greater digitisation and more networks would significantly improve situational awareness and precision-strike capabilities, and enable small units to be more lethal in future conflicts. The US Army subsequently rolled out the FBCB2 (Force XXI Battle Command Brigade and Below), Blue Force Tracker, and started to replace its tactical network capabilities. Tactical and operational-level Unmanned Aerial Vehicles (UAVs) became more ubiquitous during this period as well.[55]

At the operational level, US military innovation efforts focused on the experimentation and implementation of two key concepts: *Network-Centric Warfare* (NCW) and *Effects-Based Operations* (EBO). Both concepts essentially aimed at exploiting emerging military technologies in order to attain novel 'information-superiority' and precision-firepower capabilities. However, their ambitious visions stirred a new wave of debates that questioned their validity, reliability, and applicability. In particular, after eight years of conceptual development, EBOs became the focal point of criticism for the complex terminology and fragmented templates that aimed to predict outcomes of actions in any operational environment.[56] Its critics argued that EBOs are impossible to implement in a dynamic security environment with an infinite number of variables – EBOs could never accurately anticipate nor measure reactions of complex systems (i.e. political systems), which are highly adaptive or have different strategic cultures and behavioural parameters. In 2008, the Joint Forces Command (JFCOM) headed by Marine Gen. James Mattis issued a memorandum discarding the concept.[57] Once again, notwithstanding the military-technological developments of the era, the ambitious strategic and operational objectives behind defence transformation have failed or have been only partially implemented.

Fifth RMA wave: Hybrid warfare & modernisation-plus

From the mid-to-late 2000s, the vision of defence transformation projected an ambitious and diversified agenda for a major military change, which

---

[53] William Donnelly, *Transforming an Army at War: Designing the Modular Force 1991–2005* (Washington DC: Center for Military History 2007), 27–63.
[54] Micah Zenko, 'Millennium Challenge: The Real Story of a Corrupted Military Exercise and its Legacy', *War on the Rocks Commentary*, 5 November 2015.
[55] John Sloan Brown, *Kevlar Legions: The Transformation of the United States Army 1989–2005* (Washington DC: United States Army, Center of Military History 2012), 1.
[56] Milan Vego, 'Effects-Bases Operations: A Critique', *Joint Forces Quarterly* 41/2 (2006), 51–57.
[57] James Mattis, 'USJFCOM Commander's Guidance for Effects-Based Operations', *Joint Forces Quarterly* 51 (2006), 106.

transcended available technological, financial, and organisational resources.[58] As Bitzinger summarised, 'the challenge for the US military has been translating the transformational vision into a credible and effective set of capabilities, strategies and organisations'.[59] In the following years, the ambitious narrative as a process of disruptive military change has culminated into a ubiquitous term, which in reality outpaced the actual implementation. Before that, there were a number of critics arguing that the RMA as a theory, process, and debate has no validity and that it has rapidly evolved 'from exposition to consideration for implementation as a US government policy' so quickly that it 'outpaced the ability of scholarship to examine its underlying premises and evidence'.[60] Defence transformation pushed these ideas further and amplified expectations in ways that far exceeded available capabilities. Accordingly, an increasing number of 'transformation critics' voiced the varying problems in the unfulfilled promises and ambiguities of an open-ended process, suggesting that the concept became an empty phrase. The rationale for 'new way of thinking and a new way of fighting' justifying virtually every defence initiative or proposal, whether RMA related or not, signalled disorientation rather than a clear strategy.[61] Transformation sceptics also cautioned about the flawed logic in solving complex strategic challenges through technology, while discarding the adaptive capacity of potential enemies or rivals. In short, defence transformation turned into a misguided idea, propelled by the military's budgetary requirements and unrealistic capability sets rather than actual policy requirements.[62]

Most importantly, however, defence transformation was challenged by the operational requirements and experiences in wars in Iraq and Afghanistan, which imposed increasing costs in the protracted counterinsurgency campaigns. These two conflicts shifted the resources, priorities and focus of the US military away from pursuing broad transformational ideas and in favour of fighting low-tech insurgents capable of inflicting significant damage. In other words, the US military became entrenched in the political, socio-economic challenges of a non-linear conflict that 'it was not prepared for, nor had it anticipated'.[63] As Robert Gates succeeded Donald Rumsfeld as Secretary of Defence in 2006, the transformation agenda, as well as the overall narrative, changed its tone from the ambitious paradigm shift to a 'shift in emphasis'.[64] This lexical turn also signalled the mounting costs of defence transformation

---

[58]*Military Innovation and Small States: Creating a Reverse Asymmetry*, 50.
[59]Bitzinger, *Transforming the US Military: Implications for the Asia-Pacific*, 12.
[60]Stephen Biddle, *The RMA and the Evidence: Assessing Theories of Future Warfare* (Alexandria, VA: Institute for Defence Analyses 1996).
[61]Lawrence Freedman, *The Transformation of Strategic Affairs* (London: International Institute of Strategic Studies 2006).
[62]Kevin Reynolds, *Defence Transformation: To What? For What?* (Carlisle: Strategic Studies Institute 2006).
[63]Shimko, *The Iraq Wars and America's Military Revolution*, 203.
[64]O'Rourke, 'Defence Transformation: Background and Oversight Issues for Congress', 7.

programmes, such as the Future Combat System (FSC) concept, which envisioned distributed and networked forces being able to coordinate and mass fires from dispersed positions on the battlefield. However, the technology was simply not developed at that time, and the funding was not available due to the ongoing Global War on Terror.[65] Taken together, as Peter Dombrowski and Andrew Ross argued, the institutionalisation and actual substance behind defence transformation visions, plans, and programs within the US military establishment reflected more of an *evolutionary change* or 'modernisation plus,' rather than a discontinuous, disruptive innovation.[66]

It is important to note, however, that the transformation narrative during this period diffused beyond the US military, and it had a profound impact on military modernisation trajectories elsewhere. Studies of RMA adoption and adaptation paths outside the US began to emerge in the late 2000s in the European (NATO) states, China, Russia, Israel, Australia, and other countries. At the same time, RMA studies focused on its impact on the global defence industry.[67] However, actual RMA-oriented adaptations, such as the Systemic Operational Design in the Israel Defence Forces in the mid-2000s, were arguably not fully implemented into the use of force, i.e. in the Second Lebanon War.[68] Many European/NATO countries also faced a range of organisational, technological, and (especially) budgetary challenges when it came to implementing network-enabled capabilities by connecting post-Cold War armament platforms.[69] Consequently, the failures to implement the IT-RMA by 2010 has diminished its importance in the military concepts development and defence planning processes, particularly in the US/NATO militaries.

Sixth AI-RMA wave: Automated warfare and strategic competition

From the early 2010s, however, the narrative of an impending 'disruptive' military-technological paradigm shift in warfare began a subtle revival, propelled by three key drivers: (1) the accelerating strategic competition for political, economic, and military-technological supremacy between world's major powers – the US, China, and to a lesser degree Russia; (2) the changing dynamics of military-technological innovation brought by the convergence of varying science and technology areas such as synthetic biology and artificial intelligence, human-machine learning and cognitive manipulation, and

---

[65] Anthony Cordesman and Paul Fredericksen, *Is Defence Transformation Affordable? Cost Escalation of Major Weapons Programs* (Washington DC: Center for Strategic and International Studies 2006).
[66] Dombrowski and Ross, 'The Revolution in Military Affairs: Transformation and the Defence Industry', 23.
[67] Richard Bitzinger, 'The Revolution in Military Affairs and the Global Defence Industry: Reactions and Interactions', *Security Challenges* 4/4 (2008), 1–12.
[68] Avi Kober, 'The Israel Defence Forces in the Second Lebanon War: Why the Poor Performance?', *Journal of Strategic Studies* 31/1 (2008), 3–40.
[69] Juha Kai Mattila, 'Engaging a Moving Organisation – Modelling a Military Enterprise with Architecture Tools', PhD Dissertation, Aalto University School of Science and Technology (2020).

between cyber and artificial intelligence; and (3) the resulting diffusion of dual-use emerging technologies, particularly autonomous and AI-enabled systems in warfare – not only in the arsenals of great powers but also in select advanced small states and middle powers. The confluence of these drivers has signalled the emergence of a new, unique AI-enabled RMA wave, i.e., the AI-RMA.

Contrary to previous IT-RMA waves, which, admittedly, utilised *some* dual-use technologies in the development of major weapons platforms and systems, the current AI-RMA wave differs in the magnitude and impact of the commercial-technological innovation as the source of military innovation.[70] In particular, the AI-RMA wave is evident in the varying 'techno-nationalist' approaches, embedded in the strategic competition between the US and China, which is conditioned by economic interdependencies as well as strategic challenges simultaneously.[71] For example, the quest for disruptive technologies found as AI systems clearly underpins China's strategy of 'military-civil fusion', which views technological innovation as the central element in generating economic competitiveness, political legitimacy, military power, and international influence. This strategy has progressively evolved over the past four decades, from Chinese defence companies engaging in civilian production to overcome resource limitations in the 1980s and 1990s, to creating and leveraging synergies between defence-commercial developments and supply chains in the 2010s and 2020s.[72]

In doing so, China's concepts of 'indigenous innovation' and 'independent innovation' have aimed to identify, absorb, digest, and reinvent technology transfers from global commercial high-technology R&D sectors to the military.[73] The strategy has accelerated the People's Liberation Army (PLA) dual-track military modernisation trajectory. On the one hand, the PLA has invested in continuous upgrades of existing or legacy weapons platforms, while simultaneously experimenting with novel technologies in the so-called domains of 'new military rivalry': outer space, near-space, cyberspace and underwater.[74] The prioritisation of these domains has led

---

[70] Michael Raska, 'Strategic Competition for Emerging Military Technologies: Comparative Paths and Patterns,' *PRISM* 8/3 (2020), 64–81.

[71] Office of the Secretary of Defence, The National Defence Strategy 2018 (Washington DC:, Department of Defence 2018); Office of the President of the US, The National Security Strategy 2017 (Washington DC: The White House 2017); Thomas Mahnken, 'A Framework for Examining Long-Term Strategic Competition Between Major Powers', *SITC Research Brief*, January 2017; Aaron L. Friedberg, 'Competing with China', *Survival* 60/3 (2018), 7–64.

[72] Mel Gurtov, 'Swords into Market Shares: China's Conversion of Military Industry to Civilian Production', *The China Quarterly* 134 (1993), 213–241; Elsa Kania, 'Innovation in the new Era of Chinese Military Power', *The Diplomat*, 25 July 2019.

[73] Tai Ming Cheung, 'Innovation in China's Defence Technology Base: Foreign Technology and Military Capabilities', *Journal of Strategic Studies* 39/5–6 (2016), 728–761.

[74] Michael Raska and Richard Bitzinger, 'Strategic Contours of China's Arms Transfers', *Strategic Studies Quarterly* 14/1 (2020), 92.

the PLA to field novel military technologies such as new ballistic missiles, hypersonic weapons, unmanned underwater drones, and many other systems and platforms designed to negate strategic and operational advantages of the US military presence in East Asia, namely 'power projection, forward presence, freedom of action'.[75] Indeed, since the late 1990s, the PLA has shifted its strategic direction and operational requirements away from a continental/territorial defence and toward projecting power in China's maritime periphery or the 'three seas' – i.e., the Yellow, East China, and South China Seas – under the narrative of protecting 'China's national sovereignty, security, and territorial integrity'.[76] Since 2016, the PLA also embarked on a series of major organisational reforms, aimed to complement PLA's ongoing military-technological transformation toward 'Intelligentised' form of warfare.[77]

In this context, the key questions in the AI-RMA debate is, firstly, whether China will be able to attain technological capabilities to project military power in the Indo-Pacific region sufficient to disrupt or degrade US forward presence, and, secondly, how the United States and its key allies, in unison with other regional powers, will respond to such changes.[78] Moreover, can the US military sustain a long-term deterrence, project power in contested areas, and mitigate escalatory risks amid growing anti-access/area denial (A2/AD) challenges, and, if so, how?[79]

While PLA analysts in the US have closely followed developments in the Chinese strategic thought and military-technological advances during the 1990s, the realisation that the US could be facing a peer competitor became apparent to its political and military leadership only after two decades of fighting counterinsurgency campaigns in Iraq and Afghanistan. In July 2009, for example, then-Secretary of Defence Robert Gates instructed military planners to explore options to 'preserve the US ability to project power and maintain freedom of action in the global commons'.[80] One of the initial attempts was the development of the Air-Sea Battle (ASB) concept,

---

[75]Taylor Fravel, 'China's New Military Strategy: Winning Informationized Local Wars,' *China Brief*, 15/13, 2 July 2015.
[76]Andrew Erickson, 'China's Modernization of its Naval and Air Power Capabilities', in Ashley Tellis and Travis Tanner (eds.) *Strategic Asia 2012–13: China's Military Challenge* (Washington DC: The National Bureau of Asian Research 2012), 60–125; Michael Chase, Jeffrey Engstrom, Tai Ming Cheung, Kristen Gunness, Scott Warren Harold, Susan Puska and Samuel Berkowitz, *China's Incomplete Military Transformation: Assessing the Weaknesses of the People's Liberation Army* (Santa Monica, CA: RAND Corporation 2015), 26.
[77]Phillip C. Saunders and Joel Wuthnow, 'China's Goldwater-Nichols? Assessing PLA Organizational Reforms', *Joint Forces Quarterly* 82, July 2016; Michael Dahm, 'Chinese Debates on the Military Utility of Artificial Intelligence', *War on the Rocks*, 5 June 2020.
[78]Chung Min Lee, *Fault Lines in a Rising Asia* (Washington DC: Carnegie Endowment for International Peace 2016), 190.
[79]Aaron Friedberg, *Beyond Air-Sea Battle: The Debate over US Military Strategy in Asia* (London: International Institute for Strategic Studies 2014), 74.
[80]Michael E. Hutchens (et.al.), 'Joint Concept for Access and Maneuver in the Global Commons: A New Joint Operational Concept', *Joint Forces Quarterly* 84, 27 January 2017.

coordinated by the joint Air-Sea Battle Office (ASBO) in the US Department of Defence.[81] The ASB concept, however, became highly controversial as it envisioned air and naval strikes on early warning and missile bases located in mainland China (designated 'Networked, Integrated Attacks-in-Depth'), which led to debates on its escalatory risks and potential outcomes for US allies.[82] In February 2015, the DOD then renamed ASB into the 'Joint Concept for Access and Manoeuvre in the Global Commons' (JAM-GC). It later shifted its development into varying inter-service 'Multi-Domain Operations' concepts – joint operations across the air, land, sea, cyber, and space domains, and the electromagnetic spectrum.[83]

However, the operational-tactical ASB debate initiated a much broader search for novel strategies, organisational and operational concepts that would exploit emerging technologies such as AI-enabled systems and autonomous weapons and ensure strategic advantages in future warfare. In 2014, for example, the US DOD launched the *Defence Innovation Initiative* (DII) as a comprehensive strategy to accelerate the absorption of emerging breakthrough technologies, primarily from the commercial sector into the military.[84] The DII called for the need to 'identify a third offset strategy that puts the competitive advantage firmly in the hands of American power projection over the coming decades.'[85] The Third Offset (3O) strategy, developed under former Deputy Secretary of Defence Robert Work, then became one of the central constructs for integrating the varying 4IR technologies into the US armed forces.[86] Its analogy followed the First and Second Offset strategies during the Cold War, designed to counter Soviet quantitative military superiority – the first through the development of nuclear weapons and delivery means, and the second through qualitative leaps in conventional military capabilities.[87] The Third Offset, in turn, aimed at extending the margin of US military-technological superiority in a strategic competition with China and Russia.

At present, the US military is experimenting with select command and control and weapons systems with varying levels of autonomous functions, while rethinking ways and means to exploit commercially driven innovation.

---

[81]Norton Schwartz, 'Remarks to the National Defence University Distinguished Lecture Program,' 15 December 2010.
[82]Friedberg, *Beyond Air-Sea Battle: The Debate over US Military Strategy in Asia*, 80–90.
[83]Tom Greenwood and Pat Savage, 'In Search of a 21st-Century Joint Warfighting Concept', *War on the Rocks Commentary*, 12 September 2019.
[84]Timothy Walton, 'Security the Third Offset Strategy – Priorities for the Next Secretary of Defence', *Joint Forces Quarterly* 82/3 (2016), 6–15.
[85]Chuck Hagel, 'Memorandum – The Defence Innovation Initiative', Office of the Secretary of Defence, 15 November 2014.
[86]Cheryl Pellerin, 'Deputy Secretary Discusses Third Offset, First Organisational Construct,' *Department of Defence News*, 21 September 2016, http://www.defence.gov/News/Article/Article/951689.
[87]Robert Martinage, *Toward a New Offset Strategy: Exploiting US Long-Term Advantages to Restore US Global Power Projection Capability* (Washington DC: Center for Strategic and Budgetary Assessments 2014).

Notwithstanding the classified nature of many of these programmes, select priority research and development areas have been noted in published official budgetary statements, including the development of AI-systems and autonomous weapons in various human-machine type collaborations – i.e. AI-enabled early warning systems and command and control networks, space and electronic warfare systems, cyber capabilities, lethal autonomous weapons systems, and others.[88] These technologies have also gradually permeated into future warfare experimentation and capability development programmes, including DARPA's Mosaic Warfare, Army Futures Command, Air Force Warfighting Integration Capability, Office of Naval Research, and Joint Artificial Intelligence Centre.[89]

At the same time, the diffusion of AI-enabled RMA technologies, including additive manufacturing (3D printing), nanotechnology, space and space-like capabilities, artificial intelligence, and drones, are not confined solely to the great powers.[90] The AI-RMA wave is also reflected in defence innovation trajectories of select advanced small states and middle powers, such as Australia, France, United Kingdom, Singapore, Israel, South Korea and others.[91] These states seek to develop niche 4IR technologies to advance not only their defence capabilities but also economic competitiveness, political influence and status in the international arena.[92] Singapore is a prime example of a small state actively pursuing the research and development of AI-enabled systems in defence through strategic collaborations with leading research entities on global defence industries, as well as local small and medium enterprises. Facing a widening spectrum of threats coupled with increasing demographic and manpower limitations, the 'next-generation Singapore Armed Forces (SAF)' transformation efforts envision leveraging 4IR technologies in nearly all aspects of military operations and planning. Some of the ongoing programmes include using data analytics for servicing the Republic of Singapore Air Force's fleet of fighter jets, battlefield instrumentation analytics systems for the Army, autonomous underwater vehicles for mine detection in shallow waters, development of unmanned watchtowers for

---

[88]Cheryl Pellerin, 'Work: Human-Machine Teaming Represents Defence Technology Future,' *Department of Defence News*, 8 November 2015, http://www.defence.gov/News/Article/Article/628154/work-human-machine-teaming-represents-defence-technology-future.

[89]Benjamin Jensen and John Paschkewitz, 'Mosaic Warfare: Small and Scalable are Beautiful', *War on the Rocks*, 23 December 2019. Sydney J. Freedberg Jr., 'Inside Army Futures Command: CFT Chiefs Take Charge,' *Breaking Defence*, 14 August 2018; Arnold W. Bunch Jr and Jerry Harris Jr, 'Presentation to the House Armed Services Committee: Air Force, Force Structure and Modernization Programs,' Department of the Air Force, 12 April 2018, 14.

[90]T.X. Hammes, 'Technologies Converge and Power Diffuses: The Evolution of Small, Smart, and Cheap Weapons', *CATO Institute Policy Analysis* 786, 27 January 2016.

[91]Andreas Krieg and Jean-Marc Rickli, *Surrogate Warfare: The Transformation of War in the Twenty-First Century* (Washington DC: Georgetown University Press 2019), 85–116.

[92]Itai Barsade and Michael Horowitz, 'Artificial Intelligence Beyond the Superpowers,' *Bulletin of the Atomic Scientists*, 16 August 2018.

naval and coastal surveillance, and many other programmes.[93] How militaries such as the SAF interact with commercial science and technology ecosystems, while adopting and adapting novel technologies in their defence innovation trajectories, has become another critical feature in the ongoing AI-RMA wave.

Conclusion

From the Military-Technical Revolution conceptions by Soviet strategic theorists in the 1980s, IT-RMA narratives and debates have evolved over five consecutive waves, primarily in the strategic and operational context of the US military modernisation trajectory. These initial five waves focused mainly on integrating digital technologies into existing conventional weapon systems and organisational force structures to achieve an 'order of magnitude' change in military effectiveness. While many military innovations during this era, such as concepts of Network-Centric Warfare, have matured, the ambitious narratives of impending 'transformation' have nearly always surpassed available technological, organisational, and budgetary capabilities. In contrast, the current (sixth) AI-driven RMA wave is progressing along multiple lines simultaneously, albeit in varying paths and patterns: in the strategic competition between China, Russia and the US, which abbreviates the margins of US military-technological superiority; in the 4IR technological breakthroughs that occur primarily in the commercial arena and that inspire militaries to leverage their military potential; and along the niche defence innovation trajectories of advanced small states and middle powers that see opportunities to offset their strategic challenges and constraints through novel technologies. The AI-RMA wave also differs in the magnitude and impact of human-machine interactions in warfare, in which algorithms increasingly shape human decision-making, and future combat is envisioned in the use of AI-enabled autonomous weapons systems.

Consequently, the AI-RMA wave does not reflect a mere continuation of *'modernisation-plus'* wave; it signifies a real disruptive shift in warfare – in the framework of new or different instruments (technology), practices (doctrines and operational concepts), to the formation of new organisational force structures.[94] While the AI-RMA wave may affect select countries and regions disproportionately, its technological reach coupled with an ongoing strategic competition is sufficiently broad to require a rethinking of weapons development and R&D, defence budgetary processes, defence contractors as well as tip of the spear of operational and warfighting domains and

---

[93]Michael Raska, 'Singapore's Next-Frontier Defence Innovations', *The Straits Times*, 27 June 2018.
[94]Tai Ming Cheung, Thomas Mahnken, Andrew Ross, 'Frameworks for Analysing Chinese Defence and Military Innovation,' *SITC Policy Brief* 27 (2011), 1–4.

concepts, alliances and strategic partnerships. In doing so, the AI-RMA reflects novel strategic and operational challenges, particularly in the deployment of automated and autonomous systems and human-machine teaming, that propel new questions and debates ranging from future military budget priorities to issues of AI governance and ethics. Ultimately, the ramifications of the AI-RMA marks new opportunities and risks for international cooperation by exposing limitations of established paradigms in the ways and means of using force.

Acknowledgment

The author would like to thank Richard Bitzinger, Ian Bowers, Chung Min Lee, Zoe Stanley-Lockman, Katarzyna Zysk, and anonymous reviewers for their insightful comments and advice on this article, and for making this Special Issue special.

Disclosure statement

The author reported no potential conflict of interest.

ORCID

Michael Raska http://orcid.org/0000-0002-8283-2438

Bibliography

Adams, Thomas, *The Army After Next: The First Postindustrial Army* (Westport, CT: Praeger 2006).
Adamsky, Dima, 'Through the Looking Glass: The Soviet Military-Technical Revolution and the American Revolution in Military Affairs', *Journal of Strategic Studies* 31/2 (2008), 257–94.

Adamsky, Dima, *The Culture of Military Innovation: The Impact of Cultural Factors on the Revolution in Military Affairs in Russia, the US, and Israel* (Palo Alto, CA: Stanford University Press 2010).
Allen, Greg and Taniel Chan, 'Artificial Intelligence and National Security', *Belfer Center for Science and International Affairs*, 6 Jul. 2017.
Barsade, Itai and Michael Horowitz, 'Artificial Intelligence beyond the Superpowers', *Bulletin of the Atomic Scientists*, 16 Aug. 2018.
Biddle, Stephen, *The RMA and the Evidence: Assessing Theories of Future Warfare* (Alexandria, VA: Institute for Defence Analyses 1996).
Bitzinger, Richard, *Transforming the US Military: Implications for the Asia-Pacific* (Barton: Australian Strategic Policy Institute 2006).
Bitzinger, Richard, 'The Revolution in Military Affairs and the Global Defence Industry: Reactions and Interactions', *Security Challenges* 4/4 (2008), 1–12.
Blaker, James, *Understanding the Revolution in Military Affairs: A Guide to America's 21st Century Defence* (Washington DC: Progressive Policy Institute 1997).
Boot, Max, *War Made New Technology: Warfare and the Course of History, 1500 to Today* (New York: Gotham Books 2006).
Brown, John Sloan, *Kevlar Legions: The Transformation of the United States Army 1989–2005* (Washington DC: United States Army, Center of Military History 2012).
Bunch, Arnold W., Jr. and Jerry Harris Jr., 'Presentation to the House Armed Services Committee: Air Force, Force Structure and Modernization Programs', Department of the Air Force, 12 Apr. 2018.
Burnett, Mark et. al., 'Advanced Materials and Manufacturing - Implications for Defence to 2040', *Defence Science and Technology Group Report*, Australia Department of Defence, 2018. https://www.dst.defence.gov.au/sites/default/files/publications/documents/DST-Group-GD-1022.pdf
Chase, Michael, Jeffrey Engstrom, Tai Ming Cheung, Kristen Gunness, Scott Warren Harold, Susan Puska, and Samuel Berkowitz, *China's Incomplete Military Transformation: Assessing the Weaknesses of the People's Liberation Army* (Santa Monica, CA: RAND Corporation 2015).
Cheung, Tai Ming, 'Introduction', in Tai Ming Cheung (ed.), *Forging China's Military Might: A New Framework for Assessing Innovation* (Baltimore, MD: Johns Hopkins University Press 2014), 1–15.
Cheung, Tai Ming, 'Innovation in China's Defence Technology Base: Foreign Technology and Military Capabilities', *Journal of Strategic Studies* 39/5–6 (2016), 728–61.
Cheung, Tai Ming, Thomas Mahnken, and Andrew Ross, 'Frameworks for Analysing Chinese Defence and Military Innovation', *SITC Policy Brief* 27 (2011), 1–4.
Cooper, Jeffrey, 'Another View of the Revolution in Military Affairs', in John Arquilla and David Ronfeldt (eds.), *Athena's Camp: Preparing for Conflict in the Information Age* (Santa Monica, CA: RAND 1994), 99–140.
Cordesman, Anthony and Paul Fredericksen, *Is Defence Transformation Affordable? Cost Escalation of Major Weapons Programs* (Washington DC: Center for Strategic and International Studies 2006).
Cummings, M. L., 'Artificial Intelligence and the Future of Warfare', *Chatham House Research Paper*, 26 Jan. 2017.
Dahm, Michael, 'Chinese Debates on the Military Utility of Artificial Intelligence', *War on the Rocks*, 5 Jun. 2020.
DARPA, 'Strategic Technology Office Outlines Vision for Mosaic Warfare', *DARPA News*, 4 Aug 2017. https://www.darpa.mil/news-events/2017-08-04.

Davis, Zachary, 'Artificial Intelligence on the Battlefield', *PRISM* 8/2 (2019), 114–31.
Department of the Army HQ, *The Soviet Army: Operations and Tactics - Field Manual 100-2-1* (Washington DC: Department of Defence 1984).
Doder, Dusko, 'Ousted Soviet Chief of Staff Returns to Scene as Author', *The Washington Post*, 10 Jun. 1985.
Dombrowski, Peter and Andrew Ross, 'The Revolution in Military Affairs: Transformation and the Defence Industry', *Security Challenges* 4/4 (2008), 13–38.
Donnelly, William, *Transforming an Army at War: Designing the Modular Force 1991–2005* (Washington DC: Center for Military History 2007).
Erickson, Andrew, 'China's Modernisation of Its Naval and Air Power Capabilities', in Ashley Tellis and Travis Tanner (eds.), *Strategic Asia 2012–13: China's Military Challenge* (Washington DC: The National Bureau of Asian Research 2012), 60–125.
Evans, Paul, 'Techno-Nationalism in China-US Relations: Implications for Universities', *EAI Background Brief* 1527, 30 Apr. 2020.
Fravel, Taylor, 'China's New Military Strategy: Winning Informationized Local Wars,' *China Brief*, 15/13, 2 Jul. 2015.
Freedberg, Sydney, Jr., 'Inside Army Futures Command: CFT Chiefs Take Charge', *Breaking Defence*, 14, Aug. 2018.
Freedman, Lawrence, *The Transformation of Strategic Affairs* (London: International Institute of Strategic Studies 2006).
Freitas, Sara and Hugo Silva, 'José Almeida and Eduardo Silva, 'Hyperspectral Imaging for Real-Time Unmanned Aerial Vehicle Maritime Target Detection'', *Journal of Intelligent and Robotic Systems* 90 (2018), 551–70.
Friedberg, Aaron, *Beyond Air-Sea Battle: The Debate over US Military Strategy in Asia* (London: International Institute for Strategic Studies 2014).
Friedberg, Aaron L., 'Competing with China', *Survival* 60/3 (2018), 7–64.
Friedman, George and Meredith Friedman, *The Future of War: Power, Technology, and American Dominance in the 21st Century* (New York: Crown 1996).
Gray, Colin, *Strategy and History: Essays on Theory and Practice* (London: Routledge 2006).
Greenwood, Tom and Pat Savage, 'In Search of a 21st-Century Joint Warfighting Concept', *War on the Rocks Commentary*, 12 Sept. 2019.
Gurtov, Mel, 'Swords into Market Shares: China's Conversion of Military Industry to Civilian Production', *The China Quarterly* 134 (1993), 213–41.
Hagel, Chuck, 'Memorandum - The Defence Innovation Initiative', Office of the Secretary of Defence, 15 Nov. 2014.
Hammes, T.X., 'Technologies Converge and Power Diffuses: The Evolution of Small, Smart, and Cheap Weapons', *CATO Institute Policy Analysis* 786, 27 Jan. 2016.
Horowitz, Michael, 'The Promise and Peril of Military Applications of Artificial Intelligence', *Bulletin of the Atomic Scientists*, 23 Apr. 2018.
Hutchens, Michael E. (et.al.), 'Joint Concept for Access and Maneuver in the Global Commons: A New Joint Operational Concept', *Joint Forces Quarterly* 84, 27 Jan. 2017.
International Institute for Strategic Studies, 'Quantum Computing and Defence', in IISS, *The Military Balance 2019* (London: Routledge 2019), 18–20.
James, Andrew, 'Emerging Technologies and Military Capability', in Richard Bitzinger (ed.), *Emerging Critical Technologies and Security in the Asia-Pacific* (London: Palgrave Macmillan 2016), 6–21.
Jensen, Benjamin and John Paschkewitz, 'Mosaic Warfare: Small and Scalable are Beautiful', *War on the Rocks*, 23 Dec. 2019.
Kania, Elsa, 'Innovation in the New Era of Chinese Military Power', *The Diplomat*, 25, 2019.

Kipp, Jacob, 'The Russian Military and the Revolution in Military Affairs: A Case of the Oracle of Delphi or Cassandra?', *US Foreign Military Studies Office Paper*. 1995.

Kober, Avi, 'The Israel Defence Forces in the Second Lebanon War: Why the Poor Performance?', *Journal of Strategic Studies* 31/1 (2008), 3–40.

Krepinevich, Andrew, *The Military-Technical Revolution: A Preliminary Assessment* (Washington DC: Office of Net Assessment 1992).

Krepinevich, Andrew, 'Defence Transformation - Testimony for the US Senate Committee on Armed Services', 9 Apr. 2002.

Krieg, Andreas and Jean-Marc Rickli, *Surrogate Warfare: The Transformation of War in the Twenty-First Century* (Washington DC: Georgetown University Press 2019).

Lee, Chung Min, *Fault Lines in a Rising Asia* (Washington DC: Carnegie Endowment for International Peace 2016).

Mahnken, Thomas, 'A Framework for Examining Long-Term Strategic Competition between Major Powers', *SITC Research Brief*, Jan. 2017.

Mahnken, Thomas and James Fitzsimonds, 'Tread-Heads or Technophiles Army Officer Attitudes toward Transformation', *Parameters* 34/2 (2004), 57–72.

Martinage, Robert, *Toward a New Offset Strategy: Exploiting US Long-Term Advantages to Restore US Global Power Projection Capability* (Washington DC: Center for Strategic and Budgetary Assessments 2014).

Mattila, Juha Kai, 'Engaging a Moving Organisation - Modelling a Military Enterprise with Architecture Tools', PhD Dissertation, Aalto University School of Science and Technology. 2020.

Mattis, James, 'USJFCOM Commander's Guidance for Effects-Based Operations', *Joint Forces Quarterly* 51 (2006), 106.

Metz, Steven, 'America's Defence Transformation: A Conceptual and Political History', *Defence Studies* 6/1 (2006), 1–25.

Metz, Steven and James Kievit, *Strategy and the Revolution in Military Affairs: From Theory to Policy* (Carlisle: Strategic Studies Institute 1995).

Mitchell, Paul, *Network Centric Warfare and Coalition Operations: The New Military Operating System* (London: Routledge 2009).

Murray, Williamson, 'Thinking about Revolutions in Military Affairs', *Joint Forces Quarterly* 16 (Summer 1997), 103–11.

Murray, Williamson and MacGregor Knox, 'Thinking about Revolutions in Warfare', in MacGregor Knox and Williamson Murray (eds.), *The Dynamics of Military Revolution, 1300–2050* (Cambridge: Cambridge University Press 2001), 1–15.

National Defence Panel, *Transforming Defence: National Security in the 21st Century* (Washington DC: US Department of Defence 1997).

Naveh, Shimon, *In Pursuit of Military Excellence: The Evolution of Operational Theory* (London: Frank Cass 1996).

O'Rourke, Ronald, 'Defence Transformation: Background and Oversight Issues for Congress', *CRS Report* for Congress 322238. 2007.

Office of Soviet Analysis, 'Trends and Developments in Warsaw Pact Theater Forces 1985–2000', *National Intelligence Estimate* No. 11-14. 1985.

Office of the Joint Chiefs of Staff, 'Joint Vision 2010', US Department of Defence, Jul. 1996.

Office of the Joint Chiefs of Staff, 'Joint Vision 2020: America's Military - Preparing for Tomorrow', US Department of Defence, Jun. 2000.

Office of the President of the US, *The National Security Strategy 2017* (Washington DC: The White House 2017).

Office of the Secretary of Air Force, 'The US Air Force Transformation Flight Plan,' US Air Force Future Concepts and Transformation Division, Nov. 2003.

Office of the Secretary of Defence, 'Transformation Planning Guidance', US Department of Defence, Apr. 2003.

Office of the Secretary of Defence, *The National Defence Strategy 2018* (Washington DC: Department of Defence 2018).

Office of the Secretary of Navy, 'Sea Power 21: Projecting Decisive Joint Capabilities', US Department of the Navy, Oct. 2002.

Ogarkov, Nikolai, *Istoriya Uchit Bditelnosti* (Moscow: Voenizdat 1985).

Owens, William, 'The Emerging US System-of-Systems', *Strategic Forum* 63 (1996), 1–6.

Parker, Geoffrey, 'Military Revolution 1560-1660–A Myth?', *Journal of Modern History* 48/2 (1976), 196–214.

Pellerin, Cheryl, 'Work: Human-Machine Teaming Represents Defence Technology Future', *Department of Defence News*, 8 Nov. 2015. http://www.defence.gov/News/Article/Article/628154/work-human-machine-teaming-represents-defence-technology-future

Pellerin, Cheryl, 'Deputy Secretary Discusses Third Offset, First Organisational Construct', *Department of Defence News*, 21 Sept. 2016. http://www.defence.gov/News/Article/Article/951689

Petersen, Philip, 'The Soviet Conceptual Framework for the Application of Military Power', *Naval War College Review* 34/3 (1981), 15–25.

Petersen, Philip, 'The Modernisation of Soviet Armed Forces', *NATO's 16 Nations* 31/4 (1984), 32–38.

Raska, Michael, *Military Innovation and Small States: Creating a Reverse Asymmetry* (London: Routledge 2016).

Raska, Michael, 'Singapore's Next-Frontier Defence Innovations', *The Straits Times*, 27 Jun. 2018.

Raska, Michael, 'Strategic Competition for Emerging Military Technologies: Comparative Paths and Patterns', *PRISM* 8/3 (2020), 64–81.

Raska, Michael and Richard Bitzinger, 'Strategic Contours of China's Arms Transfers', *Strategic Studies Quarterly* 14/1 (2020), 91–116.

Reynolds, Kevin, *Defence Transformation: To What? For What?* (Carlisle: Strategic Studies Institute 2006).

Saunders, Phillip C. and Joel Wuthnow, 'China's Goldwater-Nichols? Assessing PLA Organizational Reforms', *Joint Forces Quarterly* 82, Jul. 2016.

Scharre, Paul and Michael C. Horowitz, 'An Introduction to Autonomy in Weapon Systems', Center for a New American Security, 13 Feb. 2015.

Schwartz, Norton, 'Remarks to the National Defence University Distinguished Lecture Program', 15 Dec. 2010.

Shimko, Keith, *The Iraq Wars and America's Military Revolution* (Cambridge: Cambridge University Press 2010).

Vego, Milan, 'Effects-Bases Operations: A Critique', *Joint Forces Quarterly* 41/2 (2006), 51–57.

Walton, Timothy, 'Security the Third Offset Strategy - Priorities for the Next Secretary of Defence', *Joint Forces Quarterly* 82/3 (2016), 6–15.

Watts, Barry, 'What Is the Revolution in Military Affairs?', *Northrop Grumman Analysis Center* 351 (1995), 1–6.

Zenko, Micah, 'Millennium Challenge: The Real Story of a Corrupted Military Exercise and Its Legacy', *War on the Rocks Commentary*, 5 Nov. 2015.

From closed to open systems: How the US military services pursue innovation

Zoe Stanley-Lockman

ABSTRACT
The return to strategic competition affects the US military services differently, but all are contending with the challenge of renewing their military advantage against near-peer, technologically advanced competitors. Commercially driven innovation trends simultaneously challenge the way that the US military manages technology. This article traces the pursuits to institutionalise open innovation practices inside the services to incorporate emerging technologies into their envisaged competitive advantage. Rather than treating the US military as a monolithic entity, this article assesses how new service-level organisations differ in the ways and means they pursue innovation and seeks to explain why those differences persist.

Introduction

Historically, US military-technological innovation in the second half of the 20th century spun out of administrative policies supporting the assumption that the state is the foremost driver of innovation. This assumption manifests in a US military bureaucracy that is better organised to support the research, development, testing, and acquisition of major weapons systems over many years, rather than exploit emerging, ubiquitous technologies quickly and iteratively.[1] With the accelerated diffusion and convergence of emerging technologies today, the US military is trying to orient its technology management systems toward this latter exploitation. With its call to 'out-innovate' near-peer competitors, the 2018 National Defense Strategy (NDS) provides the strategic foundations for a new examination of US military-technological efforts, which each of the services

---

[1]Audrey Kurth Cronin, *Power to the People: How Open Technological Innovation is Arming Tomorrow's Terrorists* (Oxford: Oxford UP 2020), 23–25.

is transposing in unique ways.[2] In this context, this article sheds light on the specific ways in which the US military services are modifying their models of innovation by targeting bureaucratic and administrative changes. In doing so, it asks the question: why do the military services pursue 'open' innovation in different ways?

In particular, the article builds on Henry Chesbrough and Audrey Kurth Cronin's concepts of 'closed' versus 'open' innovation systems and shows how US military services have adapted their bureaucracies to absorb emerging technologies and commercially driven innovation processes from 2014 to mid-2020.[3] In a closed-innovation system, technology flows from state-centric organisations outward, while an open- innovation system requires the state to capitalise on a broader innovation ecosystem beyond its control.[4] To analyse the conditions-setting efforts inside the US military services, this article stipulates three criteria of open innovation: cultivating systematic relationships with non-traditional vendors, nurturing in-house creativity, and prizing iterative adaptation over inflexible acquisition.

These issues are important for two primary reasons. First, how the services manage technology is a relevant variable of military innovation because bureaucratic dynamics help determine how technologies are combined and absorbed. In both closed- and open-innovation systems, technology is an enabler, rather than an endpoint, of innovation. The introduction or novel recombination of products or processes, as Tai Ming Cheung offers as a definition of innovation, often incorporates technological inventions but does not rely on the technology itself to create a competitive advantage.[5] Given the diffusion of knowledge[6] and accelerated pace of technological advancements that characterise the present 'open technological revolution,'[7] novel recombinations depend on the bureaucratic metabolism to connect technology with mission needs and overarching strategic aims.

Second, open innovation blurs the barrier between research and operations,[8] which are traditionally treated as sequential processes in a closed model of innovation. The open-innovation criteria that this article establishes disintermediate end-users from developers in the course of

---

[2]*Office of the Secretary of Defense*, 'National Defense Strategy of the United States of America: Sharpening the American Military's Competitive Edge', January 2018, 5.
[3]Cronin, *Power to the People: How Open Technological Innovation is Arming Tomorrow's Terrorists*, 17–41.
[4]Ibid., 19.
[5]Tai Ming Cheung, 'Innovation in China's Defense Technology Base: Foreign Technology and Military Capabilities', *Journal of Strategic Studies* 39/5–6 (2016), 729.
[6]Henry Chesbrough, *Open Innovation: The New Imperative for Creating and Profiting from Technology* (Boston, MA: Harvard Business School Press 2003), 43, 51.
[7]Henry Chesbrough, *Open Innovation: The New Imperative for Creating and Profiting from Technology*, 21-62; Cronin, *Power to the People: How Open Technological Innovation is Arming Tomorrow's Terrorists*, 19–20.
[8]*US Department of Defense*, 'Summary of the 2018 Department of Defense Artificial Intelligence Strategy: Harnessing AI to Advance our Security and Prosperity', 12 February 2019, 9, https://media.defense.gov/2019/Feb/12/2002088963/-1/-1/1/SUMMARY-OF-DOD-AI-STRATEGY.PDF.

capability development and deployment. As such, organisations vested in open innovation may have ostensibly little to do with force design, but still be considered significant innovation agents. Importantly, differences in how the services connect resource allocation, organisational change, technology, and strategic aims will have implications for the success of this goal. In a strategic environment where out-innovating near-peer competitors in part means out-adapting them, organisations that treat administrative concerns on par with force design may be necessary to extend the margins of an advantage.

While this article focuses on adapting to open innovation, it does not mean to suggest that the two systems are mutually exclusive, or that militaries should stop relying on the high-end military technologies that closed innovation can generate. Select elements of closed innovation remain well-suited to develop advanced military technology lacking commercial equivalents. Regardless of the integration of commercially driven or 'spin-on' technology, purely military technologies with unique operational requirements, such as stealth, cannot be expected to benefit from market forces, as an open-innovation model implies.[9]

The core argument of this paper is reflected in the divergence in the conception and implementation of open innovation within the US services. In particular, with infrastructural investments and the establishment of new outfits focused on open innovation, the Air Force is seeking to embed digitalisation in its identity and open innovation in its future competitive advantage. While the Army has placed significant stock in the establishment of a new four-star command to connect strategy and technology, it is less clear that the organisational approach to modernisation dissolves the barriers between research and operations. Meanwhile, Navy investments in open innovation are far more sparse, as partially evinced in the continued science and technology (S&T) centralisation relative to the Army and Air Force. The Marine Corps case is treated differently, owing largely to its status as a small service under the auspices of the Department of the Navy. The Marine Corps' fledgeling open-innovation investments are almost always reliant upon relationships with other entities across the Department of Defense (DoD) and are consistent with their experimentation-forward approach to transformation.

The paper is structured as follows. The theoretical framework section expands on the differences between closed and open innovation, while providing brief contours on the placement of open innovation in relation to traditional schools of military-innovation thought. The criteria of open innovation are then applied to the cases of the US Air Force, Army, Navy, and Marine Corps. In conclusion, the article comments on the connections

---

[9]Andrea Gilli and Mauro Gilli, 'Why China Has Not Caught Up Yet: Military-Technological Superiority and the Limits of Imitation, Reverse Engineering, and Cyber Espionage', *International Security* 43/3 (Winter 2018/19), 159.

between their approaches to open innovation, establishing the relative weaknesses of each approach and their implications for the ability of the United States to achieve a competitive military advantage. It should be stated clearly that the aim of this article is not to provide a comprehensive overview of *all* efforts to absorb technology in operational concepts and organisational structures, given that the majority of these efforts remain dependent on policies of closed innovation. Rather, the value this article seeks to add is a new analysis of administrative and bureaucratic change that aims to reduce US vulnerabilities and facilitate technology absorption. Furthermore, while military-innovation literature traditionally focuses on changes in the military services, scholarship on innovation developments since the issuance of the 2014 third offset strategy has more often focused on efforts in the Office of the Secretary of Defense.[10] The approach here attempts to fill the gap between traditional scholarship on innovation in the services on the one hand, and recent analysis of innovation in the US armed forces as a more monolithic entity on the other. In doing so, this article seeks to provide the basis for future studies on how new open-innovation outfits interact amongst each other, and with the incumbent S&T enterprise at large.

Debating open and closed innovation models for the military

In order to assess open-innovation efforts of the services, this section contrasts the parameters of closed and open models of innovation. The criteria discussed here are largely inspired by software practices, which serve two aims in distinguishing closed versus open systems of innovation. First, command and control (C2), mission planning, and weapons systems are all becoming increasingly software-intensive, meaning an increasing portion of US military modernisation depends on military digitalisation. Software intensiveness can be measured both in the sophistication of the software itself, as well as the number of functions the software controls in operating high-end weapons systems. Andrea Gilli and Mauro Gilli have shown how software intensiveness grows along both these vectors, contrasting the 1,000 lines of code controlling eight per cent of operations in the F-4 *Phantom* fighter bomber in the 1950s to the millions of lines of code in the F-22 *Raptor* controlling 80% of operations in the 21st century.[11] Open-innovation acquisition and sustainment models need not supplant the closed model. Yet this extent of software intensification makes clear that that the nature of contemporary innovation in software-hardware integration cannot be treated in the same manner as previous hardware-centric

---

[10]Daniel Fiott, 'A Revolution Too Far? US Defence Innovation, Europe and NATO's Military-Technological Gap', *Journal of Strategic Studies* 40/3 (2017), 425–6; Satoru Mori, 'US Defense Innovation and Artificial Intelligence', *Asia-Pacific Review* 25/2 (2018), 16–44.

[11]Gilli and Gilli, 'Why China Has Not Caught Up Yet: Military-Technological Superiority and the Limits of Imitation, Reverse Engineering, and Cyber Espionage', 151.

innovation. Second, the prevailing software methodologies that the DoD is adopting today entail broader organisational and cultural change, meaning software is the gateway to a broader capability-development ecosystem that brings users closer to developers. As such, bureaucratic-management changes put in place to accommodate digital technologies can have positive second-order effects on analogue and hardware developments, though they are largely beyond the scope of this article.

Closed model of innovation

In a closed system of innovation, states are able to amass power because technology flows from state-centric organisations outward.[12] However, evidence of the state's narrowing influence on the pace and trajectory of innovation in recent decades no longer supports this assumption.[13] Maintaining an advantage in military adoption of dual-use technologies requires not just accessing the technologies themselves, but also adapting processes to be able to update them more quickly.

Derived from the assumptions of state-controlled access to technology, the closed system of innovation is set up to develop sophisticated technology from scratch, rather than recombine available technological enablers in new ways. In closed innovation, research and operations are sequential steps in what the software community refers to as 'waterfall' acquisition. Requirements definition, design, execution, testing, and release phases are carried out in strict order because the acquisition system is set up to use information from one phase to move onto the next one.[14] This strict order segregates development from production, sees testing as static, and delays feedback loops that respond to needs from military end-users. As software intensiveness increases overall, subjecting software development to these closed-innovation conditions constrains US military capability development to be determined by the slowest link.

The current closed-innovation system mandates years-long processes to set requirements for new military capabilities. Hardware included, it takes 10–15 years from writing a contract to undergoing initial production and

---

[12]Cronin, *Power to the People: How Open Technological Innovation is Arming Tomorrow's Terrorists*, 19.

[13]Many of these policies stem from different periods of military innovation, each shaped by unique concepts, processes, and debates. The point that this article attempts to make is that the bureaucracy now has to deal with the culmination of all of them, as it is easier to add new policies and regulations, than it is to remove existing ones. Elsewhere in this special issue, Michael Raska builds on the work of Colin Gray's 'waves' of the Revolution in Military Affairs, which readers may refer to for a better understanding of the factors that shaped military innovation-relevant policies in these previous waves. See: Michael Raska, 'The sixth RMA wave: Disruption in Military Affairs?' *Journal of Strategic Studies* (2020), 1-24.

[14]Shelby S. Oakley, 'Defense Acquisitions Annual Assessment: Drive to Deliver Capabilities Faster Increases Importance of Program Knowledge and Consistent Data for Oversight', *Government Accountability Office*, June 2020, 18, https://www.gao.gov/assets/710/707359.pdf.

fielding.[15] A more recent figure from the US Army places average development time as even higher – between 17–25 years.[16] Indeed, for advanced weapons systems today, the tension between software complexity and outdated software management is responsible for most delays.[17] Consequentially, government-developed technologies could already be obsolete by the time they are fielded.[18]

The closed-innovation system that has bred the commercial-military gap is mired in ossified policies governing workforce, cultural, and acquisition issues. For example, in 2017, Senator John McCain decried the rigidity of the 1980 Defense Officer Personnel Management Act as one of the main obstacles to hiring and retention,[19] which continues to hurt the talent pipeline for increasingly important competencies, such as programming and hacking.[20] DoD purchasing power has also decreased as technological innovation becomes more diffused. For instance, while the DoD purchased more than half of global semiconductors in the 1980s, its share decreased to 0.5% as of 2017.[21] Likewise, the Defense Innovation Board, an advisory board to the DoD, recently reaffirmed that the very same military software development practices initially recommended in 1987 remain equally valid today, even decades after being overlooked.[22]

For digital transformation, this system generates narrow stovepipes, like postponed security reviews to the end of the development or legal obstacles to using testing data in operations. By vertically integrating research and development into programmes, closed innovation is set up to perfect exquisite technologies, rather than align requirements with user needs.[23] With incentives geared toward maturing technology, they fall victim to the 'valley of death' prior to being fielded and used

---

[15] Jacques Gansler, *Democracy's Arsenal: Creating a Twenty-First Century Defense Industry* (Cambridge, MA: MIT UP 2011), 122–125.

[16] *Army Futures Command*, 'Command Brief Creating a New Culture of Innovation', Command Brief, 14 March 2019, https://www.slideshare.net/TheNationalGuardBure/army-futures-command.

[17] Gilli and Gilli, 'Why China Has Not Caught Up Yet Military-Technological Superiority and the Limits of Imitation, Reverse Engineering, and Cyber Espionage', 151.

[18] Noah M. Spataro, 'FY2018 NIAC Consolidated Report: Lean Startup Approach to Capability Development: Evolving Small Batch Innovation for Dual-use Technologies', *Naval Innovation Advisory Council*, 1 August 2018, 3.

[19] John McCain, 'Opening Statement by SASC Chairman John McCain at Hearing on DoD Nominations', Office of Senator John McCain, 14 November 2017, https://www.mccain.senate.gov/public/index.cfm/floor-statements?ID=05DCC73A-F9F2-44E8-A75F-236003222AF2.

[20] Patrick Bell and Jan Kallberg, 'The Death of the Cyber Generalist', *United States Army War College War Room*, 8 June 2018, https://warroom.armywarcollege.edu/articles/death-of-cyber-generalist/.

[21] Eric Schmidt, Robert Work, 'First Quarter Recommendations', *National Security Commission on Artificial Intelligence* (March 2020), 59.

[22] J. Michael McQuade et al., 'Software is Never Done: Refactoring the Acquisition Code for Competitive Advantage', *Defense Innovation Board*, 3 May 2019, https://media.defense.gov/2019/May/01/2002126690/-1/-1/0/SWAP%20EXECUTIVE%20SUMMARY.PDF.

[23] Thomas W. Haduch, 'Maintaining the U.S. Army Research, Development and Engineering Command Prototype Integration Facilities', *Defense Acquisition UP*, May 2014, 7, https://www.dau.edu/training/career-development/sscf/Documents/T.%20HaduchSSCF2014SRPOPSECFINAL.pdf.

adaptively in relation to changing mission needs.[24] Programme budgeting also means that infrastructure investments are duplicated across C2 and weapons systems. For software, this means re-inventing the wheel to create bespoke platforms inside each weapons programme.[25] This not only prevents the services from benefitting from economies of scale, but also increases the lead time to develop mission software.

Open model of innovation

In an open model of innovation, advances in data-driven and other emerging technologies are the driving forces for changes to technology management. With hardware turning over in less than 36 months and software technology cycles lasting days or weeks, generations of digital technologies eclipse closed-innovation timelines.[26] Indeed, if measuring time with Moore's Law, computational power may quadruple in the amount of time it takes to define requirements for military systems, let alone begin acquisition. As such, an open-innovation ecosystem aims to make the business model of military-technology adoption more responsive to changing mission needs and accelerated technology lifecycles. This entails fighting against the deeply inculcated culture of inflexibility of military bureaucracies.[27] Indeed, the track record for systematising military adaptation reveals a delicate balance between flouting bureaucracy and succumbing to it. Failing to walk this tightrope means short-circuiting military adaptation before it can culminate in innovation. On one side of the tightrope, informal networks can be successful at tackling narrow issues, but ultimately fail to reach formal adoption. Nina Kollars' study on gun truck adaptation has shown how lessons from informal networks can be forgotten, despite their proven utility on the battlefield, if not institutionalised into military practices such as manuals or designs.[28] On the other side, the successes of informal networks can fail when overly formalised. Jon Lindsay's study on the organic development of the FalconView software suite, created for the F-16 in the 1990s, exemplifies precisely this issue.[29] FalconView inspired a formal acquisition

---

[24]Ibid.
[25]Eric Lofgren, The Last Frontier of Acquisition Reform: The Budget Process, *Conference Paper, Proceedings of the Seventeenth Annual Acquisition Research Symposium*, 13-14 May 2020 (Monterey, CA), 8. Naval Postgraduate School, 8.
[26]Spataro, 'FY2018 NIAC Consolidated Report: Lean Startup Approach to Capability Development: Evolving Small Batch Innovation for Dual-use Technologies', 32.
[27]While this article primarily deals with institutional change, cultural factors are closely related. Culture is more often cited as a constant that helps explain change (or resistance to it), rather than it is a malleable factor. See: Peter R. Mansoor and Williamson Murray (eds), *The Culture of Military Organizations* (Cambridge, UK: Cambridge UP 2019).
[28]Nina A. Kollars, 'War's Horizon: Soldier-Led Adaptation in Iraq and Vietnam', *Journal of Strategic Studies* 38/4 (2015), 529–53.
[29]Jon R. Lindsay, *Information Technology and Military Power* (Ithaca, NY: Cornell UP 2020), 109–35.

programme thanks to its popularity with an organically developed community of users. Yet, the instinct to programmatise FalconView's organic successes did not work because it retrofitted mission-planning software successes into the existing bureaucratic management, rather than adapting the bureaucracy to accommodate the user-driven successes.[30] In both the analogue and digital cases, informal innovation practices hit ceilings when not bureaucratised, regardless of their success in the course of operations.

Open innovation essentially entails adapting technology management to not fall into either of these traps. This means focussing on setting conditions to adapt faster than inflexible military bureaucracies currently allow. For software-intensive capability development, in particular, three criteria are relevant to the services' attempts to institutionalise open innovation: systematic efforts to broaden the national-security innovation ecosystem, infrastructural investments to capitalise on in-house creativity, and iterative software improvements to increase security and respond to mission needs.

First, to close the commercial-military gap, the DoD has sought to cultivate relations with a broader national-security innovation base that extends beyond the traditional defence industry. Efforts to spin commercial and dual-use technology into the US military date back to the 1990s,[31] but recent forays evince a more systematic approach. Systematising a broader national-security innovation ecosystem means that organisations have the explicit mission, authority, and resources to connect non-traditional vendors with warfighter needs. Relatedly, bureaucratic adaptation offers mechanisms to sidestep closed-innovation stovepipes. As Michael Horowitz describes, military organisations invest in 'change assets' when they perceive the need to respond to changes in the character of war.[32] These change assets inherently run against the grain of prevailing policies – here, the closed-innovation paradigm – because bureaucracies do not innovate in their natural state.[33] Because the closed-innovation system offers few entry points for non-traditional vendors, military adaptation toward an open model of innovation includes organisations and networks of innovators circumventing bureaucracy to bring onboard commercial and academic partners unfamiliar with military red tape. For instance, Other Transaction Authorities (OTAs) are contracting vehicles outside of the Federal Acquisition Regulations that help bypass red tape and prototype more quickly. The increased usage of OTAs aims to benefit startups, small companies, and other entrants without having to encounter the cumbersome Federal Acquisition Regulations. As

---

[30]Ibid.
[31]Fiott, 'A Revolution Too Far? US Defence Innovation, Europe and NATO's Military-Technological Gap', 425–6.
[32]Michael C. Horowitz, *The Diffusion of Military Power: Causes and Consequences for International Politics* (Princeton, NJ: Princeton UP 2010), 33.
[33]Stephen P. Rosen, *Winning the Next War: Innovation and the Modern Military* (Ithaca, NY: Cornell UP 1991), 2–5.

explored below, these workaround solutions are useful to begin relationships with non-traditional vendors, but do not assure that open innovation is sustained.

Second, administrative change and investments in the 2010s have focussed on setting the conditions for the US military services to profit from in-house creativity. Given the focus on software in this article, cloud and edge computing are described here as the primary infrastructural investments for open innovation. Open innovation favours the promotion of general-purpose tools that seek to enable transformation across and between programmes. By investing in infrastructure, the US is cultivating a 'platform ecosystem' for use across the enterprise, rather than inside of specific programmes. Platform ecosystems encourage open innovation because the provision of a platform, software, and infrastructure as services encourages 'complementors' to build on top of systems with their own products, as Apple and Google allow for third-party developers that build applications for the iOS and Android operating systems.[34] In a military system of open innovation, leveraging the bureaucracy to provide a platform ecosystem means creating space for creative, informal networks to become complementors. Be they in programme offices, on bases, or at the tactical edge, these complementors revive the possibility for in-house product development. While creative, informal networks in the ranks are a constant in military innovation, this differs from closed innovation in that enterprise tools seek to formalise informal-innovation avenues not by co-opting practice, but rather by creating the infrastructure for them to flourish.

Third, open-innovation practices include aligning software development with best practices developed from the commercially driven, open-source software community. In particular, this means promoting successful technology transition by speeding up feedback loops to the tune of days and by focussing on user experience from the front end of software development. Together, these criteria help collapse the bureaucratic barriers between research and operations.[35] Closed innovation has often led to technology requiring battlefield adaptation or being ignored altogether if it does not

---

[34]Jonathan T. Eckhardt, Michael P. Ciuchta, and Mason Carpenter, Open innovation, information, and entrepreneurship within platform ecosystems, *Strategic Entrepreneurship Journal* 12 (2018), 369–91.

[35]Andrew Grissom defines military innovation as focused on operations, saying that acquisition reform and other bureaucratic practices 'are not considered legitimate innovation unless a clear link can be drawn to operational praxis.' This makes sense when technology is adopted in a sequential manner, meaning it is first acquired and subsequently deployed. The focus on digital technology in open innovation takes a different viewpoint on the importance of bureaucratic measures because this sequence does not apply to software. By making the militaries more responsive to changes to the pace and trajectory of technological change, the collapsed barriers between research and operations may mean changing the measurement of changes to operational praxis. For his definition of military innovation, see: Andrew Grissom, 'The Future of Military Innovation Studies', *Journal of Strategic Studies* 29/5 (2006), 907.

correspond with in-situ realities. In contrast to the waterfall-acquisition process seen in closed innovation, software methodologies in open innovation shorten the upfront development cycle, and instead emphasise a tail of continuous engagement with end-users. In particular, the 'DevSecOps' pipeline and 'agile' development methodology contrast with the waterfall acquisition process typical of closed innovation. DevSecOps refers to software practices wherein development, security, and operations are integrated processes, helping collapse the barriers between development and deployment by engaging with end-users early and iteratively updating software by automating and continuously monitoring all stages.[36] This goes hand in hand with the ongoing releases in agile development, in which teams of programmers, testers, and users make constant, small changes to software.[37] While adaptive acquisition provides the conditions for continuous engagement between developers and deployers, paradigmatic changes to the related talent pipeline and oversight structures may prove longer-term challenges.

Continous software monitoring and delivery are important not only to prevent delays that software bugs cause,[38] but also to create the conditions for software developers, testers, and end-users to take advantage of the low barriers to software experimentation. In contrast to waterfall acquisition and hardware developments, digital technology facilitates experimentation because it is 'combinatorically generative,' which allow users to 'intervene or create novel behaviour from existing functionality' at low cost.[39] Furthermore, as Brynjolfsson and McAfee describe, non-rivalrous digital goods benefit from close-to-zero marginal costs of reproduction, meaning that they don't expire or degrade in quality as other resources do.[40] As such, sunk infrastructural costs aside, software experimentation is predisposed toward more frequent, less expensive 'iterative loops of learning'[41] than applies to other types of military prototypes.

The move toward open innovation described here should be read with the caveat that it is not an inevitable remedy for the bureaucratic hangover of closed-innovation practices, so much as it is an unsurprising reaction in the US context, given deeply embedded connections between technology and strategy in US strategic culture. As termed by Thomas Mahnken, the

---

[36]McQuade et al., 'Software is Never Done: Refactoring the Acquisition Code for Competitive Advantage', 10.
[37]Oakley, 'Defense Acquisitions Annual Assessment: Drive to Deliver Capabilities Faster Increases Importance of Program Knowledge and Consistent Data for Oversight', 18.
[38]Gilli and Gilli, 'Why China Has Not Caught Up Yet: Military-Technological Superiority and the Limits of Imitation, Reverse Engineering, and Cyber Espionage', 151.
[39]Lindsay, *Information Technology and Military Power*, 125.
[40]Erik Brynjolfsson and Andrew McAfee, *The Second Machine Age: Work, Progress, and Prosperity in a Time of Brilliant Technologies* (New York, NY: W. W. Norton & Company 2014), 62.
[41]Chesbrough, *Open Innovation: The New Imperative for Creating and Profiting from Technology*, 56.

'technological optimism' that has animated US defence planning since 1945 manifested as particularly decisive to creating an advantage in the 1991 Gulf War.[42] While the 2014 third offset strategy set the tone for the institutional and technological investments that aim to make the US military more receptive to open innovation, its 'lack of strategic clarity'[43] prevented connections to creating an overarching advantage. Institutional changes have since found their strategic footing in the 2017 National Security Strategy, which admitted to an extended period of strategic complacency, and the complementary 2018 NDS. Together with the diffusion potential of emerging technologies, this new strategic setting underlines the relevance of contemporary attempts at military innovation in the United States.

As Cronin acknowledges, closed and open innovation can simultaneously occur, as was the case with the nuclear and information revolutions in the second half of the 20th century.[44] The current DoD technology priorities illustrate this point. Priorities such as nuclear modernisation and hypersonic weapons require a closed system of innovation, as market conditions cannot prevail and the government must assume risk. Elements of open innovation may still apply to these technology areas, for instance, with regards to dual-use components, or as seen in select software developments, as picked up in the Air Force section below. For the reasons described above, technological investments in priorities including AI, autonomy, cyber, microelectronics, biotechnology, networked communications, space, and quantum computing more certainly require a more iterative technology-management system. As such, the challenge of military innovation today is to pursue both innovation models simultaneously.

Contextualising open innovation in military innovation literature

The focus on the services in this article intentionally echoes traditional schools of thought on military innovation, which tend to focus on efforts to shape organisational structures, concepts, and technology inside military services, rather than treating armed forces as a singular establishment. Well-known case studies focus either on efforts in a single service,[45] branches

---

[42]Thomas G. Mahnken, *Technology and the American Way of War Since 1945*, (New York, NY: Columbia UP 2008), 2–5.
[43]Fiott, 'A Revolution Too Far? US Defence Innovation, Europe and NATO's Military-Technological Gap', 430.
[44]Cronin, *Power to the People: How Open Technological Innovation is Arming Tomorrow's Terrorists*, 19.
[45]Examples include the Royal Navy's HMS Dreadnought and battlefleet warfare, as well as the Royal Air Force integrated air defence. Horowitz, *The Diffusion of Military Power: Causes and Consequences for International Politics*, 142–65; Barry R. Posen, *The Sources of Military Doctrine: France, Britain, and Germany Between the World Wars*, Cornell UP (Ithaca, NY: 1986); Stephen Peter Rosen, *Winning the Next War: Innovation and the Modern Military* (Ithaca, NY: Cornell UP 1991).

within a service,[46] or relationships between the services.[47] In this context, this article looks at the service-level of open innovation, particularly as service-level attempts manifest in the creation of organisations focused on new models of technology acquisition, management, and exploitation. To varying degrees, the organisational approaches to open innovation reveal how each of the services is trying to swim against the tide of how the DoD and military departments traditionally manage technology.

Rather than ascribing to one particular school of military-innovation thought, open innovation can take lessons from each of them. The literature allows for this because the conditions of open innovation focus more on bureaucratic prerequisites for eventual doctrinal change,[48] rather than doctrine itself, and also because the shared assumptions between the four schools of thought create some overlap or co-existence of factors across scholarship.

The four schools of thought – intra-service competition, inter-service competition, civil-military relations, and organisational culture – consider the role and relationships between the military services in different ways. The first two of these schools – the inter-service model and intra-service competition – directly posit that rivalry between different organisational outfits is a key determinant of innovation. While scholars such as Stephen Peter Rosen see intra-service rivalry as the imperative to innovate,[49] inter-service proponents like Owen Cote see competition between different services as the more decisive factor.[50] Nonetheless, there can still be an interplay between these two schools; indeed, in Cote's case on interwar carrier aviation, he describes inter-service competition as an accelerant for pre-existing intra-service innovation processes.[51] The civil-military relations school notes the importance of 'military mavericks' within services to implement the vision prescribed by civilian leadership,[52] with civilian intervention as the necessary antidote to 'service parochialism' or connections and coordination between different services."[53] The last school, focusing on cultural and organisational dynamics, assesses

---

[46]Cultural dynamics or intra-service rivalry can focus on similar cases to this end, including differences between Navy (aviation, surface, subsurface) or Marine Corps (infantry, aviation, logistics) branches. See: Terry Pierce, *Warfighting and Disruptive Technologies: Disguising Innovation*, Frank Cass Publishers (New York, NY: 2004), 8.
[47]This includes the development of the Polaris and Trident II nuclear submarine-launched ballistic missiles. See: Harvey M. Sapolsky, *Polaris System Development: Bureaucratic and Programmatic Success in Government* (Cambridge, MA: Harvard UP, 1972); Owen Reid Cote Jr., 'The Politics of Innovative Military Doctrine: The US Navy and Fleet Ballistic Missiles', Doctoral dissertation, *Massachusetts Institute of Technology*, February 1996.
[48]See footnote 35.
[49]Rosen, *Winning the Next War: Innovation and the Modern Military*.
[50]Owen Reid Cote Jr., 'The Politics of Innovative Military Doctrine: The US Navy and Fleet Ballistic Missiles', cited in Pierce, Warfighting and Disruptive Technologies: Disguising Innovation, 7.
[51]ibid.
[52]Posen, *The Sources of Military Doctrine: France, Britain, and Germany Between the World Wars*.
[53]Ibid., 135, 159.

innovation prospects based on the personalities of services. As Mahnken concluded, it is the services that mould technology to shape their purposes, more than the technology shapes them.[54] Evidence supporting each of the schools of thought can be found in present open-innovation efforts, and as the contemporary innovation efforts further crystallise, it may also become the case that singular schools of thought become more associated with the individual cases of each service.[55]

This is not to minimise the differences between the military-innovation schools of thought. For instance, while overlapping needs between services make inter-service tensions inevitable, Barry Posen describes jointness as a solution that military services tend toward to solve interdependencies.[56] For proponents of the inter-service model of military-innovation, attempts by the services to remedy competition through jointness inadvertently removes the core driver of innovation itself.[57] The tensions between models also become clear when attributing innovation to civilian intervention or intra-service dynamics, as epitomised by the debates between Posen and Rosen in the 1980s-90s.[58] The cultural model, meanwhile, focuses less on the competitive dynamics between actors than the other schools. Understanding the extent to which these models are mutually exclusive is important if seeking to determine the causality of what made a historical case study successful.

Stuart Griffin characterises the way that the schools of thought 'complement and enhance' each other as problematic because it prevents them from competing as explanatory models.[59] Yet open innovation benefits from the slivers of complementarity of the models, particularly when assessing the relationships between different services. Because this article focuses on the contemporary bureaucratic changes to military technology management, the efforts are too nascent to ascribe success, let alone causality. Instead, the focus here is on the iterative nature of open innovation, as it applies to the management of digital technology in military services.[60] In particular, it seeks to build on the growing evidence of bottom-up innovation vectors[61] as well

---

[54]Mahnken, *Technology and the American Way of War Since 1945*, 219.
[55]One example that is beyond the scope of this paper is the possibility of inter-service rivalry with the emergent Space Force.
[56]Barry Posen, 'Foreward: Military doctrine and the management of uncertainty,' *Journal of Strategic Studies* 39/2 (2016), 168–9.
[57]Cote Jr., 'The Politics of Innovative Military Doctrine: The US Navy and Fleet Ballistic Missiles'.
[58]Posen, *The Sources of Military Doctrine: France, Britain, and Germany Between the World Wars*; Rosen, *Winning the Next War: Innovation and the Modern Military*.
[59]Stuart Griffin, 'Military Innovation Studies: Multidisciplinary or Lacking Discipline?', *Journal of Strategic Studies* 40/1/2 (2016), 203.
[60]Open innovation can apply to non-digital technologies, as mentioned above, although this is beyond the scope of the article.
[61]In his 2006 article, Andrew Grissom identified the lack of bottom-up literature as a gap in military innovation literature – a call which Griffin said was answered in the following decade. See: Grissom, 'The Future of Military Innovation Studies', 920; Griffin, 'Military Innovation Studies: Multidisciplinary or Lacking Discipline?', 197.

as the aforementioned impact of informal networks on military adoption of technology.[62] Open innovation seeks to build on this by describing the conditions and processes by which military services attempt to institutionalise bottom-up innovation. This is relevant for the adoption of emerging technologies today. For example, in his writing on artificial intelligence (AI), Horowitz notes that bottom-up characteristics of research and experimentation are important to contemporary innovation endeavours.[63] Indeed, open innovation builds on these dynamics by focusing on the capacity of militaries to adapt to the present rate of technological change, for AI as for other emerging technologies. By focussing on infrastructural investments and condition-setting efforts, open innovation entails the creation of bureaucratically sanctioned pathways that encourage bottom-up innovation. In permitting small or informal networks the leeway to experiment and iterate, this means the services may better capitalise on creativity and change.

Championing open innovation in the US military

The services' transposition of software policy, and open innovation at large, vary in relation to the change assets they dedicate to emerging technology adoption. These change assets can be seen as infrastructural investments, as well as the establishment of new outfits to meet new competency requirements. Assessing the services' moves to open innovation still requires these benchmarks in tandem with more traditional parameters of military innovation, such as buy-in from leadership, organisational redesign, the ability to connect technological advances to doctrine, and resource allocation.

US Air Force

In the Air Force, revamping bureaucracy aims to engrain digital engineering into the identity of the service. Open innovation manifests in connections between the Digital Air Force initiative and the recognition that air superiority may not be presumed in future, contested operational environments. The most recent Air Superiority Flight Plan describes an operational environment in 2030 in which combining domains – air, cyber, space, and the electromagnetic spectrum – is a clearer way to define the future Air Force advantage than is dominating the air domain by itself.[64] Organisational efforts to innovate inside the Air Force do not seek to distract from the central role of

---

[62]Kollars, 'War's Horizon: Soldier-Led Adaptation in Iraq and Vietnam'; Lindsay *Information Technology and Military Power*.
[63]Michael Horowitz, 'Artificial Intelligence, International Competition, and the Balance of Power', *Texas National Security Review* 1/3 (May 2018), 36–57, https://tnsr.org/2018/05/artificial-intelligence-international-competition-and-the-balance-of-power/.
[64]*Air Force Enterprise Capability Collaboration Team*, 'Air Superiority 2030 Flight Plan', 26 May 2016, https://www.af.mil/Portals/1/documents/airpower/Air%20Superiority%202030%20Flight%20Plan.pdf.

technology and airpower, but rather to adopt open innovation in a way that reinforces a broad interpretation of airpower subsuming other domains. A reflection of this, recent innovation efforts implicitly update the definition of airpower to absorb new technological frontiers. Even with communications denied or degraded, air superiority remains the service's main paradigm for exerting airpower strategically. That said, this may confront the Air Force's persisting view of airpower as strategically decisive, which has not always been met by reality, a historical trend that Daniel Lake describes in his account on Air Force culture and the role of technology.[65] This continued focus on airpower is implicit in the prevailing operational concept to which the Air Force currently ascribes: Joint All-Domain Command and Control (JADC2). With digital enablers as the glue between different domains, JADC2 seeks to offset the challenges of operating in contested environments by fusing domains and restoring fast, reliable data transmission across networks. Recent Air Force strategic documents advocate explicit connections between bureaucratic agility to strategic aims, namely to out-adapt technologically advanced, near-peer competitors.[66] Overall, the nascent Air Force innovation outfits, namely the software factories and accelerators introduced here, are relatively low-risk and inexpensive. Even with enterprise tools, scaling investments from AFWERX and other new accelerators may come to require a different approach if decentralised innovation turns to mean diluted results.

For a service whose reliance on technology is existential, digital enablers such as strategic management of data and the development of AI-enabled capabilities are seen as horizontal competencies that should permeate across the service. The Air Force approach to open innovation can be characterised as a venture to complement infrastructural investments with new, technology-centric organisations that straddle research and operations. Rather than giving S&T incumbents custody over open innovation, burgeoning networks of software factories and accelerators are emblematic of the Digital Air Force initiative. Their support for new technology-management practices is equally enabled by enterprise-wide investments, so much as it is validation that those new practices can help the Air Force absorb new technology to support longstanding airpower assumptions. With leaders including acquisition chief Will Roper, who remains an advocate for digital force transformation even after stepping down in January 2021, providing patronage to the patchwork of open-innovation outfits described below, the Air Force offers the most complete shift toward open innovation per the specified criteria. Roper

---

[65]Daniel R. Lake, *The Pursuit of Technological Superiority and the Shrinking American Military* (New York, NY: Palgrave MacMillan 2019), 101–33.
[66]Ibid.; Will Roper, 'Take the Red Pill: _The New Digital Acquisition Reality', *Department of the Air Force*, 15 September 2020.

has pushed this even further, suggesting digital engineering as the path to restoring next-generation air dominance.[67]

The ability of airmen to adapt to an open model of innovation also depends on the Air Force's investments in digital infrastructure and enterprise services. Cloud investments are critical enterprise-wide enablers for the Air Force adaptation to an open model of innovation, as they allow software developers anywhere in the Air Force can build software solutions securely. Through Cloud One and Platform One, the Air Force cloud infrastructure acts as the digital 'plumbing' for the service's DevSecOps processes. The Air Force has also been more bullish than the other services in using open-source tools. Experimentation with open-source tools is a small, but notable, step toward changing the closed-innovation cultural perception that the availability of open-source tools to everyone, including adversaries, limits their utility to maintaining technological superiority. For example, new software methodologies are entering into the Ground-Based Strategic Deterrent (GBSD) nuclear modernisation programme. The Air Force has tested its access to Platform One and awarded contracts to use DevSecOps to manage future software applications for GBSD.[68] Open-source software tools have also successfully been deployed on legacy F-16 and the forthcoming B-21, bringing the service closer to in-flight software upgrades with appropriate cybersecurity considerations.[69]

While still nascent, these military-software advancements exemplify how the Air Force can extend adaptive acquisition and sustainment to legacy platforms and high-end strategic assets that are built on assumptions of closed innovation. By using open-source tools and iterative development methodologies, they can build on state-of-the-art advancements and debug software on fast cycles, while also hardening security measures as necessary for military operations.

In the same way that infrastructural investments in open architecture allow the Air Force to use the same tools across various programmes of record, these change assets also benefit the range of disparate software developers in accelerators and software factories across the service. In these new outfits, airmen promote open innovation to connect systems and build tools across civilian-technology corridors, on Air Force bases, and inside programmes of record. Software factories are structured teams of software developers that allow tech-savvy airmen and consultants to work alongside deployed personnel to create homegrown software remedies to problems

---

[67] Roper, 'Take the Red Pill: _The New Digital Acquisition Reality'.
[68] Jason Miller, 'Air Force's game-changing approach to cloud accreditation', *Federal News Network*, 30 July 2020, https://federalnewsnetwork.com/ask-the-cio/2020/07/air-forces-game-changing-approach-to-cloud-accreditation/.
[69] Tom Krazit, 'How the U.S. Air Force Deployed Kubernetes and Istio on an F-16 in 45 days', *The New Stack*, 24 December 2019, https://thenewstack.io/how-the-u-s-air-force-deployed-kubernetes-and-istio-on-an-f-16-in-45-days/.

in the Air Force.[70] Software factories are the organisational answers to DevSecOps advocates who want to collapse the divide between software developers and end-users in the immediate term, while creating building blocks for homegrown software development that shapes Air Force digital culture in the long term. While the model software factory is Boston-based Kessel Run,[71] whose early software successes have inspired emulation in the other services, the size and format of the approximately twenty software factories are intentionally left as blank canvases so that software factories can grow inside bureaucratised programmes or cut across programmes with a broader mission focus.[72]

While some directly serve Air Force commands or user communities of specific aircraft, other software factories serve broadly defined issues related to the cyber and space domains. The scalability of these new open-innovation hubs is linked to the enterprise-wide investments in cloud and edge computing, as well as bureaucratic changes that facilitate continuous delivery and deployment. Software factories benefit from new bureaucratic mechanisms such as 'continuous authorities to operate' to de-risk software-intensive capabilities and promote experimentation that incorporates continuous feedback from deployed airmen.[73] New adaptive acquisition guidance and infrastructural investments serve as enablers for the Air Force to grow in-house digital skills in line with its missions. While promising to grow software skills horizontally across the Air Force, these software factories still swim upstream against the prevailing waterfall acquisition system.

This infrastructure also benefits the cohort of accelerators that the Air Force began establishing in 2012[74] in order to increase Air Force access to non-traditional vendors and transition technology to airmen. In addition to non-profit accelerators, AFWERX is notable as an in-house technology accelerator with senior-level support. AFWERX seeks to foster a culture of innovation amongst airmen through its decentralised networks of intrapreneurs on bases, organised in 'spark cells' that can solve tactical problems and engage in competitions to gain funding for prototypes.[75] Roper has also focused on nurturing bottom-up efforts with AFWERX, including 'Pitch Days,' where small

---

[70]Nicolas Chaillan, 'Software Factories', *US Air Force Chief Software Office*, 2020, Last accessed 11 October 2020, https://software.af.mil/software-factories/.
[71]Mark Pomerleau, 'The Air Force is all in on software', *C4ISRnet*, 12 August 2019, https://www.c4isrnet.com/battlefield-tech/2019/08/12/the-air-force-is-all-in-on-software/.
[72]Chaillan, 'Software Factories'.
[73]Barry Rosenberg, 'Fail Fast, Not Twice: DoD's Push For Agile Software Development', *Breaking Defense*, 20 June 2019, https://breakingdefense.com/2019/06/fail-fast-not-twice-dods-push-for-agile-software-development/.
[74]The Doolittle Institute was the first of the efforts, which helped stand up SOFWERX.
[75]Tony Perez and Adam Welch, 'AFWERX Spark,' ed. Brian Maue, *Empowering Next Generation Innovators and Innovations* (Arlington, VA: AFWERX, 2020), 37–49, http://afwerx.af.mil/resources/AFWERX-Book.pdf.

businesses can receive same-day contracts – previously unprecedented in defence contracting.[76]

Notably, the funding for these ventures remains small. From 2016 to 2018, OTAs represented only one per cent of total defence contracts.[77] Placing a 'large number of small bets,'[78] meaning many commitments of small-dollar requisitions, evinces a grassroots approach to use in-house creativity as an innovation input, but says little about how lessons can filter upward. Senior leadership enables tech-savvy airmen to drive innovation from the bottom up in part because the funding is not exorbitant, meaning they can be encouraged without threatening entrenched funding for major programmes. While helpful to begin partnerships with small businesses and startups, these investments may be more useful to cut costs than they will to effectuate operational or strategic changes.

US Army

The Army's approach to open innovation is also tied to newly created organisations, albeit to a different end than the patchwork of digital-oriented outfits in the Air Force. The 2018 establishment of Army Futures Command (AFC) marked the first time the Army added a new four-star command since the Training and Doctrine Command was set up in relation to the AirLand Battle concept in 1973. The establishment of AFC does not stem from a coherent vision for the future Army, but was instead stood up to determine what that the future, 'multi-domain' vision should be.[79] The new command includes efforts to transition the Army way of doing business to an open model of innovation, especially through small teams that are designed to synergise research and operations. Nevertheless, the modernisation priorities associated with the Army's future advantage can be characterised as a repackaging of existing organisational tools, rather than a discontinuous break toward open innovation.

Army organisational redesign aims to implement new concepts that exploit technology to deter and defeat near-peer competitors – a lofty transition for a service whose primary operational experience and lessons in adaptation hail from two decades of counterinsurgency operations.[80] The establishment of AFC is associated with the service's perceived need to

---

[76] *Secretary of the Air Force Public Affairs*, 'Inaugural Air Force Pitch Day: New contracts, new partners', 8 March 2019, https://www.af.mil/News/Article-Display/Article/1779609/inaugural-air-force-pitch-day-new-contracts-new-partners/.
[77] Timothy J. DiNapoli, 'DOD's Use of Other Transactions for Prototype Projects Has Increased', *Government Accountability Office*, November 2019, 9, https://www.gao.gov/assets/710/702861.pdf.
[78] Joshua Kleinholz, 'AFwerX Vegas opens new doors to innovation', *Air Combat Command*, 23 August 2017, https://www.acc.af.mil/News/Article-Display/Article/1288094/afwerx-vegas-opens-new-doors-to-innovation/.
[79] *Army Futures Command*, 'Command Brief Creating a New Culture of Innovation'.
[80] Cases on this period of adaptation often focus on the Marine Corps as well as the Army.

signpost its relevance in strategic competition, in which future operating environments depart from assumptions underriding recent Army adaptation. AFC is a high-level, highly visible effort to actively fight against learning the wrong lesson from previous conflicts, particularly by connecting organisational change to the service's stated materiel priorities.

Within AFC, Cross-Functional Teams are tackling the priorities of the Army Modernization Strategy and enablers to lower barriers between different operational domains. These are small teams that connect concept developers to the appropriate components of the technology enterprise and military end-users.[81] These small teams include more junior ranks, but remain hierarchical because they report directly to the deputy commanding generals and also their four-star general 'mentors.' Benefitting from this support patronage, the design of these Cross-Functional Teams advocates open-innovation elements by integrating expertise in acquisition, requirements, and testing with operational expertise, including in concepts and doctrine. Instead of bifurcating acquisition and requirements into reporting to the Assistant Secretary of Acquisition, Technology and Logistics and AFC, respectively, personnel now report to both entities, and Cross-Functional Teams include personnel from both sides.[82] While the Army touts success with the requirements community,[83] the success of this shift toward open innovation is unclear. For instance, as part of the Next-Generation Combat Vehicle line of effort in AFC, the Army has already had to cancel its solicitation of the Bradley replacement and downgrade its requirements into a 'wish list.'[84] Further, congressional concern that AFC is duplicating civilian S&T efforts in the Army may come to highlight intraservice tension as the new four-star command takes shape.[85]

The modernisation priorities that guide AFC, which only represent one-quarter of Army acquisition investments, and the new Cross-Functional Teams evince a new approach to move toward adaptive acquisition. However, the possibility of over-reliance on technology may come to override any success in open innovation bureaucratic adaptation in the Army. Navigating Army modernisation recalls lessons from the infamous Future Combat Systems (FCS) programme from 2003–09, which the Army cancelled after sinking billions of dollars into technology that could not be fielded,

---

[81] 'Army Directive 2017–22 (Cross-Functional Team Pilot in Support of Materiel Development', *Office of the Secretary of the Army*, 6 October 2017.
[82] Andrew Feickert and Brendan W. McGarry, 'The Army's Modernization Strategy: Congressional Oversight Considerations', *Congressional Research Service*, 7 February 2020, 9. https://www.everycrsreport.com/files/20200207_R46216_444d93a212c95fd2fba1a596d520ca263a833307.pdf.
[83] Stew Magnuson, 'AUSA NEWS: Army Futures Command Breaking Down Barriers', *National Defense Magazine*, 16 October 2019, https://www.nationaldefensemagazine.org/articles/2019/10/16/army-futures-command-breaking-down-barriers.
[84] Jon Harper, 'Army to Release New Wish List for Optionally Manned Fighting Vehicle', *National Defense Magazine*, 19 February 2020, https://www.nationaldefensemagazine.org/articles/2020/2/19/army-to-release-new-wish-list-for-optionally-manned-fighting-vehicle.
[85] Feickert and McGarry, 'The Army's Modernization Strategy: Congressional Oversight Considerations', 9.

including six years and 18 USD billion spent on 'interconnected weapons systems and warfighting software.'[86] As the Army's predominant transformation programme at the time, FCS included an operational concept that was largely dependent on technology. The concept would only function if the data systems – dependent on 49 critical jewel technologies – were properly integrated into a system of systems.[87] A decade later, the current materiel priorities include 31 technology-dependent modernisation initiatives, yet leaves unanswered whether implementation of the Army's current 'multi-domain operations' concept[88] can survive the failure of one or more of these key technological enablers.[89]

Early AFC software developments are attempting to move away from a waterfall approach. Cross-Functional Teams in particular, aim to match requirements with technology push rather than demand pull. To take the example of the Cross-Functional Team focussing on network command, control, communications, and intelligence, rapid prototyping prior to requirements definition has shortened the front end of development. Brigade combat teams will avail of the prototypes and provide feedback to be incorporated in the eventual requirements for longer-term, scaled acquisitions for the integrated tactical network.[90] This iterative approach seeks to ensure that software experimentation informs requirements prior to transitioning capabilities to programs of record. In addition to the Cross-Functional Teams, further evidence of open innovation can be seen in AFC task forces and accelerators that collaborate more with the S&T community outside Army ranks.[91] New task forces in AFC focus on shaping the future vision of the new four-star command. The Army AI Task Force undertakings include developing algorithms using a DevSecOps model,[92] as well as leading the joint 'Coeus' effort to centralise algorithmic sharing in the cloud.[93] Beyond the task force, it is notable that AFC has also

---

[86] Hans Ulrich Kaeser, 'The Future Combat System: What Future Can The Army Afford?' *Center for Strategic and International Studies*, 5 February 2009, 2, Working draft, https://csis-website-prod.s3.amazonaws.com/s3fs-public/legacy_files/files/media/csis/pubs/090205_fcsarmy.pdf.

[87] Andrew Feickert, 'The Army's Future Combat System (FCS): Background and Issues for Congress', *Congressional Research Services*, 5 May 2006, 6; Theo Farrell, Sten Rynning, and Terry Terriff, *Transforming Military Power Since the Cold War: Britain, France, and the United States, 1991–2012* (Cambridge, UK: Cambridge UP 2013), 53–9.

[88] This concept grew out of the term 'multi-domain battle' in the early-to-mid-2010s, and has since inspired the term JADC2.

[89] Feickert and McGarry, 'The Army's Modernization Strategy: Congressional Oversight Considerations', 7.

[90] This highlights a 'DevOps' approach, similar to DevSecOps. Chris Westbrook and Kathryn Bailey, 'New faces and new tech provide the right mix of know-how and speed,' *US Army*, 18 June 2020, https://www.army.mil/article/236576/new_faces_and_new_tech_provide_the_right_mix_of_know_how_and_speed.

[91] The usage of task forces to this end is not itself new. Modernization efforts in the 1990s relied on similar methods with an operational focus, as seen in previous efforts such as the Louisiana Maneuvers digitised exercises or Force XXI design.

[92] Andrew Eversden, 'The Army AI task force takes on two "key" projects', *C4ISRnet*, 10 June 2020, https://www.c4isrnet.com/artificial-intelligence/2020/06/10/the-army-ai-task-force-takes-on-two-key-projects/.

[93] Matthew P. Easley, 'Army Artificial Intelligence Task Force (AI-TF)', *US Army Futures Command*, 2019, 12–13. https://www.clsac.org/uploads/5/0/6/3/50633811/2019-easley-aiml.pdf.

established a new software factory styled after Kessel Run, which will focus broadly on software solutions that work in degraded communications environments.[94]

Similar actors are also seen to help expand partnerships to non-traditional vendors. The aforementioned Army AI Task Force is pushing broader cultural and training efforts in partnership with Carnegie Mellon University, just as the technology accelerator Capital Factory connects startups in the Austin technology corridor with AFC. Although not new, the reservist 75th Innovation Command also offers inroads for reservists working in technology companies to play a significant role 'driving concepts, capabilities and innovation.'[95] By using workaround solutions, these organisations seek to decrease the bureaucratic burden that military organisations impose on small businesses and startups.

The Army is the largest user of OTAs, partially because of its long history employing the contracting vehicle relative to the other services. This history, however, is not without drawbacks. OTAs were a more popular tool in the 1990s,[96] but also link back to the notorious FCS programme that haunts current Army modernisation attempts. The history of transitioning the FCS programme from a series of OTAs into a unified programme under the Federal Acquisition Regulations significantly increased costs and complicated system integration.[97] It remains to be seen how funding for major programmes, which still rely on traditional procurement and administrative methods, can fuse with the insurgent innovation methods and structures. Nonetheless, the more recent focus on prototyping aims to modernise the procedure for iterative, add-on capabilities, rather than culminating in a major programme, as was the case for FCS.

While the intention behind the establishment of a four-star command was to create a coherent vision of the future, it is not yet clear what precisely the Army vision of competing against near-peer competitors will entail. The stakes for this centralised organisation are high, as success means that the organisation will be empowered to carry forth its mission, and failure means a lack of alternatives for organisational capital focused on change.

---

[94] Mandy Mayfield, 'Army Futures Command Establishes "Software Factory"', *National Defense Magazine*, 21 August 2020, https://www.nationaldefensemagazine.org/articles/2020/8/21/army-futures-command-establishes-software-factory.

[95] Todd South, 'New tech from Futures Command "designed, built, tested with soldiers" to get it there faster', *Army Times*, 20 October 2019, https://www.armytimes.com/news/your-army/2019/10/21/new-tech-from-futures-command-designed-built-tested-with-soldiers-to-get-it-there-faster/.

[96] Richard L. Dunn, 'Other Transactions Contracts: Poorly Understood, Little Used', *National Defense Magazine*, 15 May 2017, https://www.nationaldefensemagazine.org/articles/2017/5/15/other-transactions-contracts-poorly-understood-little-used.

[97] Feickert, 'The Army's Future Combat System (FCS): Background and Issues for Congress', 4–5.

US Navy

Relative to the Air Force and Army, the Navy perceives less of a need to adapt its bureaucracy for open innovation. The sparse efforts described below are not connected with strategic documents in the service, nor are they linked to the overall fleet plans for the service. Despite the software connections and emphasis on unmanned systems in the Navy's distributed maritime operations concept, the bureaucratic and cultural adaptation toward open innovation finds less purchase in the Navy. Indeed, this is consistent with the Navy's history of being considered the most stubbornly traditional of the services.[98] That said, James 'Hondo' Geurts has been leading the small charge for open innovation in the Department of the Navy, serving as Assistant Secretary of the Navy for Research, Development and Acquisition from December 2017 to January 2021, and now as Under Secretary of the Navy.[99] The visible software and open-innovation efforts nevertheless face a steeper uphill climb to gain purchase in the Navy bureaucracy because of lack of perceived connections between adapting bureaucracy for digitalisation and fleet modernisation.

Formerly the Acquisition Executive for US Special-Operations Command, Geurts has tried to replicate portions of his special operations success stories in the Navy. While the vast majority of the Navy innovation enterprise remains centralised under ONR and programmes of record, Geurts has said that 'innovation and agility cannot be centralised.'[100] The sparse decentralised components that focus on open innovation are namely Naval Expeditions (NavalX) Agility cell and burgeoning software development teams inspired by Air Force software factories. Nonetheless, this anecdotal evidence of open innovation in the Navy is far less extensive than seen in the Air Force and Army cases above. Geurts stood up NavalX Agility following his success with the special operations innovation hub, SOFWERX, that he previously established.[101] With its hallmark of 'tech bridge' hubs, NavalX Agility aims to increase partnerships with academia. The number of tech bridges has doubled from six to 12 in one year, yet do not receive the same attention as other -WERX accelerators in the Air Force family.[102]

---

[98] Carl H. Builder, *The Masks of War: American Military Styles in Strategy and Analysis* (Baltimore, MD: Johns Hopkins UP 1989); Mahnken, *Technology and the American Way of War Since 1945*.

[99] Although beyond the scope of this article, it is worth noting that this role includes R&D and acquisition for the Marine Corps. His advocacy for innovation thus extends to both services: for example, in April 2020, the first team in the Marine Corps to gain accreditation for DevSecOps was a software factory-style team that reports to Geurts.

[100] James F. Geurts, 'The Department of the Navy Fiscal year 2020 Budget Request for Science and Technology Programs', *House Armed Services Committee*, 28 March 2019, 6. https://armedservices.house.gov/_cache/files/c/4/c46d8d7f-cade-4487-bae0-f87943aa205e/5AD8EA25BA971C25EF67C083034A43F2.hhrg-116-as26-wstate-geurtsj-20190328.pdf.

[101] Herman Leonard et al., 'SOFWERX: Innovation at U.S. Special Operations Command,' *Harvard Business School* Case 819-004, July 2018.

[102] *NavalXAgility*, 'Scaling Agility, Navy Doubles Tech Bridge Locations', 13 May 2020. https://www.navy.mil/submit/display.asp?story_id=112953 and Teri Carnicelli, 'Fathomwerx Lab Designated Ventura Tech Bridge for Navy's NavalX Network,' *Naval Sea Systems Command*, 14 May 2020, https://www.navsea.navy.mil/Media/News/SavedNewsModule/Article/2187535/fathomwerx-lab-designated-ventura-tech-bridge-for-navys-navalx-network/.

In-house software development teams are another new element, though on a much smaller scale relative to Air Force software factories. One fledgeling open-innovation effort is the iLoc Development team, which informally began using software to augment tactical capabilities of antisubmarine warfare aircraft in late 2015.[103] The iLoc Development team of six Navy coders[104] digitised submarine localisation, yielding both faster and more accurate results than the simplified analogue or Excel models used until the mid-2010s. More important is the impact on training, with preliminary results showing that training for P-8 *Poseidon* tactical coordinators[105] can be compressed from two years to six months thanks to iLoc's user-friendly tool.[106] This effort benefits from even less capital than its Air Force counterparts. For instance, the team does not have a cloud server which would otherwise facilitate scaling of the software tools beyond the P-8 user community. Indeed, with regards to infrastructural investments, the Navy acquisition command also uses the Air Force's Platform One.[107] The Navy's migration of its Enterprise Resource Planning system to the cloud is notable for the acquisition and workforce management of 72,000 users across six commands.[108] The connections to military capability development are not as direct as the other services' cloud investments that seek to connect advanced military weapons to the cloud for use at the tactical edge. Overall, the sustainability of these fledgeling efforts depends on procedural buy-in which is currently unassured beyond Geurts.

Attachment to a single senior leader may threaten the continuity of efforts beyond his tenure in the Navy, particularly in the context of recent fleeting innovation efforts in the service. Indeed, James Wirtz has warned that Chiefs of Naval Operations (CNO) may not have a unified view on how accelerated technology affects the Navy's grasp on seapower.[109] For instance, the Navy Task Force Innovation that then-Secretary of the Navy Ray Mabus established in January 2014 appears to have stalled out.[110] In 2016, the CNO Admiral John Richardson dissolved the Strategic Studies

---

[103] Sean Lavelle, 'The Navy's Kessel Run', *US Naval Institute*, 3 January 2019, https://blog.usni.org/posts/2019/01/03/the-navys-kessel-run.

[104] This number refers to coders who dedicated their spare time and has fluctuated. As of late 2019, the Navy has employed two full-time coders to work on the iLoc platform, which now comprises 25 software tools for P-8 operators.

[105] These tactical coordinators manage missions, and as such, are highly trained to understand and integrate information from various software systems.

[106] Eric Lofgren, 'The future of Navy software development with Lt. Sean Lavelle', *Acquisition Talk*, 1 April 2020. Audio.

[107] AEGIS also uses Platform One. Variants of platforms that multiple services use, including the F-35, may also avail of this infrastructure.

[108] *Amazon Web Services*, 'Readying the warfighter: U.S. Navy ERP migrates to AWS', 22 January 2020, https://aws.amazon.com/blogs/publicsector/readying-warfighter-navy-erp-migrates-aws/.

[109] James J. Wirtz, 'Innovation for seapower: U.S. Navy strategy in an age of acceleration', *Defense & Security Analysis* 36/1 (2020), 89.

[110] Ray Mabus, 'Harnessing the Navy's Culture of Innovation', *Naval Science and Technology Future Force Magazine*, 7 April 2015, https://futureforce.navylive.dodlive.mil/2015/04/harnessing-the-navys-culture-of-innovation/.

Group (SSG), which was reputed as the Navy's primary 'innovation incubator' for the past 35 years.[111] His vision of the future Navy advantage was one with a larger fleet and plans to 'modernise the "punch" – the combat systems, sensors, and payloads – at the speed that technological advances allow.'[112] However, the envisioned investments in unmanned systems and AI-enabled networks to deliver this punch are not accompanied by connections between bureaucratic adaptation and strategy. While there was debate over the continued utility of the CNO SSG,[113] the lack of an institutional or procedural replacement results in a vacuum for operational concepts to be connected to sustained administrative change that can outlive single leaders. Since Admiral Michael Gilday became CNO in 2019, the Future Navy focus on a larger fleet comprising unmanned systems and a secure network that facilitates distributed operations appears largely intact, including with interest in 'tactical clouds at sea.'[114] While this interest could spawn connections with software cells, the institutional investments in open innovation remain *ad hoc*. As Wirtz writes, 'technology is available, even maturing systems are at hand, what is missing is a deliberate process to *integrate* nascent weapons into the Fleet.'[115] As such, the one-off efforts of software development and partnerships with non-traditional vendors are thus far disconnected from the way the Navy researches, acquires, and fields capability.

The exceptions to the rules of closed innovation are less scalable as a result. Another way to measure this is to link the Navy's approach to workaround solutions to push acquisition reform forward. The Department of the Navy has approached contracting vehicles outside of the Federal Acquisition Regulation with more reticence than the Army and Air Force, citing oversight concerns. Rather than capitalising on tools that other services use, the Navy created a Naval Innovation Process Adoption tool to fast-track 'lightbulb ideas,'[116] but says little

---

[111]David Adams et al., 'SSG Served as an Innovation Incubator', *US Naval Institute Proceedings* 143/4/1370, April 2017, https://www.usni.org/magazines/proceedings/2017/april/ssg-served-innovation-incubator.
[112]John Richardson, The Future Navy, Office of the Chief of Naval Operations, 17 May 2017, https://admin.govexec.com/media/gbc/docs/pdfs_edit/futurenavyfinal.pdf.
[113]James Stavridis, 'CNO's decision to terminate Strategic Studies Group is smart – it used to be good but lately was fiddling around', *Foreign Policy*, 8 April 2016, <https://foreignpolicy.com/2016/04/08/cnos-decision-to-terminate-strategic-studies-group-is-smart-it-used-to-be-good-but-lately-was-fiddling-around/>; Terry Pierce, 'The Navy Needs a New Engine of Innovation,' *Proceedings Magazine* 144/11/1389 (November 2018); Adams et al., 'SSG Served as an Innovation Incubator'. https://www.usni.org/magazines/proceedings/2018/november/navy-needs-new-engine-innovation
[114]Lauren C. Williams, Gilday outlines IT vision for Navy systems, FCW, 31 July 2019, https://fcw.com/articles/2019/07/31/gilday-confirmation-cyber-it.aspx.
[115]Wirtz, 'Innovation for seapower: U.S. Navy strategy in an age of acceleration', 95.
[116]Daniel Cebul, 'Office of Naval Research launches program to speed up innovation', *Defense News*, 2 April 2018, https://www.defensenews.com/digital-show-dailies/navy-league/2018/04/02/office-of-naval-research-launches-program-to-speed-up-innovation/.

about how the tool alleviates existing stovepipes or scales. From 2016 to 2018 – a time when the overall usage of OTAs more than doubled – the Department of the Navy made up less than one per cent of OTA contract obligations.[117] As such, speeding up prototypes and adapting to commercially driven innovation continues to be seen through traditional methods, with a stronger focus on programmes of record rather than onramps more prevalent in the Air Force and Army.

US Marine Corps

With regards to open innovation, the Marine Corps case requires a different approach from the other services due to its size and status under the auspices of the Department of the Navy. Indications of the Marine Corps' intended organisational change, as defined in Force Design 2030, do not primarily focus on leveraging open innovation, but instead prioritise the plentiful, conventional challenges related to logistics and re-orienting toward a primarily maritime theatre. This is consistent with the Marine Corps approach to technology that focuses on personnel over materiel, and dedicates its limited resources toward experimentation to support small unit operations.[118] Still, the service's well-documented history of experimentation and current priority to reorient toward distributed operations in contested littoral environments both provide a natural focus on C2 and software development.

In the Marine Corps, the desire to modernise C2 information technology infrastructure is linked to support of global distributed operations. In the 2017 Marine Corps Strategy for Assured C2, then-Commandant Robert Neller described how traditional data storage is an operational liability, writing that "reach-back" models are too slow and are most susceptible to service outages during times of network segregation, especially at the tactical edge.'[119] The Deputy Commandant for Information confirmed enterprise C2 as a top priority in January 2020, so as to align cyber, signals intelligence, and electronic warfare capabilities under a single entity focussed on information operations.[120] This priority relates to the two prevailing Marine Corps operational concepts – Expeditionary Advanced Base Operations and Littoral Operations in a Contested Environment – both of which embody the service's response to anti-access, area-denial threats (A2AD). As the Marine Corps

---

[117] As a caveat, the Army has issued an unspecified amount of OTAs on behalf of the other services. See: DiNapoli, 'DOD's Use of Other Transactions for Prototype Projects Has Increased', 10.
[118] Lake, *The Pursuit of Technological Superiority and the Shrinking American Military*, 231–32.
[119] Robert B. Neller, 'Strategy for Assured Command and Control: Enabling C2 for Tomorrow's Marine Corps, Today', *US Marine Corps*, March 2017, 4, https://www.hqmc.marines.mil/Portals/61/Marine_Corps_Strategy_for_Assured_Command_and_Control_March_2017.pdf?ver=2017-05-30-160731-940.
[120] Nathan Strout, 'The Marine Corps' 4 priorities in the information environment', *C4ISR.net*, 6 January 2020, https://www.c4isrnet.com/information-warfare/2020/01/06/the-marine-corps-4-priorities-in-the-information-environment/.

strives to disaggregate its assets and mitigate vulnerability to A2AD attacks, it is transitioning to a distributed, mobile force. This entails a business model in which data repositories and software services can be securely accessed wherever Marines are. Insofar as Marine Corps transformation encompasses digitalisation, cloud and edge computing are technological enablers for logistics and tactics in global distributed operations.

The infrastructural investments to create distributed access to information and capitalise on in-house development are, nevertheless, in tension with the lack of resources available to the Marine Corps. Many of the enterprise tools and acquisition authorities that underpin the Marine Corps' approach to digital transformation are part of the Department of the Navy bureaucracy. As such, de-siloing research and operations is inherently tied to other civilian structures inside the DoD. Truer of the Marine Corps than other services that have their own expansive research and S&T outfits, the move to open innovation is harder to isolate without the benefit of forthcoming DoD-wide infrastructural investments.[121]

Open-innovation alcoves inside the Marine Corps reflect this dependency on other structures. In mid-2019, the Marine Corps teamed with the Defense Digital Service – a software development team stood up in 2015 inside the Office of the Secretary of Defense – to create their first cloud-based product.[122] The resulting System for Operational Logistics Orders, developed in-house in 90 days, aligns with the Force Design priority of providing logistical support for distributed operations. In April 2020, a software factory-style team received accreditation to implement the DevSecOps pipeline for the Marine Corps for the first time. The resulting Operational Application and Service Innovation Site product was built in the Expeditionary Warfare Department at the Naval Information Warfare Center Atlantic, which reports to the role that Geurts occupied until January 2021. To adopt other technologies such as small unmanned aerial systems or additive manufacturing, the Marine Corps has also relied on other acquisition avenues outside the Department of the Navy, including support for OTAs from the Army and Defense Innovation Unit.[123] This dependency means the USMC has fewer onramps to build relationships with non-traditional defence companies, and needs to work collaboratively with other DoD organisations to set the conditions for intrapreneurship.

---

[121] The two most prominent near-term investments to this end are the forthcoming Joint Enterprise Defense Infrastructure and Joint Common Foundation, both housed within the Office of the Secretary of Defense.
[122] Matthew G Glavy and Brett Goldstein, 'The Battle for Mon Cala: Getting the Military to Deliver Its Own Tech Solutions', *War On The Rocks*, 20 August 2020, https://warontherocks.com/2020/08/the-battle-for-mon-cala-getting-the-military-to-deliver-its-own-tech-solutions/.
[123] Although beyond the scope of this article, another relevant contracting mechanism is the Commercial Solutions Opening.

These efforts should be contextualised with the Marine Corps' emphasis on wargaming and experimentation, particularly as they are priorities in Force Design 2030. A recognised feature of their experimentation-forward culture is the Marines' history of unleashing creativity from resource-strapped necessity. In the 2017 guidance on the C2 network, then-Commandant Neller's references to the 'bottom-up creativity' in creating software applications and to a '"build our own" mentality' are consistent with this creativity, and are contrasted against the 'build-from-scratch' vendor approaches on which current networks rely.[124] Early suggestions of an in-house, build-your-own approach date to 2012, when an Expeditionary Software Development Team deployed to develop applications in the field, therein circumventing the possibility that vendors' proprietary systems might not be interoperable with future DoD enterprise cloud investments.[125] The scalability of such expeditionary teams is hard to determine, but is notable in that it predates efforts in other services, which are presently ramping up experimentation and fielding. In 2017, Marine Expeditionary Force Information Groups were stood up to defend against threats in future joint operations in contested environments, improve management of signatures, and engrain cyber and signals capabilities into the groundwork of decision-making.[126] Yet there are only three Groups composed of only 33 Marines each, and the structure of the combatant commands is currently set up to treat information as more of an add-on capability, rather than 'combining the physical and information domains' as Force Design 2030 demands.[127] In tandem with software experimentation in wargaming at the Marine Corps Warfighting Laboratory at Quantico, these deployed units serve as a complement for the Marine Corps open-innovation push to increase in-house development, regardless of the size of its in-house S&T apparatuses. Nonetheless, these small efforts are largely subject to the pace of change toward open innovation seen in DoD civilian apparatuses.

---

[124]Neller, 'Strategy for Assured Command and Control: Enabling C2 for Tomorrow's Marine Corps, Today', 4, 11.
[125]Henry Kenyon, 'Rapid app response: Marines to embed development teams with deployed units', *GCN*, 6 February 2012, https://gcn.com/articles/2012/02/06/marine-corps-apps-embedded-development-teams.aspx.
[126]Megan Eckstein, 'Marine Corps Information Community Growing in Capability, Trying to Find Its Place in Joint Operations', *USNI News*, 7 January 2020, https://news.usni.org/2020/01/07/marine-corps-information-community-growing-in-capability-trying-to-find-its-place-in-joint-operations and Mark Pomerleau, 'Here's what the Marines' information command centers will do,' *C4ISR.net*, 6 December 2019, https://www.c4isrnet.com/information-warfare/2019/12/06/heres-what-the-marines-information-command-centers-will-do/.
[127]David H. Berger, 'Force Design 2030', *US Marine Corps*, March 2020, 3.

Conclusion

The focus on open innovation in this article aims to find a framework for technology management befitting of dual-use, emerging-technology adoption in each of the US military services. Assessments of military innovation often focus on the services when technological, operational, and organisational changes culminate in an advantage for the armed forces. Yet, the renewed focus on US military innovation in the 2010s has not yet yielded a closer look at how the organisations inside of the services are adapting to shape their future advantage. The four services are united by a common set of organisational structures that still rely overwhelmingly on outdated policies when instituting open innovation. However, their pursuits of open innovation are increasingly distinct because of their respective modernisation priorities, leadership, and institutional preferences.

The DoD sees adapting the US military model of innovation to capitalise on the open technological revolution as critical to achieving the future US military competitive advantage. While many elements of this competitive advantage will continue to be determined by closed innovation, open innovation represents a small, but growing, portion of total service-level modernisation efforts.

Between all the organisations described above, the new architecture of open-innovation outfits across the defence enterprise is not coordinated or joint in nature. Inter-service collaboration can be seen informally below the threshold of jointness, primarily in the form of co-located personnel or shared best practices, meaning that open innovation networks are diffuse and uncoordinated. Apart from examples of other services availing of the Air Force's Platform One for their own software efforts, there are few formalised practices for these innovation outfits to collaborate and adapt to a model of open innovation together. Future comparisons will have the benefit of assessing joint investments beyond the scope of this article, namely the forthcoming Joint Common Foundation and Joint Enterprise Defense Infrastructure. When implemented, these infrastructural investments may reinforce open-innovation opportunities currently supported by service-level investments in data management. More broadly speaking, future comparisons between the services' approaches to open innovation also requires understanding how the innovation constituencies overlap and interact with one another. The future competitive military advantage will depend on these interactions – not only between the services, but between factions in the services.

Between the services, the fledgeling efforts described here will have real implications for the future of interoperability, infighting about the role of commercially driven technologies to support operational concepts, and agility in the face of near-peer competitors also considering how to adopt similar technologies. As these efforts scale and the open-innovation outfits mature, the service-oriented empirics here may serve as the basis for further cases on inter- and intra-service rivalry. Indeed, given the strong focus on experimentation and emphasis on jointness in the Marine Corps, the smallest service may find itself predisposed to take advantage of the open-innovation conditions that are currently being set, even though its own resources are strained to generate the conditions themselves. Similarly, for the Air Force, whether the Space Force creates new urgency for acquisition pathways and deeper relations with non-traditional vendors may increase support for open innovation.

Further research on the institutionalisation of open innovation inside the military services could also consider the role of operational concepts as a bridge between these organisations and future doctrinal development.[128] The elevation of the Army-launched, Air Force-led JADC2 concept to the Joint Staff in December 2019 provides a preliminary path to seeing more buy-in for open innovation across the DoD. The Navy's Distributed Maritime Operations concept does not preclude buy-in to this joint concept, as seen for instance, in the reference to integrate 'the manned-unmanned force across all domains' in the Unmanned Campaign Framework.[129] Nonetheless, it does less to advance the bureaucratic and cultural ambitions embodied in open innovation. The differences are clear, for instance, in the role of cloud and edge computing as technological enablers. While JADC2 sees them as relevant to connect sensors and shooters more quickly between operational domains, Distributed Maritime Operations – and Expeditionary Advanced Base Operations – see the enablers as relevant to connect disaggregated assets in global distributed operations. Similarly, attempts to systematise relationships with non-traditional vendors suggest that commercially driven technologies and processes will be less important to the military advantages the Navy espouses.

One of the questions to judge the current attempts to forge a competitive military advantage via innovation will be whether new organisations are even necessary to institutionalise innovation. There are certainly downsides to pursuing an organisation-heavy approach, most notably the turf wars that it breeds for resources and manpower with incumbent organisations. For the Air Force in particular, which appears ahead of the other services in its approach to software, whether the diffuse nature of innovation outfits will dilute modernisation priorities remains to be seen. Regardless, without adopting aspects of an open innovation model, the US defence establishment will be constrained by 20th-century processes to address 21st-century challenges.

---

[128]Theo Farrell, 'Improving in War: Military Adaptation and the British in Helmand Province, Afghanistan, 2006–2009', *Journal of Strategic Studies* 33/4 (2010), 567–594.
[129]*Department of the Navy*, 'Unmanned Campaign Network', 16 March 2021, 6. https://www.navy.mil/Portals/1/Strategic/20210315%20Unmanned%20Campaign_Final_LowRes.pdf?ver=LtCZ-BPlWki6vCBTdgtDMA%3D%3D.

Ultimately, in comparison to the status quo of closed innovation in the services, the open innovation change assets here are niche initiatives that should be assessed as a parallel track to programme- and platform-based modernisation. When comparing the open innovation efforts to military modernisation cycles at large, funding is clearly attached to more traditional ways of doing business. With these cycles in mind, let alone the time for new doctrinal updates, operational concepts, tactics, techniques and procedures to take hold, it is too early to assess how successful the attempt to create a military innovation will be. Nevertheless, for military-innovation literature to keep pace with open innovation, the dissolution between research and operations should accelerate the measurement of outcomes. If open innovation is successful, traditional timelines that assess military innovation over the course of decades may come to be compressed to match the pace of technology absorption itself.

Acknowledgment

The author would like to thank the editors of this special issue – Michael Raska, Katarzyna Zysk, and Ian Bowers – as well as Henrik Paulsson, Maaike Verbruggen, and the anonymous reviewers for their constructive remarks.

Disclosure statement

The author reported no potential conflict of interest.

Bibliography

Adams, David *et al.*, 'SSG Served as an Innovation Incubator,' *US Naval Institute Proceedings 143/4/1370*, Apr. 2017, https://www.usni.org/magazines/proceedings/2017/april/ssg-served-innovation-incubator

Air Force Enterprise Capability Collaboration Team, 'Air Superiority 2030 Flight Plan', 26 May 2016, https://www.af.mil/Portals/1/documents/airpower/Air%20Superiority%202030%20Flight%20Plan.pdf

Amazon Web Services, 'Readying the Warfighter: US Navy ERP Migrates to AWS', 22 Jan. 2020, https://aws.amazon.com/blogs/publicsector/readying-warfighter-navy-erp-migrates-aws/

Army Futures Command, 'Command Brief Creating a New Culture of Innovation', Command Brief, 14 Mar. 2019, https://www.slideshare.net/TheNationalGuardBure/army-futures-command

Bell, Patrick and Jan Kallberg, 'The Death of the Cyber Generalist', *US Army War College War Room*, 8 Jun. 2018, https://warroom.armywarcollege.edu/articles/death-of-cyber-generalist/

Berger, David H., 'Force Design 2030', *US Marine Corps*, Mar. 2020.

Brynjolfsson, Erik and Andrew McAfee, *The Second Machine Age: Work, Progress, and Prosperity in a Time of Brilliant Technologies* (New York, NY: W. W. Norton & Company 2014).

Builder, Carl H., *The Masks of War: American Military Styles in Strategy and Analysis* (Baltimore, MD: Johns Hopkins UP 1989).

Carnicelli, Teri, 'Fathomwerx Lab Designated Ventura Tech Bridge for Navy's NavalX Network', *Naval Sea Systems Command*, 14 May 2020, https://www.navsea.navy.mil/Media/News/SavedNewsModule/Article/2187535/fathomwerx-lab-designated-ventura-tech-bridge-for-navys-navalx-network/

Cebul, Daniel, 'Office of Naval Research Launches Program to Speed up Innovation', *Defense News*, 2 Apr. 2018, https://www.defensenews.com/digital-show-dailies/navy-league/2018/04/02/office-of-naval-research-launches-program-to-speed-up-innovation/

Chaillan, Nicolas, 'Software Factories', *US Air Force Chief Software Office*, 2020. Last accessed 11 Oct. 2020. https://software.af.mil/software-factories/

Chesbrough, Henry, *Open Innovation: The New Imperative for Creating and Profiting from Technology* (Boston, MA: Harvard Business School Press 2003).

Cheung, Tai Ming, 'Innovation in China's Defense Technology Base: Foreign Technology and Military Capabilities', *Journal of Strategic Studies* 39/5–6 (2016), 728–61. DOI:10.1080/01402390.2016.1208612

Cote, Owen Reid, Jr., 'The Politics of Innovative Military Doctrine: The US Navy and Fleet Ballistic Missiles', Doctoral dissertation, Massachusetts Institute of Technology, Feb. 1996.

Cronin, Audrey Kurth, *Power to the People: How Open Technological Innovation Is Arming Tomorrow's Terrorists* (Oxford: Oxford UP 2020).

Department of the Navy, 'Unmanned Campaign Network', 16 Mar. 2021, https://www.navy.mil/Portals/1/Strategic/20210315%20Unmanned%20Campaign_Final_LowRes.pdf?ver=LtCZ-BPlWki6vCBTdgtDMA%3D%3D

DiNapoli, Timothy J., 'DOD's Use of Other Transactions for Prototype Projects Has Increased', *Government Accountability Office* GAO-20-84, Nov. 2019, https://www.gao.gov/assets/710/702861.pdf

Dunn, Richard L., 'Other Transactions Contracts: Poorly Understood, Little Used', *National Defense Magazine*, 15 May 2017, https://www.nationaldefensemagazine.org/articles/2017/5/15/other-transactions-contracts-poorly-understood-little-used

Easley, Matthew P., 'Army Artificial Intelligence Task Force (AI-TF)', *US Army Futures Command* (2019). https://www.clsac.org/uploads/5/0/6/3/50633811/2019-easley-aiml.pdf

Eckhardt, Jonathan T., Michael P. Ciuchta, and Mason Carpenter, 'Open Innovation, Information, and Entrepreneurship within Platform Ecosystems', *Strategic Entrepreneurship Journal* 12 (2018), 369–91. DOI:10.1002/sej.1298

Eckstein, Megan, 'Marine Corps Information Community Growing in Capability, Trying to Find Its Place in Joint Operations', *USNI News*, 7 Jan. 2020, https://news.usni.org/2020/01/07/marine-corps-information-community-growing-in-capability-trying-to-find-its-place-in-joint-operations

Eversden, Andrew, 'The Army AI Task Force Takes on Two 'Key' Projects', *C4ISRnet*, 10 Jun. 2020, https://www.c4isrnet.com/artificial-intelligence/2020/06/10/the-army-ai-task-force-takes-on-two-key-projects/

Farrell, Theo, Sten Rynning, and Terry Terriff, *Transforming Military Power since the Cold War: Britain, France, and the United States, 1991–2012* (Cambridge, UK: Cambridge UP 2013).

Feickert, Andrew, 'The Army's Future Combat System (FCS): Background and Issues for Congress', *Congressional Research Services*, 5 May 2006, https://www.everycrsreport.com/files/20060505_RL32888_bd0c5e4691669243ba6aacea43a6ce91c182246e.pdf

Feickert, Andrew and Brendan W. McGarry, 'The Army's Modernization Strategy: Congressional Oversight Considerations', *Congressional Research Service*, 7 Feb. 2020, https://www.everycrsreport.com/files/20200207_R46216_444d93a212c95fd2fba1a596d520ca263a833307.pdf

Fiott, Daniel, 'A Revolution Too Far? US Defence Innovation, Europe and NATO's Military-Technological Gap', *Journal of Strategic Studies* 40/3 (2017), 417–37. DOI:10.1080/01402390.2016.1176565

Gansler, Jacques, *Democracy's Arsenal: Creating a Twenty-First Century Defense Industry* (Cambridge, MA: MIT UP 2011).

Geurts, James F., 'The Department of the Navy Fiscal Year 2020 Budget Request for Science and Technology Programs', *House Armed Services Committee*, 28 Mar. 2019. https://armedservices.house.gov/_cache/files/c/4/c46d8d7f-cade-4487-bae0-f87943aa205e/5AD8EA25BA971C25EF67C083034A43F2.hhrg-116-as26-wstate-geurtsj-20190328.pdf

Gilli, Andrea and Mauro Gilli, 'Why China Has Not Caught Up Yet: Military-Technological Superiority and the Limits of Imitation, Reverse Engineering, and Cyber Espionage', *International Security* 43/3 (Winter 2018/19), 141–89. DOI:10.1162/isec_a_00337

Glavy, Matthew G. and Brett Goldstein, 'The Battle for Mon Cala: Getting the Military to Deliver Its Own Tech Solutions', *War On The Rocks*, 20 Aug. 2020, https://warontherocks.com/2020/08/the-battle-for-mon-cala-getting-the-military-to-deliver-its-own-tech-solutions/

Griffin, Stuart, 'Military Innovation Studies: Multidisciplinary or Lacking Discipline?', *Journal of Strategic Studies* 40/1/2 (2016), 196–224. DOI:10.1080/01402390.2016.1196358

Grissom, Andrew, 'The Future of Military Innovation Studies', *Journal of Strategic Studies* 29/5 (Oct. 2006), 905–34. DOI:10.1080/01402390600901067.

Haduch, Thomas W., 'Maintaining the US Army Research, Development and Engineering Command Prototype Integration Facilities', *Defense Acquisition University Press*. May 2014, https://www.dau.edu/training/career-development/sscf/Documents/T.%20HaduchSSCF2014SRPOPSECFINAL.pdf

Harper, Jon, 'Army to Release New Wish List for Optionally Manned Fighting Vehicle', *National Defense Magazine*, 19 Feb. 2020, https://www.nationaldefensemagazine.org/articles/2020/2/19/army-to-release-new-wish-list-for-optionally-manned-fighting-vehicle

Horowitz, Michael, 'Artificial Intelligence, International Competition, and the Balance of Power', *Texas National Security Review* 1/3 (May 2018), 36–57. https://tnsr.org/2018/05/artificial-intelligence-international-competition-and-the-balance-of-power/

Horowitz, Michael C., *The Diffusion of Military Power: Causes and Consequences for International Politics* (Princeton, NJ: Princeton UP 2010).

Kaeser, Hans Ulrich, 'The Future Combat System: What Future Can The Army Afford?', *Center for Strategic and International Studies*, 5 Feb. 2009. Working draft, https://csis-website-prod.s3.amazonaws.com/s3fs-public/legacy_files/files/media/csis/pubs/090205_fcsarmy.pdf

Kenyon, Henry, 'Rapid App Response: Marines to Embed Development Teams with Deployed Units', *GCN*, 6 Feb. 2012, https://gcn.com/articles/2012/02/06/marine-corps-apps-embedded-development-teams.aspx

Kleinholz, Joshua, 'AFwerX Vegas Opens New Doors to Innovation', *Air Combat Command*, 23 Aug. 2017, https://www.acc.af.mil/News/Article-Display/Article/1288094/afwerx-vegas-opens-new-doors-to-innovation/

Kollars, Nina A., 'War's Horizon: Soldier-Led Adaptation in Iraq and Vietnam', *Journal of Strategic Studies* 38/4 (2015), 529–53. DOI:10.1080/01402390.2014.971947

Krazit, Tom, 'How the US Air Force Deployed Kubernetes and Istio on an F-16 in 45 Days', *The New Stack*, 24 Dec. 2019, https://thenewstack.io/how-the-u-s-air-force-deployed-kubernetes-and-istio-on-an-f-16-in-45-days/

Lake, Daniel R., *The Pursuit of Technological Superiority and the Shrinking American Military* (New York, NY: Palgrave MacMillan 2019).

Lavelle, Sean, 'The Navy's Kessel Run', *US Naval Institute*, 3 Jan. 2019, https://blog.usni.org/posts/2019/01/03/the-navys-kessel-run

Leonard, Herman, et al., 'SOFWERX: Innovation at US Special Operations Command', *Harvard Business School* Case 819–004, Jul. 2018.

Lindsay, Jon R., *Information Technology and Military Power* (Ithaca, NY: Cornell UP 2020).

Lofgren, Eric, 'The Future of Navy Software Development with Lt. Sean Lavelle,' *Acquisition Talk* (1 Apr. 2020). Audio.

Lofgren, Eric, 'The Last Frontier of Acquisition Reform: The Budget Process', Conference Paper, Proceedings of the Seventeenth Annual Acquisition Research Symposium, 13-14 May 2020. Prepared for the Naval Postgraduate School, Monterey, CA.

Mabus, Ray, 'Harnessing the Navy's Culture of Innovation', *Naval Science and Technology Future Force Magazine*, 7 Apr. 2015, https://futureforce.navylive.dodlive.mil/2015/04/harnessing-the-navys-culture-of-innovation/

Magnuson, Stew, 'AUSA NEWS: Army Futures Command Breaking Down Barriers', *National Defense Magazine*, 16 Oct. 2019, https://www.nationaldefensemagazine.org/articles/2019/10/16/army-futures-command-breaking-down-barriers

Mahnken, Thomas G., *Technology and the American Way of War since 1945* (New York, NY: Columbia UP 2008).

Mansoor, Peter R. and Williamson Murray, (eds.), *The Culture of Military Organizations* (Cambridge: UK: Cambridge UP 2019).

Mayfield, Mandy, 'Army Futures Command Establishes "Software Factory"', *National Defense Magazine*, 21 Aug. 2020, https://www.nationaldefensemagazine.org/articles/2020/8/21/army-futures-command-establishes-software-factory

McCain, John, 'Opening Statement by SASC Chairman John McCain at Hearing on DoD Nominations', *Office of Senator John McCain*, 14 Nov. 2017, https://www.mccain.senate.gov/public/index.cfm/floor-statements?ID=05DCC73A-F9F2-44E8-A75F-236003222AF2

McQuade, J. Michael et al., 'Software Is Never Done: Refactoring the Acquisition Code for Competitive Advantage', *Defense Innovation Board*, 3 May 2019, https://media.

defense.gov/2019/May/01/2002126690/-1/-1/0/SWAP%20EXECUTIVE%20SUMMARY.PDF

Miller, Jason, 'Air Force's game-changing approach to cloud accreditation, Federal News Network', 30 Jul. 2020, https://federalnewsnetwork.com/ask-the-cio/2020/07/air-forces-game-changing-approach-to-cloud-accreditation/

Mori, Satoru, 'US Defense Innovation and Artificial Intelligence', *Asia-Pacific Review* 25/2 (2018), 16–44. DOI:10.1080/13439006.2018.1545488

NavalXAgility, 'Scaling Agility, Navy Doubles Tech Bridge Locations,' 13 May 2020, https://www.navy.mil/submit/display.asp?story_id=112953

Neller, Robert B., 'Strategy for Assured Command and Control: Enabling C2 for Tomorrow's Marine Corps, Today', *US Marine Corps*, Mar. 2017, https://www.hqmc.marines.mil/Portals/61/Marine_Corps_Strategy_for_Assured_Command_and_Control_March_2017.pdf?ver=2017-05-30-160731-940

Oakley, Shelby S., 'Defense Acquisitions Annual Assessment: Drive to Deliver Capabilities Faster Increases Importance of Program Knowledge and Consistent Data for Oversight', *Government Accountability Office*, Jun. 2020. https://www.gao.gov/assets/710/707359.pdf

Office of the Secretary of Defense, 'National Defense Strategy of the United States of America: Sharpening the American Military's Competitive Edge', Jan. 2018.

Office of the Secretary of the Army, 'Army Directive 2017–22 (Cross-functional Team Pilot in Support of Materiel Development', 6 Oct. 2017.

Perez, Tony and Adam Welch, 'AFWERX Spark', in Brian Maue (ed..), *Empowering Next Generation Innovators and Innovations* (Arlington, VA: AFWERX 2020), 37–49. https://www.afwerx.af.mil/resources/AFWERX-Book.pdf

Pierce, Terry, *Warfighting and Disruptive Technologies: Disguising Innovation* (New York, NY: Frank Cass Publishers 2004).

Pierce, Terry, 'The Navy Needs a New Engine of Innovation', *Proceedings Magazine* 144/11/1389 (Nov 2018). https://www.usni.org/magazines/proceedings/2018/november/navy-needs-new-engine-innovation

Pomerleau, Mark, 'Here's What the Marines' Information Command Centers Will Do', *C4ISR.net*, 6 Dec. 2019, https://www.c4isrnet.com/information-warfare/2019/12/06/heres-what-the-marines-information-command-centers-will-do/

Pomerleau, Mark, 'The Air Force Is All in on Software', *C4ISRnet*, 12 Aug. 2019, https://www.c4isrnet.com/battlefield-tech/2019/08/12/the-air-force-is-all-in-on-software/

Posen, Barry R., *The Sources of Military Doctrine: France, Britain, and Germany between the World Wars* (Ithaca, NY: Cornell UP 1986).

Posen, Barry R., 'Foreward: Military Doctrine and the Management of Uncertainty', *Journal of Strategic Studies* 39/2 (2016), 159–73. DOI:10.1080/01402390.2015.1115042

Raska, Michael, 'The Sixth RMA Wave: Disruption in Military Affairs?'. *Journal of Strategic Studies* (2020), 1–24. DOI:10.1080/01402390.2020.1848818

Richardson, John, 'The Future Navy', *Office of the Chief of Naval Operations*, 17 May 2017, https://admin.govexec.com/media/gbc/docs/pdfs_edit/futurenavyfinal.pdf

Roper, Will, 'Take the Red Pill: _the New Digital Acquisition Reality', *Department of the Air Force*, 15 Sept. 2020.

Rosen, Stephen Peter, *Winning the Next War: Innovation and the Modern Military* (Ithaca, NY: Cornell UP 1991).

Rosenberg, Barry, 'Fail Fast, Not Twice: DoD's Push for Agile Software Development', *Breaking Defense*, 20 Jun. 2019, https://breakingdefense.com/2019/06/fail-fast-not-twice-dods-push-for-agile-software-development/

Sapolsky, Harvey M., *Polaris System Development: Bureaucratic and Programmatic Success in Government* (Cambridge, MA: Harvard UP 1972).

Schmidt, Eric, Robert Work, *et al.*, 'First Quarter Recommendations', *National Security Commission on Artificial Intelligence* (March 2020).

Secretary of the Air Force Public Affairs, 'Inaugural Air Force Pitch Day: New Contracts, New Partners', 8 Mar. 2019, https://www.af.mil/News/Article-Display/Article/1779609/inaugural-air-force-pitch-day-new-contracts-new-partners/

South, Todd, 'New Tech from Futures Command 'Designed, Built, Tested with Soldiers' to Get It There Faster', *Army Times*, 20 Oct. 2019, https://www.armytimes.com/news/your-army/2019/10/21/new-tech-from-futures-command-designed-built-tested-with-soldiers-to-get-it-there-faster/

Spataro, Noah M., 'FY2018 NIAC Consolidated Report: Lean Startup Approach to Capability Development: Evolving Small Batch Innovation for Dual-use Technologies', *Naval Innovation Advisory Council* (1 August 2018).

Stavridis, James, 'CNO's Decision to Terminate Strategic Studies Group Is Smart — It Used to Be Good but Lately Was Fiddling Around', *Foreign Policy*, 8 Apr. 2016, https://foreignpolicy.com/2016/04/08/cnos-decision-to-terminate-strategic-studies-group-is-smart-it-used-to-be-good-but-lately-was-fiddling-around/

Strout, Nathan, 'The Marine Corps' 4 Priorities in the Information Environment', *C4ISR.net*, 6 Jan. 2020, https://www.c4isrnet.com/information-warfare/2020/01/06/the-marine-corps-4-priorities-in-the-information-environment/

US Department of Defense, 'Summary of the 2018 Department of Defense Artificial Intelligence Strategy: Harnessing AI to Advance Our Security and Prosperity', 12 Feb. 2019, https://media.defense.gov/2019/Feb/12/2002088963/-1/-1/1/SUMMARY-OF-DOD-AI-STRATEGY.PDF

Westbrook, Chris and Kathryn Bailey, 'New Faces and New Tech Provide the Right Mix of Know-how and Speed', *US Army*, 18 Jun. 2020, https://www.army.mil/article/236576/new_faces_and_new_tech_provide_the_right_mix_of_know_how_and_speed

Williams, Lauren C., 'Gilday Outlines IT Vision for Navy Systems', *FCW*, 31 Jul. 2019, https://fcw.com/articles/2019/07/31/gilday-confirmation-cyber-it.aspx

Wirtz, James J., 'Innovation for Seapower: US Navy Strategy in an Age of Acceleration', *Defense & Security Analysis* 36/1 (2020), 88–100. DOI:10.1080/14751798.2020.1712026

Artificial intelligence in China's revolution in military affairs

Elsa B. Kania

ABSTRACT
The People's Liberation Army (PLA) seeks not only to equal but also to overtake the US military through seizing the initiative in the ongoing Revolution in Military Affairs (RMA). Chinese military leaders believe the form of warfare is changing from today's 'informatised' (信息化) warfare to future 'intelligentised' (智能化) warfare. The PLA's approach to leveraging emerging technologies is likely to differ from parallel American initiatives because of its distinct strategic culture, organisational characteristics, and operational requirements. This research examines the evolution of the PLA's strategic thinking and concepts of operations, seeking to contribute to the military innovation literature by evaluating major theoretical frameworks for the case of China.

Introduction

The Chinese People's Liberation Army (PLA) regards current advances in emerging technologies, especially artificial intelligence (AI), as a unique opportunity to achieve an operational advantage.[1] Chinese military leaders believe the form of warfare is evolving from today's 'informatised' (信息化) warfare to future 'intelligentised' (智能化) warfare. In the course of that transformation, artificial intelligence (AI) is anticipated to become as critical to victory on the future battlefield as information technology is

---

[1] See, for instance, these remarks from the director of the Central Military Commission Science and Technology Commission 'Lt. Gen. Liu Guozhi: the development of military intelligentisation is a strategic opportunity for our military to turn sharply to surpass' [刘国治中将:军事智能化发展是我军弯道超车的战略机遇], CCTV News, 22 October 2017, http://mil.news.sina.com.cn/china/2017-10-22/doc-ifymzqpq3312566.shtml. See also Xi Jinping's remarks as quoted in this article: 'Scientific and technological innovation, a powerful engine for the world-class military' [科技创新, 迈向世界一流军队的强大引擎], Xinhua, 15 September 2017, http://www.gov.cn/xinwen/2017-09-15/content_5225216.htm.

today.[2] This research examines the early evolution of the PLA's strategic thinking and concepts of operations by leveraging the available open-source materials. The paper seeks to contribute to the existing literature on military innovation by applying and evaluating prominent theoretical frameworks for the case of China.

While there is a clear realist rationale for the PLA's pursuit of these emerging capabilities, the PLA's distinct priorities, strategic culture, and elements of its force structure will influence its approach to realising the potential of today's advances. Today, the PLA is exploring and experimenting with new concepts and capabilities to enhance its combat power. Chinese defence academics and military strategists are working to create new theories for intelligentised operations, seeking to determine new mechanisms for victory on the future battlefield.[3] The use of AI in wargaming and operations research can enable conceptual advancements, such as exploring new notions of human-machine coordination and integration.[4] In the process, the PLA is closely studying and adapting lessons learned from American concepts and initiatives. As this research will show, the PLA's initial efforts to develop and deploy the technologies of the fourth industrial revolution systems for a range of applications in the future operational environment could impact the balance of power in ways that risk undermining strategic stability and complicating the dynamics of deterrence in US-China military rivalry.

Review of the literature on military innovation and diffusion

This analysis first seeks to evaluate strategic rationales for the PLA's concern with AI by first raising several potential hypotheses, then reviewing factors that have enabled advances to date, and finally considering emerging indications of the prospects for progression in the stages of military innovation. The core questions that motivate this project are: how and why is the Chinese military seeking to innovate in these theories and technologies of intelligentised operations? The paper initially reviews the salient academic literature to consider the relative relevance of these potential hypotheses, informed by scholarship on military innovation. Then, I undertake a detailed discussion of the PLA's strategic thinking and programs to date.

---

[2]Pang Hongliang [庞宏亮], 'The Intelligentisation Military Revolution Starts to Dawn' [智能化军事革命曙光初现], *PLA Daily*, 28 January 2016, http://www.mod.gov.cn/wqzb/2016-01/28/content_4637961.htm.

[3]Lu Zhisheng [陆知胜], 'The Typical Style of Intelligentised Operations: Human-Machine Cooperation!' [智能化作战的典型方式：人机协同！] *PLA Daily*, 17 October 2018. http://www.81.cn/jwgz/2018-10/17/content_9315760.htm

[4]For an initial analysis of this trend, see: Elsa B. Kania, 'Learning Without Fighting: New Developments in PLA AI War-Gaming,' *China Brief*, 9 April 2019.

Realist learning

The realist frameworks for military learning predict the rapid adoption of military innovations due to the dangers of disadvantage. Against the backdrop of military competition, 'innovation and diffusion are inextricably linked,' considering militaries' tendencies to learn from each other, including in revolutionary technologies, as Goldman has observed.[5] Because security threats that arise with conflict and contention in the international system can be existential in nature, militaries tend to 'copy one another across state borders, and with good reason.'[6] This process of 'military emulation' is recognised by Resende-Santos as resulting from an international system that is inherently anarchic.

The competitive pressures force states to adopt those practices and technologies that are deemed most successful, influenced by demonstrations of the military innovations of great power militaries.[7] As a result, a high degree of similarity, even relative convergence, tends to emerge in the weapons systems, as well as military strategies, of major military powers worldwide, as Waltz has noted.[8] In peacetime, these dynamics can take the form of competitive strategies that center on the 'peacetime use of latent military power,' by which states seek to shape a competitor's calculus to advance its own interests, as Mahnken has highlighted.[9]

From this perspective, China's efforts to advance military innovation reflects a dynamic of realist learning, deeply informed by and likely tending to emulate US efforts. The relevance of realist learning can be tested based on such indicators as the extent of the PLA's focus on American initiatives, the timing and articulated rationales for the Chinese military's prioritisation of military innovation, along with the extent of direct mimicry or observed similarity between US and Chinese concepts and approaches. The explanation would predict relative congruence and tendency towards convergence between the US and Chinese initiatives, at least at first, though the extent for the long term remains to be seen.

Creative insecurity

As a related but distinct hypothesis, China's contestation of military and technological leadership in AI also could be impelled by the dynamics of 'creative insecurity.'[10] Under this paradigm, external threats serve as an

---

[5] Emily O. Goldman and Thomas G. Mahnken (eds.), *The Information Revolution in Military Affairs in Asia*, Palgrave Macmillan, 2004.
[6] João Resende – Santos, 'Anarchy and the Emulation of Military Systems: Military Organization and Technology in South America, 1870–1930,' *Security Studies* 5, no. 3 (1996): 193–260.
[7] Ibid.
[8] Kenneth Waltz, *Theory of International Relations*, Addison-Wesley, 1979.
[9] See: Thomas G. Mahnken (ed.), *Competitive Strategies for the 21st Century: Theory, History, and Practice*, Stanford University Press, 2012.
[10] Mark Zachary Taylor, *The Politics of Innovation: Why Some Countries Are Better Than Others At Science and Technology*, Oxford University Press, 2016.

impetus for rapid progress, as informed by Taylor's framework for understanding global patterns of scientific and technological innovation. In such a case, the impetus of insecurity would impact the extant balance between external threats and domestic rivalries of distributional politics, overcoming any prior obstruction to greater investments and advancement.

Pursuant to this hypothesis, Chinese leaders' decision to prioritise military innovation in AI reflects a reaction to rising external threats but would not result from or necessarily involve direct learning from the US model. From this perspective, China's pursuit of primacy in AI, among a range of emerging technologies, would be impelled by US-China strategic competition and contentious regional dynamics, which would serve as a powerful impetus to overcome prior resistance to greater investments in science and technology.

This hypothesis can be evaluated based on indicators that include changes in the Chinese leadership's threat perceptions linked to the pursuit of military innovation, signs of a resulting change in prioritisation of domestic interests, and an apparent increase in resource allocation to defence technology and innovation. However, this causal mechanism does not predict parallels between US and Chinese priorities in and approaches to innovation.

Bureaucratic and organisational dynamics

The existing literature on military innovation has often looked to relevant dynamics organisations and bureaucracies. In practice, these factors tend to result in uneven, inconsistent adoption of new technologies and strategic approaches, as Posen has noted.[11] The inter-service competition within militaries can result in variable responses to innovations, based on the implications for different organisational actors' resources and autonomy, as Coté has observed.[12] In some cases, pressures from civilians or other institutional actors within the military can also act as the necessary 'impetus, political incentive, and political opportunity' for a military's revaluation of assumptions and orthodoxies.[13]

Often, innovation even entails ideological or generational contention, such that its actualisation can require the establishment of new career paths through which to promote younger officers who have specialised in the new missions, as Rosen has argued.[14] Beyond such competition, the adoption of innovation can be constrained and conditioned by the organisational

---

[11] Barry Posen, *The Sources of Military Doctrine: France, Britain, and Germany between the World Wars*, Cornell University Press, 1986.
[12] Owen R. Cote, 'The Politics of Innovative Military Doctrine: The US Navy and Fleet Ballistic Missiles,' PhD diss., Massachusetts Institute of Technology, 1996.
[13] Ibid.
[14] Stephen Peter Rosen, *Winning the next war: Innovation and the modern military*, Cornell University Press, 1994.

capacity, including the resources and adaptability, of the military in question, according to Horowitz's framework.[15]

According to this hypothesis, bureaucratic and organisational dynamics will deeply influence China's approach to military innovation in AI, particularly over the course its continuing experimentation and implementation. As the PLA undertakes reforms that are historic and highly disruptive, the equities of the organisations at stake will extend into questions of resource allocation associated with decisions on defence science and technology.

PLA leaders may continue to debate whether to devote greater resources to traditional hallmarks of military power, such as aircraft carriers, or more to emerging technologies and capabilities. In addition, even as the PLA seeks to create a more innovative culture and to mitigate persistent shortcomings in human capital, these challenges could continue to limit its capacity to succeed in the realisation of new capabilities. This hypothesis can be evaluated based on such indicators as signs of active debate within the PLA and of competition among services.

Strategic culture

China's strategic culture, as informed by historical, 'formative ideational legacies,' continues to influence its approach to defence and military innovation.[16] As the existing literature demonstrates, variation in different militaries' adoption of new ideas and technologies can be impacted by the 'presence or absence of a cultural and ideological orthodoxy,' as well as the commitment of elites to preserving, or alternatively overturning, beliefs and practices, as Adamsky has emphasised. To a certain degree, the PLA's strategic culture is informed by traditional prioritisation of science and technology as critical to military power. The notion 'technology determines tactics' (技术决定战术) is also a salient element of the PLA's thinking that reflects this attention to technology as a decisive factor.[17]

The PLA appears to be uniquely focused on the disruptive implications of technological advancements. For instance, aspects of the Soviet Union's strategic culture, including a holistic, dialectical cognitive approach, appears to have contributed to its success in recognising dynamics of military revolution that are often discontinuous, as Adamsky has recounted. Similarly, aspects of the PLA's cognitive style could result in a similar capacity to recognise the criticality of these technologies in future warfare. As a result,

---

[15] Michael C. Horowitz, *The Diffusion of Military Power Causes and Consequences for International Politics*, Princeton University Press, 2010.
[16] Dima Adamsky, *The Culture of Military Innovation: The Impact of Cultural Factors on the Revolution in Military Affairs in Russia, the US, and Israel*, Stanford University Press, 2010.
[17] Dennis J. Blasko, '"Technology Determines Tactics„: Relationship between Technology and Doctrine in Chinese Military Thinking', *Journal of Strategic Studies* 34/3 (2011), 355–381.

the PRC approach could be distinct from and divergent relative to that of the US military.

This hypothesis predicts China's ambitions and agenda for defence and military innovation in AI will tend to be shaped by salient aspects of its strategic culture in a manner that may be complementary to the factors discussed previously. While the impact of strategic culture is difficult to evaluate, potential indicators could include the salience of traditional concepts in current writings or the emergence of distinct features in Chinese military innovation relative to the US approach. Although strategic culture appears less likely to serve as a direct causal factor, ideational influences may serve to shape the features and trajectory of Chinese defence innovation.

This relevant literature and theoretical frameworks set the baseline for this paper, which will proceed to evaluate the relative explanatory relevance of these hypotheses and provide an assessment through a structured analytical framework.

China's reactions to the new revolution in military affairs

Chinese leaders assess that a new 'Revolution in Military Affairs' is underway. These changes present urgent challenges and historic opportunities for China. The Politburo devoted a study session to new trends in global military developments and promoting military innovation in August 2014. Xi Jinping personally emphasised the emergence of this 'new RMA.' He called for China to continue to advance military innovation in order to 'narrow the gap and achieve a new leapfrogging as quickly as possible.'[18] In his remarks, Xi urged the PLA to continue striving to develop new military theories, strategy and tactics, institutions, and equipment, as well as models for management, that could fulfil its missions in an era of informatised warfare.[19] China's emphasis on leveraging science and technology to rejuvenate its military (科技兴军) is central to the Party's 'powerful military objective' (强军目标) in the 'new era.'[20]

China's national strategy of 'innovation-driven development' could transform the PLA.[21] 'Under a situation of increasingly fierce international military competition, only the innovators win,' Xi Jinping has emphasised.[22] He called

---

[18] 'Xi Jinping: Accurately Grasp the New Trend in Global Military Developments and Keep Pace with the Times, Strongly Advancing Military Innovation' [习近平:准确把握世界军事发展新趋势 与时俱进大力推进军事创新], Xinhua, 30 August 2014, http://news.xinhuanet.com/politics/2014-08/30/c_1112294869.htm.
[19] Ibid.
[20] 'Launching the Engine of Innovation for Strengthening and Rejuvenating the Military'[发动强军兴军的创新引擎 -- 军队代表委员热议科技兴军], Xinhua, 12 March 2019, http://www.xinhuanet.com/mil/2019-03/12/c_1210079238.htm.
[21] 'Scientific and technological innovation, a powerful engine for the world-class military' [科技创新,迈向世界一流军队的强大引擎].
[22] Ibid.

for China to 'aim at the frontier of global military scientific and technological developments,' urging:

> We must attach great importance to the development of strategic frontier technologies..., select the main attack direction and breach, and intensify the formation of unique advantages in some domains of strategic competition, and strive to surpass the predecessor as latecomers, turning sharply to surpass.[23]

Xi Jinping has been consistent in highlighting the importance of leveraging advanced technologies.[24] This aspiration challenges American military-technological superiority. Whether such ambitions will be realised remains to be seen, however. PLA initiatives for military innovation and modernisation are continuing to progress through planning and armaments development. These new approaches are starting to become incorporated into strategy and doctrine.

Chinese military strategy has evolved and been adjusted in response to new assessments of the form or character of conflict throughout its history.[25] The most recent revision to China's 'military strategic guideline' (军事战略方针) to 'winning informatised local wars,' was confirmed in the 2015 defence white paper, *China's Military Strategy*. This paper also discussed a 'new stage' in the global RMA as resulting from the increasing prominence and sophistication of long-range, precise, smart [*sic*, or 'intelligent,' 智能],[26] stealthy, and unmanned weapons and equipment.'[27] At that point, China was concerned about the US Third Offset Strategy, which was believed to threaten to create a new 'generational difference' (时代差) between US and PLA capabilities.[28] US initiatives influenced and provided an impetus to intensify this imperative of innovation.

The concerns of Chinese defence academics and military strategists with the potential impact of AI in future warfare have been influenced by increased awareness of the rapid progress in AI.[29] In particular, AlphaGo's defeat of Lee Sedol in the game of Go in March 2016, which appeared to demonstrate the potential advantages that AI could provide in future

---

[23]Ibid.
[24]See: 'Xi Jinping: Launching the engine of military scientific research and innovation at full speed'.
[25]For the best review of the impetus for changes in Chinese military strategy across its history, see: M. Taylor Fravel, *Active Defense: China's Military Strategy Since 1949*. Vol. 2. Princeton University Press, 2019. M. Taylor Fravel, 'Shifts in Warfare and Party Unity: Explaining China's Changes in Military Strategy.' *International Security* 42, no. 3 (2018): 37–83.
[26]Although the translation 'smart' is used in the official version of this Defence White Paper, I choose to use the translations 'intelligent' or 'intelligentised.'
[27]Mininstry of National Defense of the People's Republic of China [中华人民共和国国防部], 'China's Military Strategy' [中国的军事战略],' 26 May 2015. See also the official English translation of the white paper: http://english.gov.cn/archive/white_paper/2015/05/27/content_281475115610833.htm.
[28]See also: Li Bingyan [李炳彦], 'Major Trends in the New Global Revolution in Military Transformation and the Form of Future Warfare' [世界新军事变革大势与未来战争形态], 24 February 2016. Li Bingyan is a member of the National Security Policy Committee (国家安全政策委员会).
[29]See this series in *China Brief*, organized by Peter Wood for early analyses on these issues: 'China & the Third Offset,' https://jamestown.org/programs/cb/china-third-offset/.

Timeline of relevant milestones in Chinese military innovation (2014–2019).

2014　In May, the Department of Justice charged five Chinese military hackers from the Unit 61398 in the first of what would become a campaign of indictments as an element of efforts to 'name and shame' cyber espionage in the years to come. In August, Xi Jinping discussed the Revolution in Military Affairs in Politburo study session. In November, Secretary of Defense Hagel announced the American Defense Innovation Initiative.

2015　In April the penetration of the Office of Personnel Management by Chinese hackers is first discovered. In May, Made in China 2025 was launched, setting in motion a new era of Chinese industrial policy. Also in May, then-Secretary of Defense Ashton Carter warned China over ongoing efforts in land reclamation in the South China Sea. In September, Xi Jinping announced plans to downsize the PLA as the start of a new phase of reforms. In December, the reforms continued with the creation of the PLA Strategic Support Force, elevation and inauguration of the PLA Rocket Force, and establishment of a new headquarters for the PLA Army.

2016　In January, the PLA formally established its new joint operations command structure, which Xi Jinping visited and inspected in April, when he was first officially described as commander-in-chief. As of March, the Thirteenth Five-Year Plan officially underway. In May, the National Strategy for Innovation-Driven Development released. In August, China launched Micius, the world's first quantum satellite. In October, the National Artificial Intelligence Research and Development Strategic Plan was released by the US National Science and Technology Council. In November, Donald Trump was elected president after a campaign in which his remarks had often featured attacks on China, especially pertaining to trade.

2017　In April, President Trump hosted Xi Jinping at Mar-a-Lago. In July, The State Council released the New Generation Artificial Intelligence Development Plan. In October, Xi Jinping calls for the PLA to 'accelerate military intelligentisation' in his remarks at the 19th Party Congress. In December, the US National Security Strategy characterised China as a revisionist power.

2018　In January, the new National Defense Strategy concentrated on great power competition. In March, the Trump administration announced major tariffs against Chinese imports in response to concerns over IP theft and other 'predatory' economic behaviour, and the Chinese government's retaliatory measures starting in April marked the start of the trade war. In October, a speech by Vice President Mike Pence In December, Canada arrested Huawei executive Meng Wanzhou.

2019　In August, China's Ministry of National Defence releases China's latest national defence white paper, titled "China's National Defense in the New Era. In October, China's military parade raises concerns by highlighting new weapons systems, including drones, hypersonic missiles, and new nuclear capabilities. In December, the first reports of the coronavirus pandemic emerge from Wuhan.

command decision-making, shaped these assessments, prompting high-level attention.[30] Starting around this period, the PLA writings highlighted with increased frequency the assessment that today's 'informatised' warfare was undergoing a transformation towards future 'intelligentised' warfare, catalysed by the rapid advances in these emerging technologies, a conclusion that has since received ever more official imprimatur.[31]

---

[30] See: China Military Science Editorial Department [中国军事科学 编辑部], 'A Summary of the Workshop on the Game between AlphaGo and Lee Sedol and the Intelligentisation of Military Command and Decision-Making' [围棋人机大战与军事指挥决策智能化研讨会观点综述], *China Military Science* [中国军事科学], 2 April 2016. Note that the journal's own English language translation of the title of the workshop is not the direct or literal translation.

[31] The potential alternative spellings and translations of 智能化 include intelligent, intelligencization, smartification, and/or AI-ification. The notion of 'cognification' has also been used in English-language descriptions of a similar phenomenon. I have chosen to render this term 'intelligentisation' for consistency with some of the official translations of the term in authoritative journals, such as *China Military Science*,

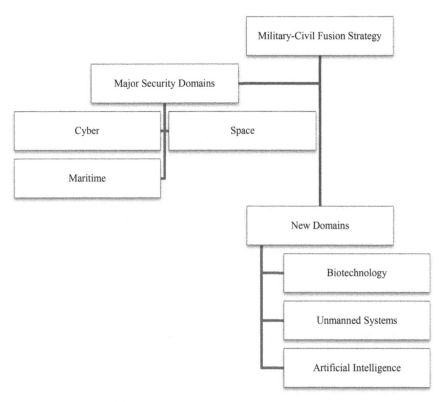

Depiction of select priorities in military-civil fusion.
Source: Author

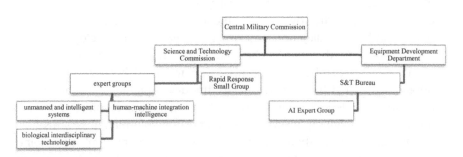

Approximate stakeholders in PRC military science, technology, and equipment.
Source: Author

---

but I am open to debating alternative translations and conceptualizations with those concerned. Not unlike 'informatization,' the notion of 'intelligentisation' is difficult to define with precision and appears to be used in a varying and sometimes somewhat inconsistent manner by PLA writings on these issues. My understanding of this concept has evolved since I first discussed it in published writing and testimony in February 2017. See also: Elsa B. Kania, 'Testimony before the US-China Economic and Security Review Commission: Chinese Advances in Unmanned Systems and the Military Applications of Artificial Intelligence – the PLA's Trajectory towards Unmanned, "Intelligentised" Warfare,' US-China Economic and Security Review Commission, 23 February 2017, https://www.uscc.gov/sites/default/files/Kania_Testimony.pdf.

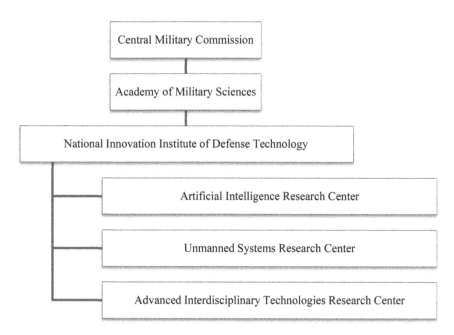

Several relevant institutions at academy of military science.
Source: Author

Writing in an authoritative commentary in August 2016, the CMC Joint Staff Department called upon the PLA to leverage the 'tremendous potential' of AI for operational command, planning and deductions, and decision support, while urging the advancement the application of big data, cloud computing, artificial intelligence, and other cutting-edge technologies to the construction of the PLA's command system for joint operations.[32] Significantly, in October 2017, in his report to the 19th Party Congress, Xi Jinping urged that the PLA, 'Accelerate the development of military intelligentisation' (军事智能化), and improve joint operations capabilities and all-domain operational capabilities based on network information systems.'[33]

This authoritative exhortation has elevated 'intelligentisation' as a guiding concept for the future of Chinese military modernisation. The PLA's apparent enthusiasm to embrace AI reflects a recognition of the potential dividends of success or leadership in this new RMA. Whereas the PLA was a spectator and latecomer to the early stages of RMA, this new RMA presents an opportunity

---

[32]CMC Joint Staff Department [中央军委联合参谋部], 'Accelerate the Construction of a Joint Operations Command System with Our Military's Characteristics [加快构建具有我军特色的联合作战指挥体系], Seeking Truth, 15 August 2016, http://www.qstheory.cn/dukan/qs/2016-08/15/c_1119374690.htm.

[33]'Xi Jinping's Report at the Chinese Communist Party 19th National Congress' [习近平在中国共产党第十九次全国代表大会上的报告].

for the PLA to perhaps emerge as the first to realise disruptive capabilities, including based on breakthroughs in new theories for intelligentisation.[34] Although the PLA continues to confront particular challenges in catching up,[35] its relative backwardness also presents the potential for certain advantages in the process of 'leapfrog development' (跨越发展) in its technological advancement.[36] In particular, the PLA possesses fewer legacy weapons and platforms and appears to be prioritising investments in next-generation weapons systems, such that it could prove capable of introducing new systems more rapidly, for instance, than the US military.

China's leaders believe AI is a strategic technology that will be critical across all dimensions of national competitiveness, with the potential to transform current paradigms of military power. Beijing's decision to prioritise AI to enhance China's economic development and military capabilities is evident across a growing number of plans, policies, and authoritative statements.[37] In July 2017, the New Generation Artificial Intelligence Development Plan elevated AI as a core priority, catalysing what has become a whole-of-nation strategic initiative.[38] Since then, this agenda has progressed at all levels of government and through the efforts of a range of stakeholders. China's AI efforts have built upon and harnessed the robust efforts of China's dynamic technology companies. This plan also discussed the implementation of a strategy of military-civil fusion (军民融合) in AI, calling for strengthening its use in military applications that include command decision-making, military deductions (e.g., wargaming), and defence equipment.[39]

Today, as Xi Jinping calls upon the PLA to pursue military innovation, such efforts are redoubling. The stakeholders that have a designated involvement

---

[34] 'Lt. Gen. Liu Guozhi: the development of military intelligentisation is a strategic opportunity for our military to turn sharply to surpass'.

[35] For an excellent academic evaluation of the challenges of catching up, see: Andrea Gilli and Mauro Gilli. 'Why China Has Not Caught Up Yet: Military-Technological Superiority and the Limits of Imitation, Reverse Engineering, and Cyber Espionage.' *International Security* 43, no. 3 (2019): 141–189.

[36] For an academic perspective on the notion of leapfrogging, see for instance: Takashi Hikino and Alice H. Amsden, 'Staying behind, stumbling back, sneaking up, soaring ahead: late industrialization in historical perspective' *Convergence of productivity: Cross-national studies and historical evidence* (1994): 285–315.

[37] See, for instance: 'Four Departments Issued a Notice Regarding the '"Internet Plus" Artificial Intelligence Three-Year Action Implementation Plan' [四部门关于印发《"互联网+"人工智能三年行动实施方案》的通知], China Government Network, 25 May 2016, http://www.miit.gov.cn/n1146290/n1146392/c4808445/content.html. 'State Council Notice on the Issuance of the New Generation AI Development Plan' [国务院关于印发新一代人工智能发展规划的通知], 20 August 2017, http://www.gov.cn/zhengce/content/2017-07/20/content_5211996.htm'MIIT's Notice Regarding the Release of the Three Year Action Plan to Promote the Development of New-Generation Artificial Intelligence Industry (2018-2020) [工业和信息化部关于印发《促进新一代人工智能产业发展三年行动计划（2018-2020年）》的通], 14 December 2017, http://www.miit.gov.cn/n1146295/n1652858/n1652930/n3757016/c5960820/content.html.

[38] For the full translation, see: Graham Webster, Rogier Creemers, Paul Triolo, and Elsa Kania, 'Full Translation: China's "New Generation Artificial Intelligence Development Plan" (2017),' https://www.newamerica.org/cybersecurity-initiative/digichina/blog/full-translation-chinas-new-generation-artificial-intelligence-development-plan-2017/.

[39] See again China's 'New Generation Artificial Intelligence Development Plan.'

in promotion and implementation of China's New Generation Artificial Intelligence Development Plan include the Central Military-Civil Fusion Development Commission Office, the Central Military Commission (CMC) Science and Technology Commission, and the CMC Equipment Development Department.[40] The PLA's Central Military Commission (CMC) Science and Technology Commission is guiding and supporting research in such 'frontier' technologies, including through a new 'rapid response small group' for national defence innovation that seeks to leverage commercial technologies.[41] The CMC Equipment Development Department, which is responsible for defence armaments development, is also funding and promoting research involving unmanned systems and artificial intelligence, including supporting dual-use technological developments with guidance from an 'AI Expert Group.'

PLA reforms and initiatives in innovation

The PLA's military reforms since late 2015 have involved historic restructuring intended to increase its capacity for military innovation.[42] In the course of these reforms, the PLA Strategic Support Force (战略支援部队) consolidated Chinese military capabilities for space, cyber, electronic, and psychological warfare. The PLASSF has been directed to undertake innovation and develop capabilities to contest new domains of military power.[43] These reforms have included the establishment of the Central Military Commission (CMC) Science and the Technology Commission (S&TC). The CMC S&TC has launched new plans, funds, and contests that concentrate on emerging technologies and promoting defence science and technological innovation.[44] In October 2017, Lieutenant

---

[40] 'New Generation AI Strategic Advisory Committee Established' [新一代人工智能战略咨询委员会成立], 21 November 2017, http://www.ia.cas.cn/xwzx/ttxw/201711/t20171121_4896939.html.
 'The New-Generation Artificial Intelligence Development Planning Promotion Office Convened a 2019 Working Conference' [新一代人工智能发展规划推进办公室召开2019年工作会议], 20 February 2019, http://www.most.gov.cn/tpxw/201902/t20190221_145137.htm.

[41] The details are available upon request.

[42] For a noteworthy commentary from Lt. Gen. Gao Jin, then president of the Academy of Military Science and later the inaugural commander of the PLA Strategic Support Force, see: 'Academy of Military Science President: Reforms Must Resolve the Restraints Upon Systematic Assurance for a Powerful Military' [军事科学院院长:改革要解决羁绊强军的体制性障碍], *PLA Daily*, 2 November 2015, http://www.chinanews.com/mil/2015/11-02/7600724.shtml.

[43] For the authoritative assessment of the PLASSF, see: John Costello and Joe McReynolds, 'The Strategic Support Force: A Force for a New Era,' National Defence University, 2 October 2018.
 See also: Elsa Kania and John Costello, 'The Strategic Support Force and the Future of Chinese Information Operations,' *Cyber Defence Review*, Spring 2018, https://cyberDefencereview.army.mil/Portals/6/Documents/CDR%20Journal%20Articles/The%20Strategic%20Support%20Force_Kania_Costello.pdf?ver=2018-07-31-093713-580.
 For primary source documentation highlighting the PLA's role in innovation, see: 'How Can the Strategic Support Force Forge New Quality Weapons' [战略支援部队如何锻造新质利器], *PLA Daily*, 11 March 2016, http://www.chinanews.com/mil/2016/03-11/7792939.shtml.

[44] For a basic description of the CMC Science and Technology Commission's mandate, see: 'Shoulder the functional mission of strengthening the military through science and technology' [肩负起科技强军

General Liu Guozhi (刘国治), director of the CMC Science and Technology Commission, emphasised the imperative of promoting intelligentisation, arguing, 'This is a rare strategic opportunity for our nation to achieve innovation surpassing and to achieve a powerful military, and it is also a rare strategic opportunity for us to achieve turning sharply to surpass (弯道超车).'[45]

The PLA's premier academic and research institutions have been tasked to prioritise innovation in disruptive and emerging technologies. During his visit to the PLA's Academy of Military Science in May 2018, Xi Jinping called for the AMS to concentrate on 'increasing the intensity of innovation in emerging domains, and strengthening the incubation of strategic, frontier, and disruptive technologies.'[46] His remarks emphasised the importance of placing innovation in a prominent position and pursuing innovation in military theories, national defence science and technology, military science and research work on organisational models. During his visit, Xi also spoke to Major General Li Deyi (李德毅), who has beena research fellow with the AMS Systems Engineering Research Institute, focusing on unmanned systems and artificial intelligence.

The PLA's National University of Defence Technology (NUDT) is considered an 'important highland for indigenous in national defence science and technologies' that is concentrating on 'developing the key technologies for national defence in the intelligent era.'[47] In particular, NUDT has built upon its existing research in automation through the Academy of Intelligent Sciences (智能科学学院), which is pursuing research that includes intelligent robotics, bionic robotics and autonomous control, such as swarm intelligence. The PLA's National Defence University has also started to explore the impact of AI in its research and teaching, including through wargaming.[48]

Concurrently, the PLA's Academy of Military Science (AMS) has transformed itself in ways that position this institution. Traditionally, AMS has been responsible for the formulation of PLA strategy and doctrine; today, AMS is also concentrating on advancing theoretical and technological innovations. Notably, the AMS has established a new National Defence Science

---

的职能使命], *PLA Daily*, 28 April 2016, http://www.mod.gov.cn/topnews/2016-04/28/content_4651316.htm.

[45]This concept (弯道超车), which often recurs in PLA writings, alludes to idea of two cars racing towards a corner, of which one cuts the turn more sharply and takes the inside track, thus passing by the other. I'm open to other suggestions on how to translate this term.

[46]'Xi Jinping: Strive to build a high-level military scientific research institution to provide strong support for the party's strong military objective in the new era' [习近平: 努力建设高水平军事科研机构 为实现党在新时代的强军目标提供有力支撑], Xinhua, 16 May 2018, http://www.xinhuanet.com/2018-05/16/c_1122843283.htm.

[47]'President Xi came to the military school for the first time' [习主席第一次到军校视察就来到这里], China Military Online, 20 March 2018, https://new.qq.com/omn/20180320/20180320A1G5SK.html .

[48]'Chief Engineer Hu Xiaofeng, General Manager of China's Bingqi Program, Delivered a Lecture: the Challenge of the Intelligentisation of Command information Systems' [中国兵棋工程总师胡晓峰少将演讲: 指挥信息系统的智能化挑战], 13 July 2016, 2016, http://chuansong.me/n/434595151184.

and Technology Innovation Research Academy (国防科技创新研究院, or 'National Innovation Institute of Defence Technology,' NIIDT, in its typical English translation).[49] NIIDT has been actively recruiting hundreds of military scientists and civilian personnel. NIIDT's Artificial Intelligence Research Center has concentrated on research in deep learning and human-machine integration.[50]

Emerging concepts of intelligentisation

The concept of intelligentisation involves the development and operationalisation of artificial intelligence and the enabling of interrelated technologies that are required for its realisation for military applications.[51] Intelligentisation is intended to build upon prior stages of mechanisation and 'informatisation,' the process through which the PLA has introduced information technology and undertaken the development of its C4ISR (command, control, communications, computers, intelligence, surveillance, and reconnaissance) capabilities.[52] For the PLA, force construction requires the simultaneous undertaking of all three processes, which may present distinct difficulties but also enables the leveraging of synergies among them.[53]

Inherently, the concept of military intelligentisation is not only about AI. Instead, it 'refers to the overall operational description of the force systems consisting of people, weapons equipment, and ways of combat,' according to one PLA scholar.[54] This new 'system of systems' consists of not only intelligent weapons but also a new military 'system of systems' that involves human-machine integration and with (artificial) intelligence in a 'leading' or dominant (智能主导) position.[55]

---

[49]'Academy of Military Science National Defence Science and Technology Innovation Research Academy – Exploring the "Matrix" Research Model to Enhance Innovation Capability' [军事科学院国防科技创新研究院 – – 探索'矩阵式'科研模式提升创新能力], PLA Daily, 2 April 2018, http://www.81.cn/jfjbmap/content/2018-04/02/content_202957.htm. See also: 'Academy of Military Science National Defence Science and Technology Innovation Research Academy Has Taken Measures to Gather Top Talents' [军科院国防科技创新研究院多措并集聚顶尖人才], China Military Network, 4 February 2018, http://webcache.googleusercontent.com/search?q=cache:WDwlAWmc6agJ:www.81.cn/jwgz/2018-02/04/content_7931564.htm+&cd=8&hl=en&ct=clnk&gl=us.

[50]'The Academy of Military Sciences has amassed and selected more than 120 urgently needed scientific research personnel from the whole military' [军事科学院面向全军集中选调120余名急需科研人才], Xinhua, 1 January 2018, http://www.xinhuanet.com/mil/2018-01/25/c_129798773.htm.

[51]This is the author's attempt to provide the simplest possible definition of the concept, and I am very open to other suggestions and interpretations.

[52]For context, see: Andrew S. Erickson and Michael S. Chase. 'Informatization and the Chinese People's Liberation Army Navy,'in Phillip Saunders, Christopher Yung, Michael Swaine, and Andrew Nien-Dzu Yang, *The Chinese Navy: Expanding Capabilities, Evolving Roles*, Washington, DC: Institute for National Strategic Studies (2011): 247–287.

[53]This concept (弯道超车), which often recurs in PLA writings, alludes to idea of two cars racing towards a corner, of which one cuts the turn more sharply and takes the inside track, thus passing by the other. I'm open to other suggestions on how to translate this term.

[54]'Experts: Military Intelligentisation Is Not Merely Artificial Intelligence' [专家: 军事智能化绝不仅仅是人工智能].

[55]Ibid.

Military learning and conceptual evolution

Chinese military science and research on the dynamics of future intelligentised operations are informed by the close study of US ways of war-fighting and are intended to 'offset' or undermine current American military advantages.[56] As an authoritative commentary in *PLA Daily* urged, 'Keep an eye on future opponents, adhere to using the enemy as the teacher, using the enemy as a guide, and using the enemy as a target ... We must develop technologies and tactics that can break the battle systems of powerful adversaries and counter the high-end combat platforms of powerful adversaries.'[57] Although the PLA has not finalised or formalised new doctrinal concepts, such as for intelligentised operations, a review of semi-authoritative and authoritative writings that are openly available can reveal initial insights about the current trajectory and continued evolution of this thinking among the community of scholars and scientists who are engaged with these issues.

The PLA's traditional concentration on devising capabilities designed to target perceived weaknesses in an adversary's ways of warfare will likely persist in conceptual and technological developments that leverage these emerging technologies. For instance, Zhang Zhanjun (张占军), a senior researcher with the Academy of Military Science's Theory and Operational Regulations Research Department,[58] who also serves as editor-in-chief of its journal *China Military Science*, wrote a lengthy commentary in October 2017 on how the PLA might compete to seize the initiative in future maritime combat, arguing, 'using new-type combat forces to fight in new domains such as networks and space, we must implement asymmetric autonomous operations.'[59]

It is noteworthy that the latest edition of *The Science of (Military) Strategy* released in 2017 by the PLA's National Defence University has added a new section on 'military competition in the domain of (artificial) intelligence' (智能领域军事竞争), in an unusual, off-cycle revision of this authoritative textbook,[60] of which Lt. Gen. Xiao Tianliang (肖天亮), who remains the vice commandant of the PLA's National Defence University, is the editor.[61] The section discusses the 'new military intelligentisation revolution' underway

---

[56] The PLA does not describe what it is doing as an 'offset' per se, but that could be the effect in practice.
[57] Ke Zhengxuan [科政轩], 'How to build a military scientific research system with our military's characteristics' [我军特色军事科学研究体系如何构建形成], *PLA Daily*, 8 August 2017, http://www.81.cn/jmywyl/2017-08/04/content_7703373.htm.
[58] This is the department that has had direct responsibility for the PLA's formulation of its equivalent to doctrine, operational regulations.
[59] Zhang Zhanjun [张占军], 'How to compete for future maritime combat initiative' [如何争夺未来海上作战主动权], *PLA Daily*, 24 October 2017, https://web.archive.org/save/http://www.xinhuanet.com/mil/2017-10/24/c_129725534.htm.
[60] The prior edition of the NDU's SMS dated back to 1999, and it is unusual for a revision of the text to occur so soon.
[61] Note: Although the 2013 edition of the Science of Military Strategy is often seen as more authoritative, it is the author's contention that the 2015 and this revised 2017 versions merit greater attention. Xiao Tianliang (ed.), *The Science of Military Strategy* [战略学], National Defence University Press, 2017.

that involves strategic competition among nations worldwide that are seeking to 'seize this new strategic commanding heights in military affairs.'

Beyond the trend of the increased prominence of intelligent unmanned systems, intelligent operational systems are expected to become 'unavoidably 'the dominant forces on the battlefield in future warfare. As a strategic guidance for the character of competition in this new frontier:

> Military intelligentisation advances new and higher requirements for armed forces construction; it is providing a rare opportunity for latecomer militaries [to undertake] leapfrog development, achieving turning sharply to surpass (弯道超车). It is necessary to actively confront the challenge of intelligentisation, planning and preparing a strategy for the development of military intelligentisation [and] seizing the commanding heights of future military competition.

As the PLA continues to concentrate on revising military policies and doctrine, these research activities may contribute to future revisions to PLA military strategic guidelines (and the next generation of the PLA's operational regulations (作战条令), which are still under development.[62] The inclusion of discussions of competition in artificial intelligence in this authoritative textbook reflects a further formalisation of the PLA's strategic thinking on the importance of military intelligentisation.

While the PLA's process of adjusting some aspects of its equivalent to doctrine remains ongoing, there are indications that new theories and concepts involving AI could be incorporated into future revisions. According to Wang Yonghua (王永华), a scholar with the Academy of Military Science's Operational Theories and Regulations Department:

> At present, to research and develop concepts of operations, it is necessary to focus research on the profound influence of such high-tech groups as artificial intelligence, big data, and Internet of Things upon the methods and routes for combat victory. [We must] research the development of changes to the winning factors of information, forces, time, space, and spirit; study the impact of the interactions of space, cyber, electromagnetic, deep sea and other spaces' with traditional combat spaces on future operations, developing new operational concepts though future combat research and design.[63]

Such ideas and concepts of operations cannot be regarded as official until their incorporated into the PLA's 'operational regulations' to inform more directly future military campaigns and training. The PLA's process of transforming concepts into doctrine has required a more formal process of evaluation and authoritative assessment, and there appear to have been delays over time. In this regard, to say that the PLA has clear policies established on

---

[62] For context, see: Elsa B. Kania, 'When Will the PLA Finally Update Its Doctrine?,' *The Diplomat*, 6 June 2017, https://thediplomat.com/2017/06/when-will-the-pla-finally-update-its-doctrine/.

[63] Wang Yonghua [王永华], 'How to get through the whole link of combat concept development?' [如何打通作战概念开发的完整链路？], China Military Network, 29 November 2018, http://www.81.cn/jwgd/2018-11/29/content_9360140.htm.

questions of autonomy and artificial intelligence would be premature. Nonetheless, this theoretical research is informative of the direction that these initiatives are taking.

There is often a recurrence of the assessment that the tempo and complexity of operations will increase to an extent, changing the role of humans on the battlefield. Already, informatised warfare has placed a premium upon competition in the domain of cognition. Future warfare is expected to demand rapid processing of information and evaluation of the operational environment.[64] Consequently, the place of humans in that endeavour could change from being 'in' the loop, to 'on' the loop, and perhaps even out of the loop.[65] There is no evidence to conclude that the PLA is likely to take humans 'out of the loop' entirely. However, there is an expectation of a future point at which 'the rhythm of intelligentised operations will be unprecedentedly accelerated,' beyond the capabilities of human cognition.[66] At the same time, PLA thinkers appear to recognise the importance of balancing human and machine elements in decision-making. This dynamic is even characterised as an important 'dialectical relationship,' as Chen Dongheng (陈东恒) and Dong Julin (董俊林) researchers with the PLA Academy of Military Science have highlighted.[67]

The promotion of intelligentisation involves and requires various supporting and interrelated technologies. For instance, cloud computing is recognised as critical to realising intelligentisation, including to improve the management of military data.[68] The recent advances in AI chips and the requisite hardware can enable improved analytic and processing capabilities 'at the edge.'[69] China's continued difficulties in the development of indigenous semiconductors could remain a significant impediment on that front. In practice, such future warfare could involve a range of intelligentised weaponry, enabled by the Internet of Things (IoT), and leveraging networked information systems that are integrated across all domains.[70] Some military scientists have emphasised 5G will be vital to enabling the process of

---

[64]Chen Hanghui [陈航辉], 'Artificial Intelligence: Disruptively Changing the Rules of the Game' [人工智能: 颠覆性改变'游戏规则'], China Military Online, 18 March 2016, http://www.81.cn/jskj/2016-03/18/content_6966873_2.htm. Chen Hanghui is affiliated with the Nanjing Army Command College. Please note that I do not assess this to be an official or entirely authoritative perspective, though I do believe that the recurrence of similar sentiments in a range of reasonably authoritative.

[65]These concepts (i.e., of humans being in, on, or out of the loop) originate in US discussions of the role of humans in decision-making, reflecting the PLA's close attention to US policies and debates.

[66]'Exploring the winning joints of intelligentised operations' [探究智能化作战的制胜关节], PLA Daily, 29 March 2018, http://military.people.com.cn/n1/2018/0329/c1011-29896429.html.

[67]Chen Dongheng [陈东恒] and Dong Julin [董俊林], 'Military Intelligence Development Should Emphasize and Seize Upon Several Dialectical Relationships' [军事智能化发展应着重把握的几个辩证关系], PLA Daily, 14 May 2019, http://www.81.cn/theory/2019-05/14/content_9502765.htm.

[68]'Exploring the winning joints of intelligentised operations' [探究智能化作战的制胜关节].

[69]'Unmanned Systems: New Opportunities the Development of Military-Civil Fusion in Artificial Intelligence' [无人系统: 人工智能军民融合发展新契机].

[70]Hao Yaohong [郝耀鸿], '5 G, One Step Closer to the Military Internet of Things' [5 G,离军事物联网更近一步], Confidential Work 《保密工作》 July 2017, http://www.cnki.com.cn/Article/CJFDTotal-

intelligentisation. Such increases in connectivity can allow for improvements in data sharing and new mechanisms for command and control.[71]

In particular, 5G is anticipated to allow for machine-to-machine communication among sensors, drones, or even swarms on the battlefield, as well as improvements in human-machine interaction.[72] As China looks to construct a more integrated information architecture, 5 G could become critical to this new 'system of systems.'[73] Ultimately, it is not AI alone but the synergies of AI as a force multiplier for a range of weapons systems and technologies, also including directed energy, biotechnology, and perhaps even quantum computing, that could prove truly transformative.

Chinese military scholars and scientists are also focused on the challenges that data presents. From a practical perspective, data, recognised as a 'pivotal strategic resource.' In July 2018, the PLA's first 'military big data forum' had been convened by the Chinese Academy of Sciences, Tsinghua University, and Chinese Institute of Command and Control in Beijing.[74] The symposium concentrated on the importance of military big data, including to emphasise ways the military could learn lessons from enterprises and government in the management of big data. For instance, Song Jie, vice president of Alibaba Cloud (Aliyun), who discussed how Alibaba had leveraged big data to achieve a major advantage relative to traditional business infrastructure.[75] At the time, He You (何友), who is director of PLA Naval Aeronautical University's Information Fusion Research Institute argued that defence competition 'is centering on cognitive advantages and decision-making advantages' that require data.[76]

Data is recognised as a critical resource for modern operations. Data is expected to become 'an important foundation for the creation of the intelligentised battlefield.' In a prominent commentary in February 2019, PLA scholar Zuo Dengyun (左登云) emphasised, 'data is the "blood" of

---

BMGZ201707033.htm. Hao Yaohong is an expert on military communications with the PLA Special Operations Academy (特种作战学院).

[71]Zhang Qingliang [张清亮] and Zhang Guoning [张国宁], '5 G Promotes the Acceleration of Military Intelligentisation' [5 G推动智能化作战提速], *China National Defence Report* [中国国防报], 12 March 2019, http://www.81.cn/gfbmap/content/2019-03/12/content_229076.htm.

[72]See: 'What is driving warfare to become more intelligentised?' [是什么在推动战争向智能化演变?], *People's Daily*, 6 November 2018. 'How does national Defence mobilization embrace the 5 G era?' [国防动员如何拥抱5 G时代], China Military Network, 27 June 2018, http://www.81.cn/gfbmap/content/2018-06/27/content_209482.htm.

[73]Hao Yaohong [郝耀鸿], '5 G, One Step Closer to the Military Internet of Things' [5 G,离军事物联网更近一步].

[74]'Big data builds the strongest "military brain"' [大数据构筑最强'军事大脑], *Qiushi*, 12 July 2018, https://web.archive.org/web/20190505163610/http://www.qsjournal.com.cn/junshiguofang/46518.html.

[75]The participation of Alibaba executives in a seminar of this nature is noteworthy and may be indicative of the company's current or intended future engagement in supporting military innovation.

[76]He You is also a professor with the Northwestern Polytechnical University, which is closely linked to military research. The propensity of influential researchers to take on many roles and multiple affiliations simultaneously could be characterized as a feature of technological development in China that contributes to easier exchange of ideas between military and technical communities.

maritime operations ... It is necessary to obtain massive amounts of information through data deposits, grasp the weaknesses of enemy systems through data mining, share the operational situation through data presentation, and open up multi-domain joint channels, activating the "sense" of "smart" network empowerment.'[77] In the future, 'without data, (you) can't (fight) a war' (无数据不战争), and the PLA is concerned with improving its collection, management, and processing of data.[78] The commercial advantage that China may have given the depth and quantity of data available to its start-ups will hardly translate into military applicability except in select use-cases.

Chinese strategic thinkers have argued the advent of AI could change the fundamental mechanisms for winning future warfare.[79] The increasing prominence of intelligent could result in 'remote, precise, miniaturised, large-scale unmanned attacks' becoming the primary method of attack, according to Yun Guanrong (游光荣) of the Academy of Military Science.[80] Considering the ways in which AI could increase the tempo, accuracy, efficiency of operations, certain Chinese military strategists even expect that '[artificial] intelligence will transcend firepower, machine power, and information power, becoming the most critical factor in determining the outcome of warfare.'[81] Potentially, superior algorithms could dispel the 'fog' of the battlefield and enable decision-making advantage, while increasing the efficiency of operations.[82] In future intelligentised operations, today's 'system of systems confrontation' could become instead a 'game of algorithms' in which algorithmic advantage is a dominant determinant of operational advantage, as Li Minghai (李明海) of the PLA's National University of Defence Technology, has anticipated.[83] At present, however, such exuberant anticipation remains premature.

With the advent of intelligentisation, the human element of conflict remains critical and potentially vulnerable. Future command decision-making could leverage the respective strengths of human and machine cognition, while leveraging a 'cloud brain' that allows for swarm and distributed decision-making, enabled by deep neural networks. AI is also expected

---

[77] Zuo Dengyun [左登云], 'Where is the road to intelligent transformation of maritime operations?' [海上作战智能化变革路在何方], *PLA Daily*, 12 February 2019. http://military.people.com.cn/n1/2019/0212/c1011-30624347.html.

[78] Liu Zhanyong [刘战勇], 'Data: The Lifeblood of Informatized and Intelligentised Warfare' [数据: 信息化智能化作战血液], *PLA Daily*, 19 February 2019, http://www.81.cn/jfjbmap/content/2019-02/19/content_227628.htm.

[79] The range of books and textbooks on the topic illustrate the PLA's interest in the topic. See, for instance: Wu Mingxi [吴明曦], Intelligent Wars [智能化战争—AI军事畅想], National Defense Industry Press (Beijing), 2020; and Shi Haiming [石海明] and Jia Zhenzhen [贾珍珍], Artificial Intelligence Disrupts Future Warfare [人工智能颠覆未来战争], People's Press (Beijing), 2019.

[80] Yun Guangrong [游光荣], 'AI Will Deeply Change the Face of Warfare' [人工智能将深刻改变战争面], *PLA Daily*, 17 October 2018, http://www.81.cn/jfjbmap/content/2018-10/17/content_218050.htm.

[81] Ibid.

[82] Ibid.

[83] 'Where is the winning mechanism of intelligent warfare?' [智能化战争的制胜机理变在哪里?]

to contribute to more far-reaching transformations that could result in the intelligentisation of logistics support, models of combat power generation, organisational mechanisms, and education and training.[84] Pursuantly, Chinese military strategists expect that new styles of operations could emerge, particularly penetrating the cognitive and information domains.

Going forward, the capability to counter or subvert an adversary's capabilities in AI could become a critical domain of competition. PLA academics and strategists have discussed options for countermeasures against adversary's military employment of AI.[85] Such measures might include interference, damage, and destruction through kinetic or non-kinetic (e.g., electromagnetic, microwave weapons) means, or even attempts to make the enemy lose control of its AI and modify its procedures.[86] In particular, 'counter-intelligentised operations' would involve to 'paralyse the enemy's artificial intelligence, this the 'brain'; cutting the enemy's combat network, this the 'nerve'; and draining the enemy's combat data, this the 'blood,' as Maj. General Li Dapeng (李大鹏) of the PLA's Naval Engineering University has argued, calling for research on such techniques as counter-swarm combat, adaptive electronic warfare, and intelligent cyber warfare.[87] The use of AI can identify weak links and important targets in an adversary's system for joint operations, including to enable assaults intended to collapse an opponent's system of systems architecture.[88]

AI/ML projects in PLA research and development

The PLA has been actively pursuing research, development, and experimentation with an array of applications of artificial intelligence in recent years. The PLA's interest in AI/ML is hardly a recent phenomenon. Chinese research and development of dual-use advances in robotics and early artificial intelligence can be traced back to the mid-1980s, at which time the 863 Plan also launched a project that involved robotics and intelligent computing.[89]

---

[84] Li Dapeng [李大鹏], 'How should we deal with the challenges of intelligent warfare' [我们该如何应对智能化战争挑战], *China Youth Daily* [中国青年报], 4 April 2019, http://www.xinhuanet.com/mil/2019-04/04/c_1210099555.htm.

[85] Zhu Qichao [朱启超], Wang Jingling [王婧凌], and Li Daguang [李大光], 'Artificial Intelligence Opens the Door to Intelligentised Warfare' [工智能叩开智能化战争大门], *PLA Daily*, 23 January 2017, http://military.china.com.cn/2017-01/23/content_40158456.htm.

[86] Chen Yufei [陈玉飞] and Xia Wenjun [夏文军], 'Intelligentised Warfare Quietly Strikes' [智能化战争悄然来袭], *PLA Daily*, 16 February 2017, http://www.81.cn/jfjbmap/content/2017-02/16/content_169593.htm.

[87] Li Dapeng [李大鹏], 'How should we deal with the challenges of intelligent warfare' [我们该如何应对智能化战争挑战].

[88] Zuo Dengyun [左登云], Gong Jia [龚佳], Huang Peirong [黄培荣], 'Why do informationized operations go to intelligized operations' [信息化作战何以走向智能化作战], *PLA Daily*, 20 September 2018, http://www.xinhuanet.com/mil/2018-09/20/c_129957478.htm. Huang Peirong is a professor at the Naval Command Academy.

[89] This program was contemporaneous with in response to the US Strategic Computing Initiative and Japan's Fifth-Generation Computing. Alex Roland, Philip Shiman, and William Aspray. *Strategic computing: DARPA and the quest for machine intelligence, 1983–1993*. MIT Press, 2002.

Certain initiatives to apply expert systems to military operations research also date back to the late 1980s and 1990s.[90] Chinese military researchers who are active in work on decision support systems, such as Major General Liu Zhong (刘忠) of the PLA's National University of Defence Technology, have been leveraging what might be considered 'AI' in their research since at least the mid-2000s.[91]

Certain initiatives in weapons development, such as the application of advanced algorithms to work on hypersonic glide vehicles can also be traced back to the mid-2000s.[92] For instance, the Chinese defence industry's attempts to make cruise and ballistic missiles more 'intelligent' build upon advances in Automatic Target Recognition (ATR) that also predate the recent concern with autonomous weapons. The swarms and suicide drones that have been already developed and subject to operational experimentation highlight

PLA support for AI has been and will be included in the PLA's plans for weapons development. The PLA Army, Navy, Air Force, Rocket Force, and Strategic Support Force are all pursuing their own service-specific projects and initiatives through their respective equipment departments and through their research institutes and partnerships. To date, each service in the PLA has started to field and deploy a number of unmanned (i.e., remotely piloted) systems, of which some have at least a limited degree of autonomy.[93]

The PLA's pursuit of military intelligentisation is intended to enhance and augment existing weapons systems, while also enabling novel capabilities. The patents, funding, and technical publications that are often openly published and demonstrated provide initial indications of the direction of these developments, and there are also certainly classified programs underway about which no or fewer details are known. The PLA should be expected to employ AI across an array of applications in all domains of warfare and a range of missions in combat and to support operations, including for maintenance, automatic target recognition, and support to command decision-making, among others.[94]

---

[90]Deborah R. Harvey and Barbara R. Felton, 'Military Operations Research in China: A Defence S&T Intelligence Study,' March 1994, DST-1820S-187-94. This document was regarded as unclassified and released in March 1998.

[91]'National University of Defence Technology's Liu Zhong: Creating a Powerful "External Brain" for Command and Control' [国防科大刘忠:为指挥控制打造强大'外脑'], People's Daily, 28 December 2015, http://military.people.com.cn/n1/2015/1228/c401735-27986608.html.

[92]For an authoritative assessment, see: Lora Saalman, 'China's Integration of Neural Networks into Hypersonic Glide Vehicles,' December 2018, https://nsiteam.com/social/wp-content/uploads/2018/12/AI-China-Russia-Global-WP_FINAL.pdf.

[93]See this report from the China Aerospace Studies Institute: Elsa Kania 'The PLA's Unmanned Aerial Systems New Capabilities for a "New Era" of Chinese Military Power,' China Aerospace Studies Institute, 8 August 2018, https://www.airuniversity.af.edu/CASI/Display/Article/1596429/the-plas-unmanned-aerial-systems-new-capabilities-for-a-new-era-of-chinese-mili/.

[94]Upon request, more details on these projects based on open sources are available from the author.

Potential challenges in chinese military innovation

While the PLA's ambitions and advances in robotics, autonomy, and a range of applications of artificial intelligence should not be dismissed or underestimated, nonetheless certain difficulties and apparent will likely impede its implementation of this agenda. Not unlike the US military or any bureaucracy, the PLA will confront constraints and challenges in the process. It remains to be seen whether attempts to overcome such impediments will prove successful, and the theoretical frameworks from the literature can contribute to our evaluation of the likely challenges.

The PLA's capacity to innovate may be impeded by bureaucratic politics and its culture as an organisation. The Chinese military, similar to any bureaucracy, has struggled to adopt and adapt new technologies that may, in some cases, present threats to existing interests. The PLA has been assessed to be an organisation that is highly hierarchical, operating in a top-down manner with a high degree of centralisation of power. These features, such as the low levels of trust often considered characteristic of authoritarian militaries, could impede more junior officers and enlisted personnel from having the opportunity to exercise initiative and experiment with new technologies and techniques.

These typical difficulties could be exacerbated by the disruption that has resulted from the significant organisational restructuring that remains ongoing. For these reasons, despite the CCP's and PLA's rhetorical commitment to innovation, its implementation may be impeded by such dynamics. Moreover, if the slowdown of China's economy constrains the resources available for military modernisation, the trade-offs between the development of new capabilities and sustainment of existing platforms could become more acute.

The PLA's capability to leverage AI could be hindered by continued challenges in talent and human capital. The PLA has attempted to overcome prior difficulties to expand the recruitment of 'high-quality' talents, including by targeting those with higher levels of education. For instance, as of spring 2019, over 2,500 colleges and universities nationwide have reportedly established recruitment workstations.[95] There have also been reforms to the PLA's personnel management to shift from 'civilian cadre' to civilian personnel, who receive benefits comparable to those of civil servants. The new rounds of recruitment for these civilian positions have aimed to attract candidates with MA and PhD degrees who have backgrounds in computer science and artificial intelligence. The PLA's actual success in recruiting and retaining those with such technical proficiencies remains to be seen. The PLA will be competing for high-tech talent against intense demands from a growing private sector.

---

[95]'Military Delegates Hotly Discussed Accelerating and Improving Innovative Development of National Defence Mobilization' [军队人大代表热议加速推进国防动员创新发展], China Military Network, 15 March 2019, https://web.archive.org/save/http://www.legaldaily.com.cn/army/content/2019-03/15/content_7802049.htm.

There are particular bottlenecks in the availability of AI talent to date that have also presented significant challenges to technology companies. The application of an approach of military-civil fusion to talent development could contribute to resolving this problem, including through dedicated programs that leverage closer collaboration with the tech sector. For instance, Beihang University has launched a new degree program in AI to which Baidu is contributing, and the Beijing Institute of Technology has also established a new program for intelligent weapons development.[96] As Chinese universities expand educational programming in AI research, and as plans and programs for the recruitment of overseas talents continue to expand, the PLA may manage to create a more sizable pool of talent to draw from. These attempts to cultivate 'first-class talent' continue, but progress will take time to realise and may prove limited in some cases.[97]

While the PLA has concentrated on increasing the realism of its training, the PLA may struggle to match the sophistication required for preparations for future warfare. The PLA's training was once highly scripted and has improved in sophistication, but further challenges will intensify considering the complexities and challenges of future intelligentised operations. Chinese military officers and researchers recognise the importance of innovation in training in response to new challenges. However, the adoption of new techniques to be incorporated into the PLA's official Outline of Military Training and Education, which was last revised in 2017, could prove challenging.[98] The PLA's experimentation with the use of virtual reality and artificial intelligence training, as well as active efforts for AI systems in wargaming, could enable improvements in realism that could facilitate preparation for actual combat, which is a critical concern considering the PLA's lack of operational experience. In particular, the complexities of managing human factors in training with complex systems could present particular challenges for the PLA.

The PLA has seemed to struggle with revising its doctrine and may confront difficulties in adopting new theories and concepts in practice. The Chinese military does not appear to have fully revised its doctrine since 1999, even though ongoing, rolling revisions that have involved some updates. The new 'fifth-generation' of operational regulations (作战条令), including campaign guidelines (战役纲要), which has been under development since 2004, was nearly, but not fully or officially, launched in 2008 at its intended completion. Despite ongoing research activities, the PLA was slow

---

[96] Artificial Intelligence Research Direction 2017 Double Certificate Master's Degree [人工智能研究方向 2017年双证硕士], http://soft.buaa.edu.cn/BuaaPublic/html/ShowNews_60_4896.html.
[97] 'A First-Class Military; New-Type Military Talent Cultivation' [一流军队，新型军事人才咋培养], *PLA Daily*, 2 January 2018, http://www.xinhuanet.com/mil/2018-01/02/c_129780635.htm .
[98] For context on the trajectory of these developments, see: Department of Defence, 'Military and Security Developments Involving the People's Republic of China 2018,' https://media.Defence.gov/2018/Aug/16/2001955282/-1/-1/1/2018-CHINA-MILITARY-POWER-REPORT.PDF.

to progress in completing and implementing these doctrinal changes, which appears to indicate a lack of consensus or institutional impediments. The apparent complications also raise questions about whether the PLA will be able to incorporate new theories and concepts of intelligentised operations into this framework in practice, such as through facilitating increasing connectivity between scientists and strategists, or could confront comparable difficulties in the process.

In this regard, while China may appear to possess a data advantage given the aggregate amount of data that it possesses as a nation, that edge may prove limited in actuality and unlikely to directly translate into a military advantage. The relative fragmentation across bureaucracies could obstruct progress. Chinese military researchers have expressed concern that there are current inadequacies in data mining, analytic processing capabilities, awareness of security and secrecy, and support of training data.[99] The PLA will have to manage practical challenges in cleaning and labelling disparate sources of data for use, which can be time and labour intensive, but these efforts could be facilitated access to cheap services for data labelling such as available in China.[100] The PLA will be required to adopt shared infrastructure, including cloud computing, to enable deployment and promote an integrated approach. However, if the inefficiencies redundancies, even corruption, that arose during the implementation of informatisation arise again in the process of intelligentisation, the PLA may be hindered from effective utilisation of these technologies.

The PLA's lack of operational experience could result in a failure to appreciate the challenges of operating highly complex automated or autonomous systems under actual combat conditions. The PLA approaches warfare through the lens of military science. Lacking operational experience in its recent history, the PLA has confronted the unique challenge of 'learning without fighting,' often based on engaging in theoretical research that examines trends and technologies. Traditionally, military innovation in peacetime has been considered particularly challenging, and the PLA is unlikely to be an exception in that regard. Nonetheless, the sense of threat and urgency that comes with facing a 'powerful adversary' appears to have overcome the inertia that often impedes change. The progress in 'actual combat' training, including confrontations between blue and red forces, could compensate for the lack of operational experience. Nonetheless, the PLA may fail to appreciate the extent to which the full complexity of warfare can extend beyond that anticipated in theories or exercises.

---

[99]Liu Zhanyong [刘战勇], 'Data: The Lifeblood of Informatized and Intelligentised Warfare' [数据: 信息化智能化作战血液], *PLA Daily*, 19 February 2019, http://www.81.cn/jfjbmap/content/2019-02/19/content_227628.htm.
[100]'Data-labeling: the human power behind Artificial Intelligence,' *Xinhua*, 17 January 2019, http://www.xinhuanet.com/english/2019-01/17/c_137752154.htm.

Whereas initial American enthusiasm about the notion of a Revolution in Military Affairs was tempered by the realities of combat and the failures of certain capabilities to materialise as anticipated, the PLA's focus on the notion of the RMA has persisted, seemingly without a comparable recalibration of expectations. For instance, certain Chinese military writings go so far as to claim that these advances could render the battlefield 'clear and transparent,' lifting or perhaps lessening the fog of war. In actuality, the advent of AI could change that fog, perhaps creating new sources of confusion and novel cognitive challenges, particularly given the likely limitations of AI. In this regard, the PLA's efforts could be undermined by 'hot thinking' on AI that is not always qualified by the 'cooler' realities.[101]

The particular ideological constraints and characteristics for the PLA as a Party army may impede or condition its development in ways that could prove unique. The PLA is a Party army, not a national military, and that reality could influence its approach to AI. Xi Jinping has consistently reiterated that the PLA must adhere to the Party's 'absolute leadership,' expanding and emphasising the importance of innovation in 'political work' that is intended to ensure that obedience. At first glance, these imperatives of capability and controllability could appear to be at odds in some cases. For instance, time dedicated to political activities is time taken away from training, and the imposition of ideological indoctrination seems unlikely to be conducive to the creativity that can enable innovation. Moreover, certain idiosyncrasies might be introduced into the PLA's approach to AI as a result of the ideological environment within which it is being developed. Some writings have called for a dialectical approach to AI or emphasised the importance of ensuring that AI possesses certain political qualities and adhere to the necessary ideological requirements, avoiding any disloyalty.[102]

Implications for US-China rivalry

As US-China military rivalry intensifies at a time of technological transformation, these trends may present new risks to strategic stability under complex geopolitical circumstances. Chinese military strategists are seeking to seize the initiative, believing 'first-class militaries design warfare, second-rate militaries are trailing in warfare, and third-rate militaries have to contend with warfare.'[103] The PLA's ambitions to be a truly world-class military imply its intention to be at the forefront of shaping and 'designing' the conditions of

---

[101]For instance, certain Chinese military writings have articulated a more skeptical perspective, and it is likely there is still some disagreement among PLA stakeholders.
[102]For translation and discussion, see: 'Intersections of Ideology with China's Approach to Military Applications of Artificial Intelligence,' https://www.battlefieldsingularity.com/musings-1/intersections-of-ideology-with-china-s-approach-to-military-applications-of-artificial-intelligence.
[103]Ke Zhengxuan [科政轩], 'How to build and form a military scientific research system with our military's characteristics' [我军特色军事科学研究体系如何构建形成].

future battlefields.[104] However, there are reasons to question and regard sceptically the PLA's capacity to realise its aspirations given the challenges that remain. Even as American observers fear that China may have surpassed the US military on some fronts, the PLA itself continues to regard it as a powerful adversary that sets the benchmark for its own advances.

Looking forward, while the disruption that AI may introduce may be the subject of exaggerated expectations in the near future, the transformations that such emerging information technologies could create in the decades to come may extend beyond anyone's anticipation. 'AI' is best considered a general-purpose enabling technology that has a diverse array of applications that cannot be characterised through a single facet. This disparate and qualitative character of how AI can enhance various military capabilities may create a degree of uncertainty that could impede assessments of relative advances. The impact on the military balance may be merely perceived, rather than adequately evaluated.

Since the contributions of AI to military power are essentially intangible, there are incentives for militaries to signal, display, and demonstrate relevant capabilities, such as swarming, in attempts to bolster deterrence, including through activities that may be intended for purposes of deception or misdirection. This trend can be exacerbated by the consistent tendency towards worst-case scenario thinking and overestimation of a potential adversary's capabilities. However, it is encouraging that military specialists and technology stakeholders in the United States and China alike appear to be cognizant on such concerns.[105] Ultimately, the frequent framing of an 'AI arms race' is also problematic,[106] insofar as this conceptualisation can be misleading and has significant limitations. As the US-China military-to-military relationship evolves going forward, there may be opportunities to progress towards greater clarity and transparency through dialogue on shared concerns of strategic stability, including questions of risk mitigation and crisis management.

Disclosure statement

No potential conflict of interest was reported by the author.

---

[104]'Xi Jinping's Report at the Chinese Communist Party 19th National Congress' [习近平在中国共产党第十九次全国代表大会上的报告], Xinhua, 27 October 2017, http://www.china.com.cn/19da/2017-10/27/content_41805113_3.htm.

[105]China Institute of Information and Communications (CAICT), 'AI Security White Paper' [人工智能安全白皮书], September 2018, http://www.caict.ac.cn/kxyj/qwfb/bps/201809/P020180918473525332978.pdf.

[106]For an excellent assessment of this issue see: Heather Roff, 'The frame problem: The AI "arms race" isn't one,' *Bulletin of the Atomic Scientists*, 29 April 2019, https://thebulletin.org/2019/04/the-frame-problem-the-ai-arms-race-isnt-one/.

Select Bibliography

'Xi Jinping's Report at the Chinese Communist Party 19th National Congress' [习近平在中国共产党第十九次全国代表大会上的报告], Xinhua, October 27, 2017.

Adamsky, Dima, *The Culture of Military Innovation: The Impact of Cultural Factors on the Revolution in Military Affairs in Russia, the US, and Israel* (Stanford CA: Stanford University Press 2010).

All-Military Military Terminology Management Committee [全军军事术语管理委员会]. *People's Liberation Army Military Terminology* [中国人民解放军军语] (Beijing: Military Science Press [军事科学出版社] 2011), 660.

Cheung, Tai Ming, Thomas G. Mahnken, and Andrew L. Ross. 'Frameworks for Analysing Chinese Defence and Military Innovation,' 2011, working paper.

China Institute of Information and Communications (CAICT), 'AI Security White Paper' [人工智能安全白皮书], September 2018.

China Military Science Editorial Department [中国军事科学 编辑部], 'A Summary of the Workshop on the Game between AlphaGo and Lee Sedol and the Intelligentisation of Military Command and Decision-Making' [围棋人机大战与军事指挥决策智能化研讨会观点综述], China Military Science [中国军事科学], April 2, 2016.

CMC Joint Staff Department [中央军委联合参谋部], 'Accelerate the Construction of a Joint Operations Command System with Our Military's Characteristics [加快构建具有我军特色的联合作战指挥体系], Seeking Truth, August 15, 2016.

Costello, John and Joe McReynolds, 'The Strategic Support Force: A Force for A New Era,' National Defence University, October 2, 2018.

Cote, Owen R., 'The Politics of Innovative Military Doctrine: The US Navy and Fleet Ballistic Missiles,' PhD diss., Massachusetts Institute of Technology, 1996.

Department of Defence, 'Military and Security Developments Involving the People's Republic of China 2018.'

Dongheng, Chen, [陈东恒] and Dong Julin [董俊林], 'Military Intelligence Development Should Emphasise and Seize upon Several Dialectical Relationships' [军事智能化发展应着重把握的几个辩证关系], *PLA Daily*, May 14, 2019.

Erickson, Andrew S. and Michael S. Chase *Informatisation and the Chinese People's Liberation Army Navy*.' Phillip Saunders, Christopher Yung, Michael Swaine, and Andrew Nien-Dzu Yang, the Chinese Navy: Expanding Capabilities, Evolving Roles (Washington, DC: Institute for National Strategic Studies 2011), 247–87.

Fravel, M. Taylor, 'Shifts in Warfare and Party Unity: Explaining China's Changes in Military Strategy', *International Security* 42/3 (2018), 37–83. doi:10.1162/ISEC_a_00304.

Fravel, M. Taylor, *Active Defence: China's Military Strategy Since 1949*. Vol. 2 (Princeton NJ: Princeton University Press 2019).

Gilli, Andrea and Mauro Gilli, 'Why China Has Not Caught up Yet: Military-Technological Superiority and the Limits of Imitation, Reverse Engineering, and Cyber Espionage', *International Security* 43/3 (2019), 141–89. doi:10.1162/isec_a_00337.

Goldman, Emily O. and Thomas G. Mahnken, eds, *The Information Revolution in Military Affairs in Asia* (New York: Palgrave Macmillan 2004).

Harvey, Deborah R. and Barbara R. Felton, 'Military Operations Research in China: A Defence S&T Intelligence Study,' March 1994, DST-1820S-187-94.

Hikino, Takashi and Alice H. Amsden, 'Staying Behind, Stumbling Back, Sneaking Up, Soaring Ahead: Late Industrialisation in Historical Perspective', *Convergence of Productivity: Cross-national Studies and Historical Evidence* (1994), 285–315.

Horowitz, Michael C., *The Diffusion of Military Power Causes and Consequences for International Politics* (Princeton NJ: Princeton University Press 2010).

Kania, Elsa B., 'Learning without Fighting: New Developments in PLA AI War-Gaming,' *China Brief*, April 9, 2019.

Kania, Elsa 'The PLA's Unmanned Aerial Systems New Capabilities for a 'New Era' of Chinese Military Power,' China Aerospace Studies Institute, August 8, 2018.

Mahnken, Thomas G, ed., *Competitive Strategies for the 21st Century: Theory, History, and Practice* (Stanford CA: Stanford University Press 2012)

Ministry of National Defence of the People's Republic of China [中华人民共和国国防部], 'China's Military Strategy' [中国的军事战略],' May 26, 2015.

Posen, Barry, *The Sources of Military Doctrine: France, Britain, and Germany between the World Wars* (Cornell NY: Cornell University Press 1986).

Resende-Santos, João, 'Anarchy and the Emulation of Military Systems: Military Organization and Technology in South America, 1870–1930', *Security Studies* 5/3 (1996), 193–260. doi:10.1080/09636419608429280.

Roff, Heather, 'The Frame Problem: The AI 'Arms Race' Isn't One,' *Bulletin of the Atomic Scientists*, April 29, 2019.

Roland, Alex, Philip Shiman, and William Aspray, *Strategic Computing: DARPA and the Quest for Machine Intelligence, 1983-1993* (Cambridge MA: MIT Press 2002).

Saalman, Lora, 'China's Integration of Neural Networks into Hypersonic Glide Vehicles', *AI, China, Russia, and the Global Order: Technological, Political, Global, and Creative* (New York 2018), 153.

Saunders, Phillip C., Arthur S. Ding, Andrew Scobell, Andrew N.D. Yang, and Joel Wuthnow, eds., *Chairman Xi Remakes the PLA: Assessing Chinese Military Reforms*, Washington DC: National Defence University Press 2019.

Taylor, Mark Zachary, *The Politics of Innovation: Why Some Countries are Better than Others at Science and Technology* (Oxford: Oxford University Press 2016).

Tianliang, Xiao, ed., *The Science of Military Strategy [战略学]* (Beijing: National Defence University Press 2017)

Wu Mingxi [吴明曦], Intelligent Wars [智能化战争—AI军事畅想], National Defense Industry Press (Beijing), 2020; and Shi Haiming [石海明] and Jia Zhenzhen [贾珍珍], Artificial Intelligence Disrupts Future Warfare [人工智能颠覆未来战争], People's Press (Beijing), 2019.

Yaohong, Hao, [郝耀鸿], '5G, One Step Closer to the Military Internet of Things' [5G,离军事物联网更近一步], Confidential Work《保密工作》, July 2017.

Yonghua, Wang, [王永华], 'How to Get through the Whole Link of Combat Concept Development?' [如何打通作战概念开发的完整链路], China Military Network, November 29, 2018.

Yunxian, Wang, [王云宪] and Li Dawei [袁大伟], 'Intelligentised Operations Require Intellientized Training' [智能化作战呼唤智能化训练], China Military Network, August 23, 2018.

⚆ OPEN ACCES

Defence innovation and the 4th industrial revolution in Russia

Katarzyna Zysk

ABSTRACT
Russia is pursuing select 4th Industrial Revolution (4IR) technologies in a drive to rapidly close the capability gaps with rivals. The transformation of warfare these technologies portend could also make Russia more vulnerable. Joining the 'technological race' seems therefore less of a choice than an existential necessity. Constrained by structural problems and lacking the resources of the US and China, however, Russia has so far struggled to leverage its ambitions within the 4IR. Yet it has also shown the ability to experiment with 4IR technologies, including hypersonics and AI, to amplify existing symmetric and asymmetric capabilities, and create interconnected systems that may provide critical advantages.

Introduction

Ahead of the vote in the Russian parliament in July 2012 on a new agency that would be tasked with pursuing breakthrough technologies, Deputy Prime Minister Dmitrii Rogozin said that 'After 20 years of stagnation it will be hard [for Russia] to catch up with the West's weapons development the ordinary way,' given the long post-Cold War inertia and decay in the defence sector.[1] Breakthrough technologies, conversely, could not only narrow the defence gap but potentially provide Russia with much-needed critical advantages in a relatively short period of time. Therefore, Rogozin argued, Russia had to establish 'a radical organisation' to aggressively pursue risky innovation projects in the most promising areas. The result, later that year, was the creation of the Advanced Research Foundation (*Fond perspektivnykh issledovanii* – FPI), which was intended to become

---

[1]Rogozin quoted in 'Predator on the prowl: Multi-billion DARPA rival set up in Russia', *RT*, 5 July 2012, https://www.rt.com/news/darpa-rogozin-army-future-technologies-529/.

a 'real predator'[2] in the effort to place Russia among global leaders in new technologies.

In addition to the expected rapid modernisation of the defence sector, Russia's intent to push forward the development of breakthrough military technologies has been driven by another central factor of defence innovation, as identified by Stephen Rosen,[3] that is its potential ability to change the character of future warfare. The reasoning is well embedded in Soviet strategic thinking about the 'military-technical revolution' and the impact of new technologies on a fundamental discontinuity in the character of warfare.[4] Likewise, contemporary Russian authorities are concerned that new, possibly disruptive technologies may alter the ways and means of achieving victory, potentially in radical ways, thus generating vulnerabilities that Russia's enemies could take advantage of.[5] Leaving the development of such technologies to adversaries threatens therefore to further widen the asymmetry of power between Russia and its perceived adversaries. This in turn could undermine strategic balance, the maintenance of which has been given top priority in Russia's foreign and defence policy in the post-Cold War era.[6] Seen from Moscow, joining the 'technological race' seems therefore less a choice than an existential inevitability. As President Putin put it bluntly: 'Those who manage to ride this technological wave will surge far ahead. Those who fail to do this will be submerged and drown.'[7]

Furthermore, the Russian government has consistently expressed an expectation that innovation in the defence sector and the massive defence acquisition programmes could generate a wave of progress that would lift not only the Russian armed forces, but also the economy by driving a nationwide technological innovation.[8] Innovation centres that Russia has been setting up are to become generators of ideas and dual-use technologies intended to fuel economic growth by creating new jobs and high-tech products to be commercialised for both domestic and foreign markets.[9] Indeed, in September 2016, Putin ordered the domestic defence industry to increase its share of civilian and dual-

---

[2] Federal'nii zakon ot 16 oktyabrya 2012 g. N 174-FZ 'O Fonde perspektivnykh issledovanii', *Rossiiskaya gazeta*, 19 October 2012, https://rg.ru/2012/10/19/fond-dok.html; 'Predator on the prowl'.
[3] Stephen Rosen, *Winning the Next War. Innovation and the Modern Military* (London: Cornell University Press, 1991), 18–21.
[4] Dima Adamsky, 'Through the Looking Glass: The Soviet Military-Technical Revolution and the American Revolution in Military Affairs', *Journal of Strategic Studies*, 31/2 (2008), 257–294; Adamsky, *The Culture of Military Innovation: The Impact of Cultural Factors on the Revolution in Military Affairs in Russia, the US, and Israel* (Palo Alto, CA: Stanford University Press, 2010).
[5] 'Shoigu prizval voennykh i grazhdanskikh uchionykh ob'edinit'sya dlya raboty nad iskusstvennym intellektom', *Voennoe obozrenie*, 14 March 2018, https://topwar.ru/137827-shoygu-prizval-voennyh-i-grazhdanskih-uchenyh-obedinitsya-dlya-raboty-nad-iskusstvennym-intellektom.html.
[6] Ivan Cheberko, 'Pochemu v Rossii ne poluchilsya analog DARPA', *RBK Daily*, 12 April 2018.
[7] Vladimir Putin, *Poslanie Prezidenta Federal'nomu Sobraniyu*, President of Russia, Moscow, 1 March 2018, http://kremlin.ru/events/president/news/56957.
[8] Interview with Dmitrii Rogozin, Life.ru, 30 January 2018.
[9] Vladimir Putin, *Poslanie Prezidenta Federal'nomu Sobraniyu*, President of Russia, Moscow, 12 December 2013, http://kremlin.ru/events/president/news/19825; Vladimir Putin, *Poslanie Prezidenta Federal'nomu Sobraniyu*, President of Russia, Moscow, 12 December 2012, http://kremlin.ru/events/president/news/17118.

purpose products from 16.8% to 30% by 2025, and up to 50% by 2030.[10] The development of breakthrough technologies is therefore seen not only as critically important to national security, but also to Russia's economic future and international standing at large.

Consequently, and since 2010 in particular, Russia has systematically increased its focus on new and potentially disruptive technologies in all major 4IR fields, including artificial intelligence (AI) and quantum computing, big data, automated decision-making, and human-machine hybrid intelligence as well as autonomous and AI-enabled unmanned systems, intelligent robotics, hypersonics, additive technology, and so-called 'weapons based on new physical principles' (*oruzhie na novykh fizicheskikh printsipakh*),[11] i.e. directed energy, radiological, genetic, electromagnetic and geophysical weapons – to name a few examples. While the effort is expected to produce new types of weapon systems, the new technologies are also being applied to strengthen the traditional pillars of Russian defence, deterrence and coercive options. i.e. nuclear capabilities, non-nuclear strategic weapons and general purpose forces, as well as asymmetric non-military methods and means.

This development has potentially far-reaching implications for the Russian armed forces and the country's international standing. Yet, Russia's pursuit of 4IR technologies has received fairly limited scholarly attention, with some notable exceptions.[12] There remains a lacuna of scholarly analysis of Russian 4IR development programmes at large, not least in the context of their military-strategic and operational implications.

This analysis aims to help fill the knowledge gap by raising and answering the following research questions: (1) what strategies does Russia apply to pursue breakthrough technologies and stimulate defence innovation, and to what extent does the research into and development of 4IR technologies have an impact on Russia's traditional state-driven, top-down innovation model; (2) to what extent do emerging technologies amplify Russian symmetric and asymmetric warfare capabilities; and (3) how do they impact Russia's position in and the key ramifications of the ongoing strategic competition?

---

[10]Denis Zhurenkov, Anton Savel'ev, 'Gosudarstvenno-chastnoe partnerstvo v nauchnoi sfere', *Oboronno-promyshlennyi kompleks*, No.1 (33) 2018.

[11]'Oruzhie na novykh fizicheskikh printsipakh', *Military Encyclopaedic Dictionary*, The Ministry of Defence of the Russian Federation, http://encyclopedia.mil.ru/encyclopedia/dictionary/details_rvsn.htm?id=13770@morfDictionary; 'Piervyi Voennyi innograd', Era technopolis, https://www.era-tehnopolis.ru/.

[12]See in particular excellent work done by Samuel Bendett (CNA) published in *Defense One, National Interest* and other outlets, e.g. 'Putin Seeks to Plug Gaps in Russia's State-Driven Tech Efforts', *Defense One*, 18 January 2020, https://www.defenseone.com/technology/2020/01/putin-calls-more-hi-tech-breakthroughs/162496/; Vasily Kashin, 'Russian perspectives on the Third Offset strategy and its implications for Russian-Chinese Defence technological cooperation', in Tai Ming Cheung and Thomas Mahnken (eds) *The Gathering Pacific Storm. Emerging US-China Strategic Competition in Defence Technological and Industrial Development*, (Amherst, New York: Cambria Press, 2018), 211–238; Keith Dear, 'Will Russia Rule the World Through AI? Assessing Putin's Rhetoric Against Russia's Reality', *The RUSI Journal*, Volume 164, 2019, Issue 5–6, 36–60.

This paper argues that despite grand ambitions, new initiatives, and modifications of the traditional defence innovation model to incorporate civilian and private-sector innovation, Russia struggles to leverage 4IR technologies due to structural and circumstantial constraints and a lack of resources relative to near-peer competitors, the US and China. Still, although an unlikely global 4IR leader, Russia has shown the ability to experiment with and exploit 4IR technologies that are being incrementally added to amplify symmetric responses and asymmetric capabilities, for instance hypersonic weapons and AI in grey-zone operations, respectively. The interconnected systems may in the future provide Russia a critical advantage on the battlefield, provided it finds the right relationship between technology and hardware on the one hand, and concepts, doctrine, and organisations on the other.

The paper is organised in two main parts. The first examines the Russian defence innovation model and strategies applied to foster innovation, including attempts to combine the traditional Russian state-dominated approach with progress being made in the civilian and private sectors, where many of the sought-after 4IR technologies are developed. The second part analyses a) the main effects of Russian defence innovation on the ongoing strategic competition, and b) selected examples of Russian 4IR technologies with their expected strategic and battlefield advantage: hypersonics (representing a continuation of missile development technology at which Russia has traditionally excelled), and the country's novel AI technology.

This study is based on primary sources, such as Russian government documents and materials, published interviews with Russian civilian officials and military brass, and discussions presented in military and civilian journals and newspapers, both government-affiliated and independent, as well as other media outlets that shed light on the context and the nature of defence innovation in Russia. The challenge of studying defence development in Russia in general, and the development of breakthrough military technologies in particular, is sensitivity of the topic. Many projects in the planning, development, and experimentation phase remain highly classified and are kept out of public view. Occasional leaks provide some information about the direction of development, the interest level of Russian authorities, and the possible impact of defence innovation on Russian military strategy and warfare. Some programmes presented by the Russian authorities are designed to produce a particular signal effect, though the reality in such cases does not always match the overambitious rhetoric that is employed. To overcome the limitations inherent in open-source research, this article aims to base its assertions on a critical assessment of a variety of unrelated sources from within and outside the government. Unless otherwise stated, all translations from Russian to English are by the author.

The Russian 4IR defence innovation model

Theo Farrell and Terry Terriff have identified three key drivers of military change: pressure from the senior leadership that could induce changes in culture; emulation of other professional militaries; and an external shock.[13] While in the case of Russia the latter is less evident, there is little doubt that the Russian state's top political and military leadership has been a key driver behind the effort to accelerate the development of 4IR technologies.

The trend has been strengthened under the rule of Vladimir Putin, with the expansion of the state and centralisation of many Russian industries and companies (e.g. United Shipbuilding Corporation, United Aircraft Corporation) causing the public sector's share of the economy to reach approximately 70%. As all central schools of military innovation argue, military organisations, being extensive bureaucracies, are not only tough to change but are designed not to change and therefore have to be strong-armed to accept change and innovation[14] – a dynamic evident in the Russian approach. Furthermore, Russian emulation of innovation processes adopted by other militaries is also evident, not only in the priorities identified, but in the very innovation model Russia seeks to adapt to its own environment.

Strategies

The basic Russian innovation model for developing breakthrough technologies consists of creating state-driven 'radical innovation centres' or 'technoparks' (also called technopolises, futuropolises, or innopolises) aimed at fostering conditions seen as necessary to enable innovation. Russia has established several such centres in the civilian and defence sectors since 2011. In order to draw on breakthrough technologies being developed also in the civilian and private sectors, the Russian government creates military-civilian collaborative platforms to maximise the generation and exchange of ideas and expertise, and to increase the state's access to talent. As the Russian authorities argue, the foundation for Russia's potential to become one of the global leaders in the development and use of AI[15] is based on its strong intellectual tradition and high level of education in science, technology, engineering and mathematics (STEM) across the population – strengths broadly considered to be conducive to high-tech development.[16]

The use of emulation processes, i.e. imitating the methods and means of warfare[17] and the innovation paths taken by other militaries, is another

---

[13] Theo G. Farrell and Terry Terriff, *The Sources of Military Change: Culture, Politics, Technology* (Boulder, CO: Lynne Rienner, 2002).
[14] Adam Grissom, 'The future of military innovation studies', *Journal of Strategic Studies* (2006) 29:5, 919; Rosen, *Winning the Next War*.
[15] Ukaz Prezidenta Rossiiskoi Federatsii ot 10.10.2019 g. № 490: O razvitii iskusstvennogo intellekta v Rossiiskoi Federatsii, President of Russia, http://www.kremlin.ru/acts/bank/44731.
[16] Ukaz Prezidenta Rossiiskoi Federatsii ot 10.10.2019 g.
[17] Farrell and Terriff, *The Sources of Military* Change, 5.

important feature of Russian defence innovation. One of the flagship innovation centres, the Advances Research Foundation (FPI),[18] has been broadly compared in Russia, including by then President Dmitrii Medvedev, to the US DARPA,[19] and preceded by the Skolkovo Innovation Centre referred to as the Russian Silicon Valley.[20] The stated purpose of the FPI is to pursue R&D of cutting-edge technologies, primarily for the needs of the defence sector.[21] While it is too early to make a conclusive assessment of the FPI's performance, its record of achievement is mixed.

The establishment of the FPI did not immediately lead to new ideas. Some of the FPI's most widely publicised projects were in fact developed by others earlier, including the Fedor robot (developed by the Russian State Corporation for Space Activities – Roskosmos); liquid breathing technology (experimented with in the Soviet Union since the 1980s); and robots for energy resource exploration on the continental shelf (developed by the Rubin Central Design Bureau for Marine Engineering). However, the programmes pursued by the FPI have gradually expanded. In addition to AI, unmanned autonomous systems and automated decision-making, researchers are working on quantum computing and technology for processing information based on superconducting qubits ('Liman'), 3D printing of polymetallic products ('Matrix'), and additive technology in the aircraft industry ('Tantal'). FPI R&D programmes also focus on a means of monitoring near-earth space ('Horizon'), a detonation ramjet/engine for high-speed aircraft, a reusable rocket, a means of individual camouflage and protection ('Tavloga'), intelligent robotics, and exoskeletons. The scope and developmental stage of these programmes vary significantly. The Marker unmanned ground combat vehicle (UGV),[22] which among other functions is set to combine the ability of autonomous navigation with interaction with other unnamed systems, has been under development since March 2018 and has already been tested in a range of conditions, including in 2020.[23]

While the FPI pursues civilian and dual-use programmes, in 2018 Russia created a 'military Skolkovo': an innovation technopolis called Era that explicitly seeks to develop technology for the Russian armed forces.[24] According

---

[18]Fond perspektivnykh issledovanii, https://fpi.gov.ru.
[19]'Medvedev rasschityvaet, chto fond proryvnykh issledovanii ispol'zuet opyt DARPA', homepage of the United Russia party, 1 October 2012, https://er.ru/news/91312/.
[20]Interview with Andrei Grigorev in *Natsional'naya oborona*, No. 6, 2020, https://oborona.ru/includes/periodics/maintheme/2015/0126/164814981/detail.shtml.
[21]Ibid.; FPI, https://fpi.gov.ru.
[22]FPI Projects, https://fpi.gov.ru/projects/; see also 'FPI ne sostyazaetsya s amerikanskim DARPA, zayavil zamgendirektora', *Ria novosti*, 5 February 2020; FPI, https://fpi.gov.ru; 'V Rossii nachalis' raboty po sozdaniyu pervoi mnogorazovoi rakety', *Ria novosti*, 28 February 2020; 'FPI: Rossiya mozhet voiti v pyaterku liderov po kvantovym vychisleniyam', *Ria novosi*, 29 November 2019.
[23]'Kak chelovek: v Rossii ispytyvayut boevogo robota', *Gazeta.ru*, 29 June 2020, https://www.gazeta.ru/army/2020/06/29/13135063.shtml.
[24]Ukaz Prezidenta Rossiiskoi Federatsii ot 25.06.2018 g. № 364: O sozdanii Voennogo innovatsionnogo tekhnopolisa 'Yera' Ministerstva oborony Rossiiskoi Federatsii, President of Russia, 25 June 2018, http://

to the Russian MoD, Era was created to reduce the time from scientific discovery to implementation in the form of military weapons and equipment as well as to provide advanced training of personnel for defence industry enterprises and military research institutes.[25]

Era is to become 'a base for the development and pioneering of a model of the interaction of scientific, educational, and industrial organisations', with an objective of assembling some 2,000 military scientists.[26] Its priority R&D fields include AI, small spacecraft, robotics, automated control and IT systems, computer science and computer engineering, pattern recognition, information security, hydrometeorological (meteorological) and geophysical support, energy sufficiency, nanotechnology, and bioengineering. Other priorities are weapons based on new physical principles, meaning electromagnetic, radiological, genetic, geophysical and directed energy weapons such as the Peresvet land-based mobile combat laser system, which some believe may be used for air and missile defence.[27]

Officially, the weapon system has been on combat duty in five missile divisions of the Strategic Missile Forces since December 2019, though it is being further developed to enhance its qualities and strength.[28] Russia is also working on completing the design and development of other directed energy systems, such as tactical laser weapons for destroying unmanned aerial vehicles (UAVs) and lightly protected surface targets.[29] Other laser systems are already in use to protect airborne defence systems of Russia's strategic, tactical and army aviation forces from ground-to-air and air-to-air missiles with optical homing heads.[30]

The Era technopolis model is a combination of laboratories, engineering centres, and 'open spaces' equipped with the most advanced equipment specifically designed for promising military scholars and members of

---

kremlin.ru/acts/bank/43213; 'Strel'bovye ispytaniya boevogo robota "Marker" proidut v 2020 godu', *Voenno-promyshlennyi kurer*, 21 November 2019; Zhurenkov, Savel'ev, 'Gosudarstvenno-chastnoe partnerstvo v nauchnoi sfere'.

[25]'Voennyi innovatsionnyi tekhnopolis "Yera"', Ministry of Defence of the Russian Federation, 5 March 2020, http://mil.ru/era/about.htm; Inna Sidorkova, 'Voennoe "Skolkovo": zachem Shoigu stroit tekhnopolis v Anape', *RBC News*, 13 March 2018, https://www.rbc.ru/politics/13/03/2018/5a9e82869a7947860d0516ca.

[26]*Vladimir Putin posetil Voenno-innovatsionnyi tekhnopark YeRA*, President of Russia, 22 November 2018, http://kremlin.ru/events/president/news/59179.

[27]While its missions are shrouded in secrecy, the Russian MoD describe its task as providing cover for operations of the Russian mobile ground missile systems. 'Prezident RF: Boevyye lazery uzhe postupayut na vooruzhenie voisk', *Rossiiskaya gazeta*, 1 March 2018; 'Piervyi Voennyi innograd'; *Vladimir Putin posetil Voenno-innovatsionnyi tekhnopark*.

[28]'Verkhovnyi Glavnokomanduyushchii Vooruzhennymi Silami Rossii Vladimir Putin prinyal uchastie v rasshirennom zasedanii Kollegii Minoborony', Russian Ministry of Defence, 24 December 2019, https://function.mil.ru/news_page/country/more.htm?id=12268217@egNews; 'Nachal'nik General'nogo shtaba Vooruzhennykh Sil Rossiiskoi Federatsii general armii Valerii Gerasimov vstretilsya s predstavitelyami Voenno-diplomaticheskogo korpusa, akkreditovannymi v Rossii', Russian Ministry of Defence, 18 December 2019, https://function.mil.ru/news_page/country/more.htm?id=12267331@egNews; 'Vooruzhennye sily Rossiiskoi Federatsii osnashchayutsya innovatsionnymi vidami oruzhiya osnovannymi na novykh fizicheskikh printsipakh', Ministry of Defence of the Russian Federation, 8 January 2020, https://function.mil.ru/news_page/country/more.htm?id=12270004@egNews.

[29]'Vooruzhennye sily Rossiiskoi Federatsii osnashchayutsya innovatsionnymi vidami'.

[30]Ibid.

academia.[31] The objective is to create a strong link between theory and practice in order to integrate all stages of the product generation cycle: from idea to limited-scale testing.[32] Hence, according to Deputy Defence Minister General Pavel Popov, representatives of Russia's top arms manufacturers, including branches of major corporations such as Kalashnikov and Sukhoi, will co-locate with private companies and research teams.[33] Era partners, for instance, with a range of military and civilian actors, including the Sozvezdie concern, which is the leading developer and manufacturer of electronic warfare, communication and electronic countermeasures systems and equipment, and the renowned Kurchatov Institute, the largest interdisciplinary laboratory in Russia. It hosts a substantial share of Russia's nuclear physics facilities and pursues cutting-edge technologies such as nanotechnology, biotechnology, IT, cognitive technology, next-generation nuclear power systems, plasma physics and tokamaks, as well as information and communication technologies and systems.[34] According to official data, 257 organisations cooperate with the Era technopolis, 80% of which are enterprises of the Russian military-industrial complex, while 18% are scientific institutions and two per cent are non-profit organisations.[35]

'Science cities' with a high concentration of scientists and an R&D infrastructure are not a new phenomenon in Russia. In the Soviet Union, such 'naukogrady' were numerous and some have survived to the present day. However, the current model, while building on that experience, introduces a novel element: cooperation of the state military and civilian branches with the private sector. Traditionally, military research communities have been separate from the business sector. This relatively new development appears in part to emulate the US model of public-private and business-academic research as well as government/military-private sector cooperation, while maintaining state control.[36] Other experts discern possible inspiration from the Chinese model of innovation, with science and technology parks linked to the campuses of large military universities.[37]

Russia has applied a similar innovation model to create the intellectual and physical infrastructure needed to facilitate development of 'the crown jewel' of 4IR technology: artificial intelligence. In addition to the AI-focused R&D taking place at the FPI and Era (which has been tasked with developing 'smart weaponry' equipped with AI systems),[38] Russia also aims to exploit AI developed in the

---

[31] 'Voennyi innovatsionnyi tekhnopolis 'Yera' sozdan v sootvetstvii s Ukazom Prezidenta Rossiiskii Federatsii ot 25 iyunya 2018 g. № 364', Russian Ministry of Defence, http://mil.ru/era/about.htm.
[32] Ibid.
[33] 'Sovet po razvitiyu Voennogo tekhnopolisa "YeRA" obsudil proekt strategii, predlozhennyi Kurchatovskim institutom', Russian Ministry of Defence, 25 May 2019, https://function.mil.ru/news_page/organizations/more.htm?id=12232894@egNews.
[34] The partners of Era, https://www.era-tehnopolis.ru/partners/.
[35] 'Voennyi innovatsionnyi tekhnopolis "Yera"'.
[36] Poslanie Prezidenta Federal'nomu Sobraniyu, 2018.
[37] Dear, 'Will Russia Rule the World Through AI?'; Sidorkova, 'Voennoe "Skolkovo"'.
[38] 'Oruzhie razuma: rossiiskii put' k Voennomu iskusstvennomu intellektu', Izvestiya, 22 November 2018.

civilian sector. Indeed, several private Russian AI developers have received a degree of international recognition, including VisionLabs: founded in 2012 and located at the Skolkovo Innovation Centre, it specialises in facial recognition for banking and retail.[39] The FaceN algorithm, focused on neural networks and developed by NTechLab, won first place in a 2015 world championship for facial recognition technologies.[40] Another example is the Neural Networks and Deep Learning Lab at the Moscow Institute of Physics and Technology, which was selected to compete in the Amazon Alexa Prize 'Socialbot Grand Challenge' in 2019.[41]

Hence, the Russian authorities are creating public-private consortiums to facilitate collaboration between the private high-technology sector and civilian academic institutions on the one hand and military and security institutions on the other.[42] Participants include AI labs at Russia's leading universities, such as Moscow State University, the Higher School of Economics, the Russian Academy of Sciences, the iPavlov Conversational Intelligence and Dialog Agents project, the above-mentioned Moscow Neural Networks and Deep Learning Lab,[43] the National Centre for Cognitive Technologies at the Information Technologies, Mechanics and Optics University in Saint Petersburg.[44] The National Research Nuclear University has been working on an AI programme called Virtual Actor, developed to be capable of situational and emotional intelligence and of adapting to human psychology, behaviour and emotions.[45]

The Russian MoD has shown an interest in developing both theoretical AI research and AI implementation as well as war games with a broad spectrum of scenarios to determine the impact of AI models on the changing character of warfare at the tactical, operational and strategic level.[46] One expression of the state's focus on AI development is the 'National Strategy for the Development of Artificial Intelligence for the period until 2030'.[47] Signed by President Putin in October 2019, the strategy announces key objectives in investment, R&D,

---

[39]'VisionLabs unveils Russia's first smart home face recognition system', *Skolkovo News*, 5 April 2018, https://sk.ru/news/b/news/archive/2018/04/05/visionlabs-unveils-russia_1920_s-first-smart-home-face-recognition-system.aspx.
[40]'Russian Startup N-Tech.Lab Upstaged Google in Face Recognition', *Prnewswire*, 16 December 2015, https://www.prnewswire.com/news-releases/russian-startup-n-techlab-upstaged-google-in-face-recognition-562635061.html.
[41]'Dream Team', the Neural Networks and Deep Learning Lab at Moscow Institute of Physics and Technology, http://deeppavlov.ai/dream_alexa.
[42]'Shoigu prizval Voennykh i grazhdanskikh uchenykh sovmestno razrabatyvat' robotov i bespilotniki', Russian MoD, 14 March 2018, https://tass.ru/armiya-i-opk/5028777.
[43]'Dialogs with conversational AI', iPavlov project's home page, https://ipavlov.ai.
[44]'AI Is for Active Involvement ... of Russian Students in Artificial Intelligence Research', *Russian Academic Excellence Project*, Ministry of Science and Higher Education of the Russian Federation, 20 December 2019, https://5top100.ru/en/news/115622/?sphrase_id=16842.
[45]'Kak razvivaetsya iskusstvennyi intellekt v Rossii', *Agit Polk*, 18 December 2018, https://agitpolk.ru/3918-kak-razvivaetsya-iskusstvennyj-intellekt-v-rossii/.
[46]'Konferentsiya "Iskusstvennyi intellekt: problemy i puti ikh resheniya – 2018"', Russian Ministry of Defence, 14–15 March 2018, http://mil.ru/conferences/is-intellekt.htm.
[47]Ukaz Prezidenta Rossiiskoi Federatsii ot 10.10.2019.

education and training, and seeks to improve the coherence of the state's approach to implementing AI programmes across a range of sectors.[48]

To satisfy the growing need for AI specialists and foster conditions needed to attract talented youth, Russia is testing various strategies to train and retain new generations of specialists.[49] A large number of higher education institutions offer not only professional AI training but also participation in actual development projects commissioned by the universities' corporate partners, including Gazprom Neft, MTS (a telecoms operator) and Sberbank (a banking and finance giant), Russian Railways, Rosseti (a power grid operator), the Skolkovo Institute of Science and Technology, and others.[50] Another example of this trend is a cooperation agreement signed by the FPI and the Russian Ministry of Science and Higher Education aimed at facilitating the creation of new scientific schools and centres of competence focused on breakthrough R&D.[51]

Limitations

While in most cases the development of Russian 4IR technologies is relatively new and still a work in progress, several aspects of Russian defence innovation strategies may constrain further advancement. These include a preference for domestic rather than foreign supply chains; a low level of innovation across the economy; insufficient and unpredictable project funding; long-standing structural problems in the defence industry; and worrying trends in the educational base. The Russian economic model as a whole and spill-over effects from the country's foreign policies generate additional impediments.

As Russia was entering its rapid period of sweeping modernisation in the early 2000s, former Defence Minister Anatolii Serdyukov and former Chief of the General Staff Nikolai Makarov (both 2007–12) attempted to offset some of Russia's technological backwardness by purchasing selected capabilities abroad, such as Israeli drones, Italian infantry vehicles and small arms, German combat training centres for brigades and smaller units, and French Mistral amphibious assault ships.[52] The purchases were important not only to rapidly provide capabilities that were lacking, but to partake in the latest Western technological achievements in ways that would expedite the modernisation of Russia's domestic defence industry, thus saving years of home-grown development.[53]

---

[48]Ibid.
[49]'AI Is for Active Involvement ...'; 'Konferentsiya "Iskusstvennyi intellekt'.
[50]Ibid.
[51]'Minobrnauki i FPI podpisali soglashenie o sotrudnichestve po proryvnym razrabotkam', *Tass*, 9 July 2019, https://nauka.tass.ru/nauka/6645611.
[52]Katarzyna Zysk, 'Managing Military Change in Russia', in J. I. Bekkevold, I. Bowers, M. Raska (eds), *Security, Strategy and Military Change in the 21st Century: Cross-Regional Perspectives* (London: Routledge, 2015).
[53]Interview with Vladimir Vysotskii, *Moscow Defence Brief*, 2010/1; see also the same topic discussed in *RIA Novosti*, 31 July 2011.

This policy, however, was largely reversed in 2013 when the new military leadership, including Defence Minister Shoigu and Chief of the General Staff Valerii Gerasimov promised to favour domestic production over foreign manufacturers. Apart from pressure from the defence industry lobby, the move was driven by the concern that Russia could become excessively dependent on advanced foreign technology.[54] To accelerate modernisation of the defence industry, the government has assisted with such incentives as tax relief, low-interest loans, and help in obtaining key components of major weapons systems.

Prospects for defence innovation have also been undermined by spill-over from the consequences of Russia's foreign policy, such as Western sanctions and freezes in defence cooperation imposed in response to Russia's annexation of Crimea in 2014. This has further limited Russia's access to Western technology and slowed military modernisation in several strategically important fields, exposing areas in which Russia has remained dependent on foreign components, including Ukrainian gas turbine engines, German diesel power units, and dual-use technology and electronic components for Russian weapons and satellites purchased from the United States, France and Germany.[55] While Russia has launched a programme to support the development of domestic import substitutes, and has found some components in China, it takes time and resources to develop them. Higher prices and lower quality may be the result, along with a number of accidents that have occurred during testing.[56]

Progress, therefore, has been uneven, notwithstanding the full weight of the government's political and financial support. The low level of innovation in Russia's overall economy has not helped. The country does have several innovative sectors, including the space industry, parts of the defence sector, and IT services, and there are a range of successful firms (NtechLab, Kaspersky Lab, Yandex and Sberbank to name a few). Yet in 2019 Russia ranked 46th in the Global Innovation Index, down from 43rd in 2016 and 45th in 2017.[57] Russia's effort to spur innovation by expanding the governmental sector does not constitute a solid foundation for innovation. Labour productivity in state-owned Russian industries and companies is estimated to be much lower than

---

[54]Zysk, 'Managing Military Change in Russia'.
[55]'The strengths and weaknesses of Russia's military', *Deutsche Welle*, 7 April 2018,
   https://www.dw.com/en/the-strengths-and-weaknesses-of-russias-military/a-43293017. The sanctions have not been 'waterproof', however, as some material from Germany was delivered to the Russian defence industry even after the sanctions were imposed; see Yuri Lobunov, 'Germany – a partner of the Russian military?', *Intersection*, 13 July 2016, http://intersectionproject.eu/article/security/germany-partner-russian-military.
[56]'Skorbnaya zhivuchest', *Kommersant*, 23 July 2019, https://www.kommersant.ru/doc/4039718; cf. Gustav Gressel, 'The sanctions straitjacket on Russia's defence sector', Commentary, The European Council on Foreign Relations, 13 February 2020, https://www.ecfr.eu/article/commentary_the_sanctions_straitjacket_on_russias_defence_sector.
[57]*Global Innovation Index 2018*, https://www.globalinnovationindex.org/gii-2018-report#; *Global Innovation Index 2019* https://www.globalinnovationindex.org/analysis-indicator.

in the private sector and is more than 30% below the national average.[58] As state industries rely on preferential state funding, they have limited incentive to invest in innovation and create a competitive environment. Crucial decisions are also more likely to have political rather than commercial objectives.[59]

Despite the state's large-scale effort to improve the future pool of specialists in new technologies, some data suggest the Russian educational system is no longer the solid basis for high-tech development that it was in the Soviet era. While Russia is ranked fourth in the OECD's 2019 global index of education, less than one per cent of Russia's graduates earned a degree in IT, communication or other forms of technology. The Moscow State University – considered Russia's highest ranked computer science research institution – was listed 43rd globally in 2017, 60th in 2018, and 78th in 2019.[60]

This challenge is exacerbated by another central problem affecting the Russian military-industrial complex, namely a decline in professional expertise and the human resources available to it. Highly qualified employees are on average more than 50 years of age; 70% of research personnel with a doctoral degree are over 60, and about half of those are actually over 70.[61] The share of specialists under 30 is less than four per cent.[62] According to Andrei Ilnitskii, adviser to the Russian MoD, more than half of the 1300 enterprises of the Russian military-industrial complex are experiencing personnel shortages.[63] A worsening of the economic situation increases the risk of further brain drain, as shown by a public opinion survey conducted by the Levada Centre in December 2019: as living standards continue to fall and economic opportunities decrease, more than half of Russians between the ages 18 and 24 consider moving abroad permanently.[64]

The Russian innovation programmes struggle, furthermore, with insufficient and unpredictable funding. The protracted economic crisis in Russia, including periods of stagnation and low-level recession since 2014, has put R&D funding under further pressure, limiting the scope and pace of the development programmes. The annual budget of the FPI, for example, has amounted to USD 50–60 million per year, compared to the USD 3.4 billion allocated for

---

[58]Martin Russell, *Seven economic challenges for Russia. Breaking out of stagnation?* European Parliamentary Research Service, July 2018, 4.
[59]Ibid.
[60]Dear, 43–44.
[61]Andrei Ilnitskii, adviser to the Russian MoD, presentation at international scientific conference 'Human capital in digital economy', Russian New University, 18 February 2018, https://www.rosnou.ru/pub/diec/assets/files/IlnitskiyAM.pdf.
[62]Prof. V.A. Tsvetkov, *Oboronno-promyshlennyi kompleks Rossii: problemy i perspektivy razvitya*, lecture at the second conference 'The Economic Potential of Industry in the Service of the Military-Industrial Complex', Moscow, 9–10 November 2016, Financial University Under the Government of the Russian Federation, http://www.ipr-ras.ru/appearances/tsvetkov-opcconf-2016.pdf.
[63]Ilnitskii, 'Human capital in digital economy'.
[64]'Emigratsionnye nastroieniya', Levada Center, 26 November 2019, https://www.levada.ru/2019/11/26/emigratsionnye-nastroeniya-4/.

DARPA in 2019.[65] In 2017 the FPI budget actually decreased from RUB 3.8 billion to RUB 3.4 billion RUB. Ambitions to boost FPI spending significantly in the coming years have not been matched with funding.[66] Indeed, the presidential decree establishing the Era technopolis stipulated that its key innovation projects are to be financed not only from the MoD budget, but also the FPI budget.[67] Additionally, the Russian defence industry continues to struggle with the spectre of long-standing structural problems such as pervasive corruption.

Other factors behind Russia's poor economic performance include excessive dependence on natural resources, an unfavourable business environment and low levels of foreign investment, all aggravated by the weak rule of law and deficient intellectual property rights. The Russian political system is additional constraint on economic development. On the one hand it permits relatively rapid decision-making, so that grand initiatives like the creation of a military technopolis require only a stroke of the presidential pen. The system's procedural efficiency, however, is undermined by pervasive corruption, red tape and heavy-handed bureaucratic control, all of which obstruct the generation and implementation of innovative projects. Sergey Guriyev, chief economist at the European Bank for Reconstruction and Development, argues that economic recovery will be impossible unless Russia radically reduces the state's role in the economy and protects property rights.[68]

An assessment by the International Monetary Fund dated August 2019 concluded that the Russian authorities have put in place a relatively strong macroeconomic policy that has reduced uncertainty and helped to minimise the consequences of external shocks such as Western sanctions and low energy prices.[69] The World Bank points out that unemployment remains at a historically low level (4.5%), and the Russian banking sector has remained largely stable. A typical Russian citizen was 1.8 times richer in 2017 than in 2000. Russia has also continued to diversify exports, albeit slowly; it remains dominated by energy exports, which accounted for 65% of total exports in 2018 (compared to 59% in 2017).[70]

---

[65] DARPA, Budget, https://www.darpa.mil/about-us/budget.
[66] Aleksei Nikol'skii, Svetlana Bocharova, 'Novoe litso Voennykh innovatsii', *Vedomosti*, 26 February 2018; 'Byudzhet Fonda perspektivnykh issledovanii na 2018 godu ostanetsya prezhnim', *Ria Novosti*, 6 July 2016, https://ria.ru/20160706/1459588542.html; DARPA, Budget, https://www.darpa.mil/about-us/budget.
[67] Ukaz Prezidenta Rossiiskoi Federatsii ot 25.06.2018 g.
[68] Sergey Guriyev, *Only radical reforms can stop Russian economic stagnation*, RaamopRusland/Window to Russia, 26 August 2019,
   https://www.raamoprusland.nl/mission-statement-window-to-russia/188-mission-statement-window-to-russia.
[69] *Russian Federation: 2019 Article IV Consultation-Press Release; Staff Report*, IMF, 2 August 2019, https://www.imf.org/en/Publications/CR/Issues/2019/08/01/Russian-Federation-2019-Article-IV-Consultation-Press-Release-Staff-Report-48549.
[70] *Weaker Global Outlook Sharpens Focus on Domestic Reforms*, 42nd issue of the Russia Economic Report, World Bank, 4 December 2019, http://documents.worldbank.org/curated/en/782731577724536539/Weaker-Global-Outlook-Sharpens-Focus-on-Domestic-Reforms.

However, long-term growth prospects are expected to be modest due to structural constraints and sanctions. Domestic investment has remained low, at 20–22% of GPD, while foreign investment has fallen substantially and capital flight has accelerated. From 2014 to 2018, foreign investment declines in Russia reached USD 320 billion, or about 4% of GDP per year.[71] Structural reforms are needed to increase long-term growth and reduce the risk of stagnation. This means reducing the state's role in the economy, reducing regulations, and strengthening institutions, to name but a few key actions.[72] Yet structural reforms are not on the government's agenda to any sufficient degree. It is unknown how long Russia can pay for and sustain its defence innovation efforts, military modernisation, and high level of military activity at home and abroad, and without risking domestic political stability. The economic impact of the Covid-19 pandemic, combined with a further fall in energy prices, has sent shockwaves across the Russian state,[73] heightening uncertainty about the future of the defence innovation programmes.

Strategic context and battlefield advantages of 4IR capabilities

Overall, Russia does not appear to have a strong foundation in terms of factors considered to be enablers of R&D, including favourable economic, business, educational, industrial and legal environment that are conducive to stimulating innovation.[74] Does that mean the Russian defence innovation model is doomed to failure? And to what extent may Russia's advantages and driving forces help it to achieve success in selected, high-priority fields seen as key to a successful strategic competition? The section below places Russia's pursuit of 4IR development in the broader strategic context, then examines two examples of high-priority Russian R&D programmes: hypersonics and AI.

Strategic context of Russian 4IR development

The Russian authorities view the technological race as a central element in the ongoing great power competition, one that could potentially produce a game-changing, war-winning advantage. Given its long-standing perceived vulnerability to US/NATO military-technological superiority, Russia has sought to match some existing Western military capabilities symmetrically. Initially, in the 1990s and early 2000s, Russia had to compete from a position

---

[71] Sergey Guriyev, Only radical reforms can stop Russian economic stagnation.
[72] Russian Federation, IMF; *Weaker Global Outlook*.
[73] Heli Simola, 'Russian economy hit by COVID-19 and oil market turmoil', *Bank of Finland Bulletin*, Blog, 15 May 2020, https://www.bofbulletin.fi/en/blogs/2020/russian-economy-hit-by-covid-19-and-oil-market-turmoil/.
[74] Dear, 'Will Russia Rule the World Through AI?', 36–60.

of dramatic inferiority in conventional forces and a widening gap between the capabilities of its domestic military-industrial complex and those of its Western rivals. The Russian defence sector went through an extensive physical decline, suffering the dwindling attention of top political leadership, a national economic crisis, and insufficient material and human resources.[75]

As a result, the Russian leadership focused initially on stake-raising strategies based on the only significant capability available at the time – nuclear weapons. The idea was to ramp up the risks to competitors, so that any action to threaten Russia would be rejected in advance as prohibitively costly and likely ineffective. Russia's subsequent renewal and fielding of an increasingly diverse nuclear arsenal, its delivery systems and supporting infrastructure, were accompanied by doctrinal revisions that have elevated the role of nuclear weapons. Military doctrines (including from 2000, 2010 and 2014) have maintained clauses permitting Russia the first use of nuclear weapons in a conventional conflict.[76]

However, the advances of the sweeping military modernisation programme launched in 2008 have increasingly enabled Russia to invest in strategies of denial, aimed to convince competitors that it would be impossible to translate military means into political ends at an acceptable cost.[77] Russia has managed to level out its military decline and partially rebuild innovation capability by constructing the foundations of advanced new technological development programmes. It has gradually increased the role and significance of non-nuclear defence and deterrence in its military doctrine and strategy. Its well-established missile technology, including the development of hypersonics, is at the heart of this change. Long-range high-precision ballistic and cruise missiles, followed by hypersonic boost-glide vehicles and cruise missiles that are under development, constitute the backbone of Russia's non-nuclear defence and deterrence, as highlighted in the 2010 military doctrine, subsequently elevated to the strategic level in its update from 2014.[78]

Despite the largely successful military modernisation programme, Russia has been unable to engage in full-spectrum symmetrical competition. Its military technology remains inferior to that of the US and NATO, and China is likely to be an increasing challenge in the long run. Hence, Russia has simultaneously pursued both symmetrical and asymmetrical means and

---

[75]Zoltan Barany, *Democratic Breakdown and the Decline of the Russian Military* (Princeton University Press, 2007); Anne C. Aldis, Roger N. McDermott, eds, *Russian military reform 1992–2002*, (London: Frank Cass, 2003); Dale R. Herspring, 'Undermining Combat Readiness in the Russian Military, 1992–2005 , *Armed Forces & Society*, Vol. 32 (2006), 513–531.

[76]Voennaya doktrina Rossiiskoi Federatsii, Nezavisimoe Voennoe Obozrenie, 22 April 2000; Voennaya doktrina Rossiiskoi Federatsii, President of Russia, 5 February 2010, http://kremlin.ru/supplement/461; Voennaya doktrina Rossiiskoi Federatsii, Security Council of the Russian Federation, 26 December 2014, http://www.scrf.gov.ru/security/military/document129.

[77]Thomas Mahnken, A Framework for Examining Long-Term Strategic Competition Between Major Power, SITC Research Brief, January 2017, 2.

[78]Voennaya doktrina 2010; Voennaya doktrina, 2014.

methods of warfare. The objective has been to undermine or circumvent the opponent's military-technological superiority and exploit its vulnerabilities, preferably in a cost-effective manner politically and economically. This means, among other efforts, experimenting with selected 4IR technologies that are seen as both force enablers and force multipliers for Russia's traditional military (nuclear and non-nuclear) as well as non-military defence, deterrence and coercive options.

The case of hypersonics and AI: Strategic and battlefield advantages

One of key 4IR fields in which Russia has made significant progress and which is exerting an impact on the strategic environment, strengthening Russia's overall ability to compete, has been hypersonic technology.[79] Progress on that front stands in contrast to Russian AI development. Although the strategic importance of AI is appreciated, Russia is far from being a global AI leader, a fact the Russian authorities themselves acknowledge.[80] Still, AI technology has been a major preoccupation of the top political and military leadership inasmuch as so many other key 4IR technologies rely on it, including autonomous weapon systems, automated decision-making, human-machine hybrid intelligence, intelligent robotics, and harvesting and exploiting big data. Like hypersonics, AI is already having an operational impact as a force enabler and multiplier in all three main pillars of Russian defence and military strategy (nuclear, non-nuclear, non-military) discussed below.

Hypersonic technology

Russia has succeeded in following a consistent missile development pathway since the 1980s, making the country a global leader in two cutting-edge 4IR technologies: hypersonic boost-glide vehicles and hypersonic cruise missiles. This distinction was preceded by the development of a substantial arsenal of long-range land-, sea- and air-launched precision strike cruise and ballistic missiles (e.g. Kh-555/Kh-55SM, Kh-101/Kh-102, Kalibr, Iskander-K, Iskander-M and SSC-8/9M729) that allow Russia to engage land targets across Europe and large parts of Asia from international waters or Russian airspace, in addition to delivering them as anti-ship cruise missiles. The missiles' ranges, stealth capability, high subsonic speed and low-altitude flight profile are intended to strain the enemy's ability to defend effectively.[81] The ground-launched missiles, able

---

[79]Dean Wilkening, 'Hypersonic Weapons and Strategic Stability', *Survival*, 61:5, 2019, 129–148; Robert O. Work and Greg Grant, *Beating the Americans at Their Own Game: An Offset Strategy with Chinese Characteristics*, CNAS Report, June 2019.
[80]Ukaz Prezidenta Rossiiskoi Federatsii ot 10.10.2019 g.
[81]Robert Dalsjö, Christofer Berglund, Michael Jonsson, Bursting the Bubble. Russian A2/AD in the Baltic Sea Region: Capabilities, Countermeasures, and Implications (Stockhold: FOI, March 2019).

to reach European cities with little warning, are mobile and thus harder to detect and destroy.[82]

As a result, the growing role of non-nuclear deterrence in Russian strategic thinking has fuelled long-standing speculation among Russian and Western experts about the imminent shift in the major share of missions of the Russian strategic deterrence from the nuclear to the non-nuclear domain. Indeed, the Russian General Staff assumes that the production and deployment of long-range high-precision weapons, in particular hypersonics, 'will make it possible to transfer a major part of missions of strategic deterrence from the nuclear to the non-nuclear sphere'.[83] Defence Minister Shoigu has promised that Russia will have 'full non-nuclear deterrence' by means of a fourfold expansion of the number of non-nuclear strategic weapons by 2021.[84]

However, any such transition is still in the future and depends on when and if Russia's economy will allow the acquisition of a large number of such weapons along with a credible intelligence support system – i.e. an improved C2ISTAR infrastructure (command and control plus intelligence, surveillance, target acquisition and reconnaissance) that can effectively locate targets from longer distances, not least mobile targets.[85]

The development of hypersonic technology highlights the continued critical importance of nuclear forces and strategic stability in Russia's military doctrine and strategy. The Russian authorities' – and President Putin's – *idée fixe* has been to render useless any Western strategic air and ballistic missile defences that may reduce the vulnerability of the US strategic nuclear forces and thus undermine the strategic balance.[86] While some experts claim the development of hypersonics for this reason would be a solution to a non-existent problem,[87] the Russian authorities have, nonetheless, consistently pointed to it as one of the main reasons for the high priority attached by Russia to the development of hypersonic technologies.[88]

---

[82] Interview with NATO Secretary General Jens Stoltenberg, *Spiegel International*, 2 April 2019, https://www.spiegel.de/international/world/interview-with-nato-secretary-general-stoltenberg-u-s-100-percent-behind-us-a-1260690.html.

[83] 'Vystuplniye nachal'nika General'nogo shtaba Vooruzhennykh Sil Rossiiskoi Federatsii generala armii Valeriya Gerasimova na otkrytom zasedanii Kollegii Minoborony Rossii', Moscow, 7 November 2017, Russian Ministry of Defence, http://function.mil.ru/news_page/country/more.htm?id=12149743@egNews.

[84] 'Ministr oborony Rossii provel ustanovochnuyu lektsiyu kursa "Armiya i obshchestvo"', Russian Ministry of Defence, 12 January 2017, https://function.mil.ru/news_page/world/more.htm?id=12108199@egNews&_print=true.

[85] Dalsjö, Berglund, Jonsson, *Bursting the Bubble*.

[86] Putin's statement on US missile defences at the International Economic Forum, St. Petersburg, June 2016: 'Putin's warning', https://www.youtube.com/watch?v=kqD8IIdIMRo.

[87] Andrew W. Reddie, 'Hypersonic missiles: Why the new "arms race" is going nowhere fast', *Bulletin of the Atomic Scientists*, 13 January 2020, https://thebulletin.org/2020/01/hypersonic-missiles-new-arms-race-going-nowhere-fast/.

[88] Russia's preoccupation with extending range has also been behind projects such as the nuclear-powered nuclear cruise missile Burevestnik, which is to have an 'unlimited range'; *Poslanie Prezidenta Federal'nomu Sobraniyu*, 2018; official channel of the Russian Ministry of Defence, published on 19 July 2018, https://www.youtube.com/watch?v=okS76WHh6Fl.

These weapons systems aim to provide an innovative solution by evading missile defences with advanced speed and manoeuvrability, thus being inherently difficult to shoot down. Apart from their speed in excess of five times the speed of sound, dramatically reducing warning time, one of the key advantages of hypersonic boost glide vehicles and cruise missiles is the difficulty of accurate attack assessment by the adversary until late in the vehicles' trajectories. This is due to their significant manoeuvrability that allows them to divert to targets that may be 'hundreds of kilometres to either side of their initial trajectory'.[89] These new strike systems, developed to reach heavily defended, high-priority targets, have qualities that also make them a demanding target for US battle networks because they are moving through 'near space' – an operational domain that is not well covered by US sensors.[90]

In December 2019, Russia announced deployment of the first hypersonic boost-glide vehicles: the Avangard intercontinental ballistic missile system.[91] Two other hypersonic missile systems appear to be in advanced development phases: the sea and ground-launched high supersonic to hypersonic cruise missile 3K22 Tsirkon[92] (range approximately 500–1,000 km, Mach 4.5–6) and Kh-47 M2 Kinzhal air-launched ballistic missile (range over 2,000 km, Mach 10).[93] The introduction of hypersonic boost-glide vehicles and cruise missiles, especially when conventionally armed, could have a profound effect on strategic stability. As defence against them may be prohibitively high, it may increase the likelihood of offence dominance in a conventional strike. This, in turn, may create problems of crisis instability and arms-race instability with profound implications for the global strategic environment.[94] The head start Russia has in development, with China not far behind (followed by India and France), has therefore been a source of a concern in US policy circles, where symmetric and asymmetric responses are being considered.[95]

Artificial intelligence

AI development has been a top priority on Russia's 4IR development list and is being pursued with an increasing sense of urgency.[96] Defined in the

---

[89]This is also a major difference between ballistic missiles (which are inherently hypersonic) and non-ballistic hypersonic weapons, Wilkening, 'Hypersonic Weapons and Strategic Stability', 131, 137.
[90]Work and Grant, Beating the Americans at Their Own Game.
[91]'Russia proceeds with Avangard hypersonic missile production according to schedule', *Tass*, 2 July 2019; '"Okazalis" v "Avangarde": kak i gde budut razvorachivat' novuyu sistemu', *Izvestiya*, 4 November 2018; 'Shoigu zayavil, chto rossiiskie voennye skoro poluchat novoe giperzvukovoe i lazernoe oruzhie', *Tass*, 18 June 2019.
[92]'Vladimir Putin raskryl kharakteristiki rakety "Tsirkon"', *Rossiiskaya gazeta*, 20 February 2019.
[93]'Perspektivy robotizatsii rossiiskih vooruzhenii', *Ria novosti*, 9 February 2016.
[94]Wilkening, 'Hypersonic Weapons and Strategic Stability'.
[95]Rebecca Kheel, 'Russia, China eclipse US in hypersonic missiles, prompting fears', *The Hill*, 27 March 2018, https://thehill.com/policy/defense/380364-china-russia-eclipse-us-in-hypersonic-missiles-prompting-fears.
[96]'Putin rasskazal, kto mozhet stat' vlastelinom mira', *TV Zvezda*, 1 September 2017, Russian Ministry of Defence, https://tvzvezda.ru/news/vstrane_i_mire/content/201709011425-qb2f.htm.

Russian AI strategy as 'technological solutions capable of mimicking human cognition and performing intellectual tasks similarly to, or better than, humans',[97] the technology is expected to have possibly game-changing impact on both the military and civilian sectors.

Russia views AI development in terms of a long-term strategic competition and a potentially winning solution in several fundamental ways. First, AI systems may strengthen the socio-economic foundation of Russian power by massively transforming the national economy. Putin has argued that in the coming decades additional global GDP growth due to the introduction of AI could be 1.2% annually, i.e. twice the economic impact of information technology at the beginning of the 21st century.[98] Similarly, Minister for Economic Development Maksim Oreshkin sees the integration of AI as possibly leading to a significant increase in labour productivity by 2030.[99] German Gref, former Minister of Natural Resources and subsequently CEO of the thriving Sberbank, also anticipates positive nationwide effects from the integration of new economic or financial solutions based on AI.[100] Such development would be highly welcome given the poor long-term economic projections for Russia issued by the IMF and the World Bank.[101]

Second, the urge to push ahead with AI development stems from its possible impact on the trajectory of future warfare and the ways and means of victory, broadly considered one of the main drivers of defence innovation in general.[102] AI-enabled systems could create a more effective, less expensive strategy to compete asymmetrically with the United States when symmetrical competition, outside a few selected fields, is not within Russia's reach.[103]

Third, the Russian authorities see AI development not only in terms of the potentially immense opportunities, but also as a source of new vulnerabilities in national, technological and economic security.[104] Putin and other influential leaders, such as Gennadii Osipov, director for the AI programme at the Institute of Artificial Intelligence at the Russian Academy of Sciences, argue that employing AI in information systems and to link non-military and military technologies may give an adversary critical superiority, providing victory in any conflict even before its official eruption. AI could therefore have a destabilising effect by undermining the strategic balance.[105]

---

[97] Ukaz Prezidenta Rossiiskoi Federatsii ot 10.10.2019 g.
[98] Quoted in 'Oreshkin: iskusstvennyi intellekt pomozhet povysit' proizvoditel'nost' truda', *Ria novosti*, 4 September 2019.
[99] Ibid.
[100] 'Gref schitaet, chto razvitie iskusstvennogo intellekta sposobno sil'no izmenit' Rossiyu', *Tass*, 17 October 2019.
[101] Russian Federation: 2019 Article IV Consultation-Press Release; Weaker Global Outlook.
[102] Rosen, Winning the Next War.
[103] Bytev Aleksei, Smirnova Lyudmila, 'Udarnye intellekty. Chelovek ukhodit s polya boya', *Voenno-promyshlennyi kuryer*, 24 September 2019.
[104] 'Shoigu prizval Voennykh i grazhdanskikh uchenykh'.
[105] Cheberko, 'Pochemu v Rossii ne poluchilsya analog DARPA'.

Despite the possible game-changing qualities of AI and its potential to radically alter future warfare, its development and application in Russia to date appears more incremental than revolutionary. Notably, AI is being tested and applied as a force enabler and force multiplier for traditional symmetric and asymmetric military and non-military methods and means, such as the nuclear capability, non-nuclear strategic and general purpose forces, and non-military measures.

For instance, Russia is experimenting with turning AI technology into a battlefield advantage in several fields, including unmanned aerial vehicles (UAV), unmanned underwater vehicles (UUV), ground-based robotic systems, unmanned boats and other innovative combat systems.[106] Such exploitation of AI extends to nuclear missions, as demonstrated by the development of the nuclear-powered and nuclear-armed UUV Poseidon, likely tasked with destroying infrastructure, carrier groups and other high-value targets.[107] Some sources indicate that other projects are underway, including the application of AI to control various air defence systems, including S-300, S-400, and Pantsir.[108]

Likewise, AI is being applied to enhance the combat effectiveness of other traditional weapons to minimise personnel losses.[109] Russian drone development, though progressing at a slower pace than the authorities initially hoped for? is one example.[110] In 2013, the General Staff promised domestically produced drones by 2020, investing more than USD 900 million (about RUB 5 billion) for the purpose.[111] Although the domestic industry has been struggling to attain the objective, it has advanced in developing Israeli-licenced surveillance drones and manufacturing unmanned vehicles for surveillance, reconnaissance and target acquisition, though with limited range and endurance (e.g. Forpost-M, Forpost-R',[112] or Orlan-10[113]). As of May 2020, however, Russia still lacked assault drone capability, considered a major vulnerability.[114] However, the development appears to be moving forward (e.g. Al'tius/Al'tair heavy UAV, Okhotnik attack

---

[106]'Rossiiskie bespilotniki vedut kruglosutochnyi kontrol' v Sirii, zayavil Shoigu', *Ria novosti*, 27 September 2017.

[107]'Istochnik: zavodskie khodovye ispytaniya "Poseidona" nachnutsya letom 2019 goda', *Tass*, 10 February 2018.

[108]Aleksandr Kruglov, Aleksei Ramm, Yevgenii Dmitriev, 'Sredstva PVO ob'yedinyat iskusstvennym intellektom', *Izvestiya*, 2 May 2018.

[109]'Vooruzhennye sily Rossiiskoi Federatsii osnashchayutsya innovatsionnymi vidami oruzhiya'.

[110]'MO potratilo 5 mlrd rub. na bespilotniki, no rezul'tata net – Popovkin', *Ria novosti*, 7 April 2010.

[111]Vladimir Popovkin, quoted in: Mikhail Sergeyev, 'Nebesnyi dolgostroi', *Rossiiskaya gazeta*, 25 February 2013; 'Genshtab dolozhil o real'nykh rezul'tatakh Voennoi reformy', *Odnako.org*, 14 February 2013.

[112]'Minoborony RF poluchit 10 novyh bespilotnikov "Forpost-R"', *TV Zvezda*, 5 February 2020, https://tvzvezda.ru/news/opk/content/2020251520-QDjSl.html.

[113]'Bespilotniki "Orlan-10" nachali razvedku nad Voennym skladom pod Achinskom', *Ria novosti*, 3 March 2020; 'Dron – v stroi: "Orlan-30" naidet tseli dlya artillerii', *Izvetsiya*, 2 October 2019; 'Do kontsa goda v VVO postupit partiya bespilotnykh letatel'nykh apparatov "Orlan-10"', Ministry of Defence of the Russian Federation, 16 December 2019, https://function.mil.ru/news_page/country/more.htm?id=12267088@egNews.

[114]'Top 10 military innovations novelties Russian defense industry Army-2018 Moscow Region Russia', *DefenceWebTV*, published on 28 August 2018, https://www.youtube.com/watch?v=nvT_sKTD7p0.

UAV).[115] Russia has also shown an interest in swarm technology, which, if successfully developed, could provide Russia with a significant edge on the battlefield.[116]

Russian AI-enabled technologies also aim to strengthen the basis for asymmetric competition in both the military and non-military domains. In the view of the Russian MoD, the position of leading states in today's information society is largely determined by their level of development in information technologies, primarily those of cognitive analysis and decision support at various levels of management.[117]

The Russian General Staff attaches critical importance to winning and holding information superiority and influencing the cognitive-psychological domain, seen as key in any contemporary conflict. Influence operations and other forms of AI-enabled and AI-augmented 'information confrontation' (*informatsionnoe protivoborstvo*)[118] exploiting new forms and roles of information and social interaction are set to play an increasingly prominent role in Russia's military strategy.[119] Sergei Chvarkov, professor at the Russian Academy of Military Sciences, points that cyber weapons have several critical advantages and in some cases may be many times more effective than physical destruction by conventional weapons; moreover, threats and attacks in the information sphere are hard to retaliate against.[120]

The exploitation of big data is likely to play a significant role in enhancing existing and creating new means of confrontation. It requires creating an infrastructure and conditions for big data harvesting, considered by the Russian authorities? a key factor in AI development. To this end, the Russian national AI strategy clearly states that priority in accessing big data will be given to state actors.[121]

Russia has also demonstrated interest in combining new technologies, such as AI and drones, in order to augment traditional methods of influence operations such as disinformation, demoralisation and propaganda. Specially developed Russian drones and cell site simulators have been able to impersonate cell phone towers with the objective of intercepting, jamming, spoofing or broadcasting tailored content on civilian mobile phones belonging to the opposing side. Russia has tested such systems in operations in Eastern

---

[115]'Istochnik soobshchil ob ispytaniyakh prototipa BLA "Al'tius" so sputnikom', *Ria novosti*, 20 January 2020; Oleg Falichev, 'Smozhet li okhotit'sya "Okhotnik"?' *Voenno-promyshlennyi kuryer*, 14 April 2020.

[116]'Vysshii bespilotazh: Voennye vpervye otrabotali deistviya udarnykh grup dronov', *Izvestiya*, 7 November 2019. See also Jörgen Elfving, 'Ryska obemannade farkoster – Det västliga försprånget inhämtat?', KrVA Handlingar och Tidskrift nr 2–2020.

[117]'Shoigu prizval voennykh i grazhdanskikh uchenykh ob"edinit'sya dlya raboty nad iskusstvennym intellektom', *Voennoe obozrenie*, 14 March 2018, https://topwar.ru/137827-shoygu-prizval-voennyh-i-grazhdanskih-uchenyh-obedinitsya-dlya-raboty-nad-iskusstvennym-intellektom.html.

[118]'Informatsionnoe protivoborstvo', *Military Encyclopaedic Dictionary*, The Ministry of Defence of the Russian Federation, http://encyclopedia.mil.ru/encyclopedia/dictionary/details.htm?id=5221@morfDictionary.

[119]See also Sergei Chvarkov, professor at the Russian Academy of Military Sciences, 'Nauka o voine – neobkhodimost' ili dan' mode?', *Nezavisimoe voennoe obozrenie*, 20 February 2020.

[120]Chvarkov, 'Nauka o voine'.

[121]Ukaz Prezidenta Rossiiskoi Federatsii ot 10.10.2019 g.

Ukraine and Syria by delivering content to cell phones of opposing fighters. Based on information harvested from the smartphones, the projected content was intended to harass, intimidate and undermine morale, for instance by revealing seemingly compromising details about the adversary's commanders or divulging knowledge about soldiers' own families. Such methods have also been used against NATO soldiers deployed in the Baltic republics as a part of NATO's Enhanced Forward Presence, apparently for similar influence operation purposes.[122]

Furthermore, Russia has been investing in counter-network capabilities that could disrupt or degrade the backbone of the US and NATO information technology-enabled warfare, critical infrastructures (C4ISR), including space-based systems, command and operational networks, and other complex technological warfare enablers that developed countries depend on. The Russian Aerospace Forces, created in 2015, integrate the previously separated offensive and defensive capabilities, including air defence, missile defence, offensive electronic warfare, anti-space capabilities (such as anti-satellite missiles and manoeuvring space robots),[123] and directed energy weapons, such as the abovementioned Peresvet.[124] They are likely to play key role in crisis and conflict, including regional war scenarios.

Conclusions

Driven by the top political and military leadership and partly emulating other militaries, Russia has systematically increased its focus on 4IR technologies. The pace of development has been mixed, with advancement in selected key areas. The achievements appear to have strengthened the basic foundations of Russian defence and military strategy, providing a broader spectrum of options in defence, deterrence and escalation management. To date, 4IR development has not produced a fundamental change in the character of

---

[122]'"We are watching you": Russia accused of sending threatening texts to British troops', *The Telegraph*, 15 October 2019; 'Electronic warfare by drone and sms', *Digital Forensic Research Lab*, Atlantic Council, 18 May 2017, https://medium.com/dfrlab/electronic-warfare-by-drone-and-sms-7fec6aa7d696; 'Reports suggest Russia engages in psychological warfare in Avdiyivka – media', UNIAN Information Agency, 1 February 2017, https://www.unian.info/war/1754086-reports-suggest-russia-engages-in-psychological-warfare-in-avdiyivka-media.html; Thomas Grove, Julian E. Barnes, Drew Hinshaw, 'Russia Targets NATO Soldier Smartphones, Western Officials Say', *The Wall Street Journal*, 4 October 2017; Keir Giles, 'Time to Shed More Light on Russian Harassment of NATO Forces' Families', *Expert Comment*, Chatham House, 14 August 2019, https://www.chathamhouse.org/expert/comment/time-shed-more-light-russian-harassment-nato-forces-families; 'Russian Harassment of NATO Personnel, Families: The Next Chapter in Information Warfare?', *Military.com*, 3 September 2019, https://www.military.com/daily-news/2019/09/03/russian-harassment-nato-personnel-families-next-chapter-information-warfare.html.

[123]According to several sources, including the US Space Command, Russia tested such missiles in mid-April 2020, 'Russia tests direct-ascent anti-satellite missile', US Space Command, Department of Defence, 16 April 2020, https://www.spacecom.mil/MEDIA/NEWS-ARTICLES/Article/2151611/russia-tests-direct-ascent-anti-satellite-missile/.

[124]'Minoborony RF razmestilo boevyye lazery v mestakh dislokatsii', *Nezavisimaya gazeta*, 19 July 2018; 'Na boevoe dezhurstvo zastupili "Peresvety"', *Krasnaya zvezda*, 5 December 2018.

Russian warfare. Rather, it has been a process of an incremental evolution, with gradual improvements in symmetrical and asymmetrical methods and means of warfare. That said, the development of 4IR technologies may be non-linear, and the occurrence a breakthrough that could revolutionise Russia's warfighting capability and its ability to compete cannot be excluded.

Russia has made attempts to modify its traditional top-down, state-driven innovation model by building a bridge to the civilian and private sectors. It remains to be seen whether the state will provide sufficient support for 4IR development through all stages of the product generation cycle: from idea to limited-scale testing and production. Structural and circumstantial constraints on this process have been numerous, and Russia lags behind the United States and China in particular. While Russia has emulated elements of US and possibly Chinese technological innovation pathways, the idiosyncrasies of the Russian defence innovation model and the broader political, economic and legal ramifications, have produced different outcomes. Problems such as centralised and inefficient bureaucracies, weak intellectual property rights and rule of law, poor investment climate, pervasive corruption, and insufficient funding are among the problems that hinder swift progress in fields that are particularly dependent on creating a breeding ground for creativity and the free exchange of ideas.

Furthermore, Russia's slow economic growth, discouraging long-term socioeconomic prospects and spill-over effects from its own foreign policy have limited access to foreign technology, knowhow, supplies, and investments. Domestic policies, such as the state's tightening of control over the Internet and its tendency to take over, punish or ban companies for non-compliance (e.g. Telegram, VKontakte, LinkedIn) may have a further dissuasive effect on Russian and foreign investors.[125]

Given the current set of circumstances, Russia appears an unlikely global leader in 4IR technologies. The question, however, is to what extent such technologies are necessary to satisfy the needs and objectives of Russian defence policy and military strategy as well as the country's ability to successfully compete with other great powers. Despite the relatively limited scope and modest progress of its 4IR programmes, Russia has demonstrated a willingness and an ability to rapidly exploit some of the new technological gains as they emerge, by integrating AI, for example, to enhance nuclear, non-nuclear and non-military capabilities and missions. The interconnected systems that Russia is creating – combining advanced pre-4IR technologies with such features as artificial intelligence, autonomous systems, and

---

[125] Alena Epifanova, *Deciphering Russia's 'Sovereign Internet Law'*, DGAP Analysis No. 2, 2020, German Council on Foreign Relations, https://dgap.org/en/research/publications/deciphering-russias-sovereign-internet-law; Justin Sherman, Samuel Bendett, 'Putin Takes Another Step in Bid to Control Russia's Internet', *Defense One*, 8 April 2020, https://www.defenseone.com/ideas/2020/04/putins-latest-step-his-bid-control-russias-internet/164467/.

quantum computing – may provide a sharpened edge on the battlefield, if not the critical advantage that the Russian top leadership is ultimately pursuing.

One notable Russian advantage is that ethical and moral considerations related to military applications of AI and autonomous weapons systems will likely not emerge as a major factor constraining further development. While the Russian authorities promise to develop ethical norms covering the interaction between humans and AI, they simultaneously argue that excessive regulation can hamper the pace of AI development and implementation in Russia, thus undermining the country's chances in the ongoing technological competition.[126] In Russia's pursuit of AI technology, therefore, the national interest is likely to remain a higher priority than privacy and human rights. In this context, state-controlled and state-driven innovation in Russia can provide an advantage as limitations on harvesting large amounts of data are unlikely to get in the way of creating the infrastructure and conditions conducive to AI development. Similar logic applies to Russia's stance on Lethal Autonomous Weapons Systems: although Russia argues for inserting humans in the decision-making process, the country has rejected a proposition to create an international body capable of limiting the sovereign rights of states in the process of building and testing such technologies.[127]

Even if successful in generating some breakthroughs, the Russian military organisation's ability to translate newly achieved technological prowess into battlefield advantage will remain in question. For innovation to occur, it has to be significant in scope and impact, and it must alter how the armed forces operate while substantially increasing their battlefield effectiveness.[128] As Robert Work argues, having 'the best technology is not enough' in a successful political-military-technology competition. The key is the relationship between technology and hardware on the one hand, and concepts, doctrine, and organisations on the other,[129] i.e. a change in operational praxis. In other words, a successful military modernisation is not defined by technology and hardware alone, but requires changes in organisation and force deployment while anticipating the implications of new technologies for future warfare. Following the development of 4IR in Russia and tracking what Russia can invent, develop and successfully deploy is an issue requiring further research. As Russia continues to field existing and emerging 4IR technologies, another important topic on the future research agenda should be the extent to which Russia can take advantage of the new technologies by

---

[126] Ukaz Prezidenta Rossiiskoi Federatsii ot 10.10.2019 g.
[127] Justin Haner, Denise Garcia, 'The Artificial Intelligence Arms Race: Trends and World Leaders in Autonomous Weapons Development', *Global Policy*, Vol. 10, Issue 3, September 2019, 331–337.
[128] Grissom, 'The future of military innovation studies', 907.
[129] Work and Grant, Beating the Americans at Their Own Game.

creating the optimal relationship between technology and operational concepts.

Disclosure statement

No potential conflict of interest was reported by the author.

ORCID

Katarzyna Zysk http://orcid.org/0000-0002-9862-3112

Bibliography

Adam, Grissom, 'The Future of Military Innovation Studies', *Journal of Strategic Studies* 29/5 (2006), 905–34. doi:10.1080/01402390600901067.
'AI Is for Active Involvement ... of Russian Students in Artificial Intelligence Research', *Russian Academic Excellence Project*, Ministry of Science and Higher Education of the Russian Federation, 20 Dec. 2019, https://5top100.ru/en/news/115622/?sphrase_id=16842
Aldis, Anne C and McDermott Roger N. McDermott Roger (eds), *Russian Military Reform 1992–2002* (London: Frank Cass 2003).
Aleksandr, Kruglov, Ramm Aleksei, and Dmitriev Yevgenii, 'Sredstva PVO Ob"yedinyat Iskusstvennym Intellektom', *Izvestiya*, 2 May 2018.
Aleksei, Bytev and Smirnova Lyudmila, 'Udarnye Intellekty. Chelovek Ukhodit S Polya Boya', *Voenno-promyshlennyi kuryer*, 24 Sept. 2019.
Aleksei, Nikol'skii and Bocharova Svetlana, 'Novoe Litso Voennykh Innovatsii', *Vedomosti*, 26 Feb. 2018.

Alena, Epifanova, *Deciphering Russia's 'Sovereign Internet Law'*, DGAP Analysis No. 2, 2020, German Council on Foreign Relations. https://dgap.org/en/research/publica tions/deciphering-russias-sovereign-internet-law

Andrei, Ilnitskii, 'Human Capital in Digital Economy', Russian New University, 18 Feb. 2018, https://www.rosnou.ru/pub/diec/assets/files/IlnitskiyAM.pdf

'Byudzhet Fonda Perspektivnykh Issledovanii Na 2018 Godu Ostanetsya Prezhnim', 6 Jul. 2016, https://ria.ru/20160706/1459588542.html

Dean, Wilkening, 'Hypersonic Weapons and Strategic Stability', *Survival* 61/5 (2019), 129–48. doi:10.1080/00396338.2019.1662125.

Denis, Zhurenkov and Savel'ev Anton, 'Gosudarstvenno-chastnoe Partnerstvo V Nauchnoi Sfere', *Oboronno-promyshlennyi kompleks*, No.1 (33), 2018.

Dima, Adamsky, 'Through the Looking Glass: The Soviet Military-Technical Revolution and the American Revolution in Military Affairs', *Journal of Strategic Studies* 31/2 (2008), 257–94. doi:10.1080/01402390801940443.

Dima, Adamsky, *The Culture of Military Innovation: The Impact of Cultural Factors on the Revolution in Military Affairs in Russia, the US, and Israel* (Palo Alto, CA: Stanford University Press 2010).

Federal'nii zakon ot 16 oktyabrya 2012 g. N 174-FZ 'O Fonde perspektivnykh issledovanii', *Rossiiskaya gazeta*, 19 Oct. 2012. https://rg.ru/2012/10/19/fond-dok.html

'FPI: Rossiya Mozhet Voiti V Pyaterku Liderov Po Kvantovym Vychisleniyam', *Ria novosi*, 29 Nov. 2019.

Global Innovation Index, 2018, 2019, https://www.globalinnovationindex.org

Gustav, Gressel, 'The Sanctions Straitjacket on Russia's Defence Sector', Commentary, The European Council on Foreign Relations, 13 Feb. 2020, https://www.ecfr.eu/article/commentary_the_sanctions_straitjacket_on_russias_defence_sector

Heli, Simola, 'Russian Economy Hit by COVID-19 and Oil Market Turmoil', *Bank of Finland Bulletin*, Blog, 15 May 2020, https://www.bofbulletin.fi/en/blogs/2020/russian-economy-hit-by-covid-19-and-oil-market-turmoil/

Herspring, Dale R., 'Undermining Combat Readiness in the Russian Military, 1992–2005', *Armed Forces & Society* 32/4 (2006), 513–31. doi:10.1177/0095327X06288030.

'Informatsionnoe Protivoborstvo', *Military Encyclopaedic Dictionary*, The Ministry of Defence of the Russian Federation, http://encyclopedia.mil.ru/encyclopedia/dictionary/details.htm?id=5221@morfDictionary

Inna, Sidorkova, 'Voennoe "Skolkovo": Zachem Shoigu Stroit Tekhnopolis V Anape', *RBC News*, 13 Mar. 2018, https://www.rbc.ru/politics/13/03/2018/5a9e82869a7947860d0516ca

Interview with Andrei Grigorev in *Natsional'naya oborona*, No. 6, 2020, https://oborona.ru/includes/periodics/maintheme/2015/0126/164814981/detail.shtml

Interview with Dmitrii Rogozin, *Life.ru*, 30 Jan. 2018.

'Istochnik Soobshchil Ob Ispytaniyakh Prototipa BLA "Al'tius" so Sputnikom', *Ria novosti*, 20 Jan. 2020.

Ivan, Cheberko, 'Pochemu V Rossii Ne Poluchilsya Analog DARPA', *RBK Daily*, 12 Apr. 2018.

Jörgen, Elfving, 'Ryska Obemannade Farkoster – Det Västliga Försprånget Inhämtat?', KrVA Handlingar och Tidskrift nr 2-2020.

Justin, Haner and Garcia Denise, 'The Artificial Intelligence Arms Race: Trends and World Leaders in Autonomous Weapons Development', *Global Policy* 10/3 (Sept. 2019), 331–37. doi:10.1111/1758-5899.12713.

'Kak Razvivaetsya Iskusstvennyi Intellekt V Rossii', *Agit Polk*, 18 Dec. 2018, https://agitpolk.ru/3918-kak-razvivaetsya-iskusstvennyj-intellekt-v-rossii/

Katarzyna, Zysk, 'Managing Military Change in Russia', in J. I. Bekkevold, I. Bowers, and M. Raska (eds.), *Security, Strategy and Military Change in the 21st Century: Cross-Regional Perspectives* (London: Routledge 2015), 155–177.

Keir, Giles, 'Time to Shed More Light on Russian Harassment of NATO Forces' Families', *Expert Comment*, Chatham House, 14 Aug. 2019, https://www.chathamhouse.org/expert/comment/time-shed-more-light-russian-harassment-nato-forces-families

Keith, Dear, 'Will Russia Rule the World through AI? Assessing Putin's Rhetoric against Russia's Reality'. *The RUSI Journal* 164/5–6 (2019), 36–60. doi:10.1080/03071847.2019.1694227.

'Konferentsiya "Iskusstvennyi intellekt: Problemy i puti ikh resheniya – 2018"', Russian Ministry of Defence, 14–15 Mar. 2018, http://mil.ru/conferences/is-intellekt.htm

Martin, Russell, *Seven economic challenges for Russia: Breaking out of stagnation?* European Parliamentary Research Service, Jul. 2018.

'Ministr Oborony Rossii Provel Ustanovochnuyu Lektsiyu Kursa "Armiya I Obshchestvo"', Russian Ministry of Defence, 12 Jan. 2017, https://function.mil.ru/news_page/world/more.htm?id=12108199@egNews&_print=true'

'Minoborony RF Poluchit 10 Novyh Bespilotnikov "Forpost-r"', *TV Zvezda*, 5 Feb. 2020, https://tvzvezda.ru/news/opk/content/2020251520-QDjSl.html

'Minoborony RF Razmestilo Boevye Lazery V Mestakh Dislokatsii', *Nezavisimaya gazeta*, 19 Jul. 2018.

'Na Boevoe Dezhurstvo Zastupili "Peresvety"', *Krasnaya zvezda*, 5 Dec. 2018.

'Nachal'nik General'nogo Shtaba Vooruzhennykh Sil Rossiiskoi Federatsii General Armii Valerii Gerasimov Vstretilsya S Predstavitelyami Voenno-diplomaticheskogo Korpusa, Akkreditovannymi V Rossii', Russian Ministry of Defence, 18 Dec. 2019, https://function.mil.ru/news_page/country/more.htm?id=12267331@egNews

Oleg, Falichev, 'Smozhet Li Okhotit'sya "Okhotnik"?' *Voenno-promyshlennyi kuryer*, 14 Apr. 2020.

'Oruzhie Na Novykh Fizicheskikh Printsipakh', *Military Encyclopaedic Dictionary*, The Ministry of Defence of the Russian Federation, http://encyclopedia.mil.ru/encyclopedia/dictionary/details_rvsn.htm?id=13770@morfDictionary

'Oruzhie Razuma: Rossiiskii Put' K Voennomu Iskusstvennomu Intellektu', *Izvestiya*, 22 Nov. 2018.

'Perspektivy Robotizatsii Rossiiskih Vooruzhenii', *Ria novosti*, 9 Feb. 2016.

'Predator on the Prowl: Multi-billion DARPA Rival Set up in Russia', *RT*, 5 Jul. 2012, https://www.rt.com/news/darpa-rogozin-army-future-technologies-529/

'Prezident RF: Boevye Lazery Uzhe Postupayut Na Vooruzhenie Voisk', *Rossiiskaya gazeta*, 1 Mar. 2018.

'Putin Rasskazal, Kto Mozhet Stat' Vlastelinom Mira', *TV Zvezda*, 1 Sept. 2017, Russian Ministry of Defence, https://tvzvezda.ru/news/vstrane_i_mire/content/201709011425-qb2f.htm

Reddie Andrew, W., 'Hypersonic Missiles: Why the New "Arms Race" Is Going Nowhere Fast', *Bulletin of the Atomic Scientists*, 13 Jan. 2020, https://thebulletin.org/2020/01/hypersonic-missiles-new-arms-race-going-nowhere-fast/

Robert, Dalsjö, Berglund Christofer, and Jonsson Michael, *Bursting the Bubble. Russian A2/AD in the Baltic Sea Region: Capabilities, Countermeasures, and Implications* (Stockhold: FOI Mar. 2019).

Rosen, Stephen Peter, *Winning the Next War: Innovation and the Modern Military* (London: Cornell University Press 1991).

'Rossiiskie Bespilotniki Vedut Kruglosutochnyi Kontrol' V Sirii, Zayavil Shoigu', *Ria novosti*, 27 Sept. 2017.

'Russia Tests Direct-ascent Anti-satellite Missile', US Space Command, Department of Defence, 16 Apr. 2020, https://www.spacecom.mil/MEDIA/NEWS-ARTICLES/Article/2151611/russia-tests-direct-ascent-anti-satellite-missile/

Russian Federation: 2019 Article IV Consultation-Press Release; Staff Report, International Monetary Fund, 2 Aug. 2019, https://www.imf.org/en/Publications/CR/Issues/2019/08/01/Russian-Federation-2019-Article-IV-Consultation-Press-Release-Staff-Report-48549

Samuel, Bendett, 'Putin Seeks to Plug Gaps in Russia's State-Driven Tech Efforts', *Defense One*, 18 Jan. 2020, https://www.defenseone.com/technology/2020/01/putin-calls-more-hi-tech-breakthroughs/162496/

Sergei, Chvarkov, 'Nauka O Voine – Neobkhodimost' Ili Dan' Mode?', *Nezavisimoe voennoe obozrenie*, 20 Feb. 2020.

'Shoigu Prizval Voennykh I Grazhdanskikh Uchienykh Ob"edinit'sya Dlya Raboty Nad Iskusstvennym Intellektom', *Voennoe obozrenie*, 14 Mar. 2018, https://topwar.ru/137827-shoygu-prizval-voennyh-i-grazhdanskih-uchenyh-obedinitsya-dlya-raboty-nad-iskusstvennym-intellektom.html

'Sovet Po Razvitiyu Voennogo Tekhnopolisa "Yera" Obsudil Proekt Strategii, Predlozhennyi Kurchatovskim Institutom', Russian Ministry of Defence, 25 May 2019, https://function.mil.ru/news_page/organizations/more.htm?id=12232894@egNews

'Strel'bovye Ispytaniya Boevogo Robota "Marker" Proidut V 2020 Godu', *Voenno-promyshlennyi kurer*, 21 Nov. 2019.

Theo Farrell and Terry Terriff, *The Sources of Military Change: Culture, Politics, Technology* (Boulder, CO: Lynne Rienner 2002).

Thomas, Mahnken, 'A Framework for Examining Long-Term Strategic Competition between Major Power', SITC Research Brief, Jan. 2017.

Tsvetkov, V.A., *Oboronno-promyshlennyi kompleks Rossii: problemy i perspektivy razvitya*, lecture at the second conference 'The Economic Potential of Industry in the Service of the Military-Industrial Complex', Moscow, 9–10 Nov. 2016, Financial University Under the Government of the Russian Federation, http://www.ipr-ras.ru/appearances/tsvetkov-opcconf-2016.pdf

Ukaz Prezidenta Rossiiskoi Federatsii ot 10.10.2019g. № 490: O razvitii iskusstvennogo intellekta v Rossiiskoi Federatsii, President of Russia, http://www.kremlin.ru/acts/bank/44731

Ukaz Prezidenta Rossiiskoi Federatsii ot 25.06.2018g. № 364: O sozdanii Voennogo innovatsionnogo tekhnopolisa "Yera" Ministerstva oborony Rossiiskoi Federatsii, President of Russia, 25 Jun. 2018, http://kremlin.ru/acts/bank/43213

'V Rossii Nachalis' Raboty Po Sozdaniyu Pervoi Mnogorazovoi Rakety', *Ria novosti*, 28 Feb. 2020.

Vasily, Kashin, 'Russian Perspectives on the Third Offset Strategy and Its Implications for Russian-Chinese Defence Technological Cooperation', in Tai Ming Cheung and Thomas Mahnken (eds.), *The Gathering Pacific Storm: Emerging US-China Strategic Competition in Defence Technological and Industrial Development* (Amherst, New York: Cambria Press 2018), 211–38.

'Verkhovnyi Glavnokomanduyushchii Vooruzhennymi Silami Rossii Vladimir Putin Prinyal Uchastie V Rasshirennom Zasedanii Kollegii Minoborony', Russian Ministry of Defence, 24 Dec. 2019, https://function.mil.ru/news_page/country/more.htm?id=12268217@egNews

Vladimir, Putin, *Poslanie Prezidenta Federal'nomu Sobraniyu*, Moscow, 12 Dec. 2012, http://kremlin.ru/events/president/news/17118

Vladimir, Putin, *Poslanie Prezidenta Federal'nomu Sobraniyu*, Moscow, 12 Dec. 2013, http://kremlin.ru/events/president/news/19825

Vladimir, Putin, *Poslanie Prezidenta Federal'nomu Sobraniyu*, Moscow, 1 Mar. 2018, http://kremlin.ru/events/president/news/56957

'Vladimir Putin Posetil Voenno-innovatsionnyi Tekhnopark 'Yera,' President of Russia, 22 Nov. 2018, http://kremlin.ru/events/president/news/59179

'Vladimir Putin Raskryl Kharakteristiki Rakety "Tsirkon"', *Rossiiskaya gazeta*, 20 Feb. 2019.

Voennaya doktrina Rossiiskoi Federatsii, Nezavisimoe voennoe obozrenie, 22 Apr. 2000.

Voennaya doktrina Rossiiskoi Federatsii, President of Russia, 5 Feb. 2010, http://kremlin.ru/supplement/461

Voennaya doktrina Rossiiskoi Federatsii, Security Council of the Russian Federation, 26 Dec. 2014, http://www.scrf.gov.ru/security/military/document129

'Voennyi Innovatsionnyi Tekhnopolis "Yera" Sozdan V Sootvetstvii S Ukazom Prezidenta Rossiiskii Federatsii Ot 25 Iyunya 2018 G. № 364', Russian Ministry of Defence, http://mil.ru/era/about.htm

'Vooruzhennye Sily Rossiiskoi Federatsii Osnashchayutsya Innovatsionnymi Vidami Oruzhiya Osnovannymi Na Novykh Fizicheskikh Printsipakh', Ministry of Defence of the Russian Federation, 8 Jan. 2020, https://function.mil.ru/news_page/country/more.htm?id=12270004@egNews

'Vysshii Bespilotazh: Voennye Vpervye Otrabotali Deistviya Udarnykh Grup Dronov', *Izvestiya*, 7 Nov. 2019.

'Vystuplniye Nachal'nika General'nogo Shtaba Vooruzhennykh Sil Rossiiskoi Federatsii Generala Armii Valeriya Gerasimova Na Otkrytom Zasedanii Kollegii Minoborony Rossii', Russian Ministry of Defence, Moscow, 7 Nov. 2017, http://function.mil.ru/news_page/country/more.htm?id=12149743@egNews

Weaker Global Outlook Sharpens Focus on Domestic Reforms, 42nd issue of the Russia Economic Report, World Bank, 4 Dec. 2019, http://documents.worldbank.org/curated/en/782731577724536539/Weaker-Global-Outlook-Sharpens-Focus-on-Domestic-Reforms

Work, Robert O. and Greg Grant, 'Beating the Americans at Their Own Game: An Offset Strategy with Chinese Characteristics', CNAS Report, Jun. 2019.

Zoltan, Barany, *Democratic Breakdown and the Decline of the Russian Military* (Princeton: Princeton University Press 2007).

4IR technologies in the Israel Defence Forces: blurring traditional boundaries

Yoram Evron

ABSTRACT
This paper explores how Fourth Industrial Revolution (4IR) technologies obscure the traditional boundaries associated with the military realm. As the first examination of the conditions underlying the assimilation of 4IR technologies in Israel's armed forces, this paper makes several contributions. It expands the knowledge on the military assimilation of 4IR technologies and describes the interaction between military doctrine and technology using current evidence. It also enriches the evolving discussion on the strategic effect of emerging technologies. Finally, it demonstrates how emerging technologies involve neither straightforward spinoff or spin-on processes but a reciprocal transfer of know-how between the military and civilian sectors.

Introduction

The assimilation of Fourth Industrial Revolution technologies (4IR) in the Israel Defence Forces (IDF) has coincided with a profound doctrinal change in the military that began in the late 1990s.[1] The underlying logic of the new doctrine is the replacement of extensive ground manoeuvres and seizure of large amounts of enemy territory with precise, lethal operations against the enemy's critical capabilities in wartime and between wars. While 4IR technologies have not been the driving force behind the new operational concept, they have enabled it and moved it forward.[2] As Cheung and others have

---

[1] The term 'military doctrine' is dubbed 'operational concept' in Israel's military terminology. In this paper these terms are used interchangeably when referring to Israel and the IDF. Similarly, 4IR technologies are occasionally referred to as emerging technologies and these two terms are used interchangeably as well.

[2] On the role of technology in military innovation see Barry R. Posen, *The Sources of Military Doctrine: France, Britain, and Germany between the World Wars* (Ithaca: Cornell University Press 1984), 35, 54–55; Andrew Krepinevich, 'Cavalry to Computer: The Pattern of Military Revolutions', *The National Interest* 37 (1994), 30–42; I. B. Holley, *Technology and Military Doctrine: Essays on a Challenging Relationship* (Maxwell: Air University Press 2004); Dmitry Adamsky, *The Culture of Military Innovation: The Impact of Cultural Factors on the Revolution in Military Affairs in Russia, the US, and Israel* (Stanford: Stanford University Press 2010), 7. For a different view, which assigns technological innovation a central place in military innovation, see Warren Chin, 'Technology, War and the State: Past, Present and Future', *International Affairs* 95/4 (2019), 765–83.

argued, technology is the most visible component of military innovation, 'yet, new technology is rarely the *sine qua non* of military innovation'.[3] In the case of Israel, it was the country's political and strategic conditions that drove the IDF's doctrinal change. 4IR technologies simply facilitated and shaped it. In particular, they allowed the IDF to carry out more frequent, yet limited, accurate operations at long range and with a smaller number of casualties. In doing so, these technologies, which some have characterized as leading to 'the blurring of lines between the physical, digital and biological spheres,'[4] also blurred some of the traditional operational distinctions related to the military realm. In particular, they allowed military doctrines and operations that obscured the distinction between war and ceasefires, the frontlines and the home front, and combat and non-combat units.[5]

The operational dimension is not the only one where 4IR technologies blur traditional military-related boundaries. The same happens in the area of procurement. 4IR technologies involve in-depth scientific research and rapid technological developments.[6] Obviously, the defence establishment lacks the capacity to develop the entire range of these technologies and associated products itself. Therefore, it relies increasingly on technologies developed by civilian organizations for the civilian market.[7] This process, known as technology spin-on (or spin-in), has already been associated with emerging technologies and contemporary military innovation.[8] However, the Israeli case supports observations that the deployment of civilian 4IR technologies in the armed forces is not a linear process, but a complex one where know-how transfers reciprocally between the military and civilian sectors.[9] Thus, the spillover of military technology to the civilian sector in the form of technology spinoffs has been a major force behind the creation of

---

[3] Tai Ming Cheung, Thomas G. Mahnken, and Andrew L. Ross, 'Frameworks for Analyzing Chinese Defense and Military Innovation,' in Tai Ming Cheung (ed.), *Forging China's Military Might: a New Framework for Assessing Innovation* (Baltimore: Johns Hopkins University Press 2014), 23.
[4] Clement Wee Yong Nien, Tay Cheng Chuan, and Ho Jin Peng, 'At the Leading Edge: the RSAF and the Fourth Industrial Revolution', *Pointer: Journal of the Singapore Armed Forces* 44/2 (2018), 2. See also Klaus Schwab, *The Fourth Industrial Revolution* (New York: Crown Business 2017), 8.
[5] Recently, Tristan A. Volpe highlighted one particular form of this feature, the growing difficulty in distinguishing between civilian and military motives. Tristan A. Volpe, 'Dual-use Distinguishability: How 3D-printing Shapes the Security Dilemma for Nuclear Programs', *Journal of Strategic Studies* 42/6 (2019), 814–40.
[6] Schwab, *The Fourth Industrial Revolution*, 50–61.
[7] Michael Brzoska, 'Trends in Global Military and Civilian Research and Development (R&D) and their Changing Interface', *Proceedings of the International Seminar on Defence Finance and Economics* 19 (2006).
[8] Michael Raska, 'Strategic Competition for Emerging Military Technologies: Comparative Paths and Patterns', *Prism* 8/3 (2019), 67; Marcus Schulzke, 'Drone Proliferation and the Challenge of Regulating Dual-Use Technologies', *International Studies Review* 21/3 (2019), 497–517; Volpe, 'Dual-use Distinguishability'; Filippo Sevini et al., 'Emerging Dual-Use Technologies and Global Supply Chain Compliance', in *IAEA Symposium on International Safeguards*, Vienna 2018; Ronald L. Sandler (ed.), *Ethics and Emerging Technologies* (New York: Palgrave Macmillan 2014), especially chs. 18–19.
[9] Chin, 'Technology, War and the State', 770–71.

a flourishing civilian hi-tech sector, which, in turn, becomes an important source of technology for the defence establishment.

Taking place in the strategic, operational, and material areas, the blurring of the traditional lines between the military and the civilian may have far-reaching strategic, political, and economic implications, both inside and outside the country. Among other things, it may impact the perceptions of politicians about the role of military force, promote new modes of civilian-military interaction, broaden the diversity of targets and threats, and affect cooperation between states. In examining these developments in detail, I explore the IDF's assimilation of 4IR technologies by focusing on the following questions. How do technological developments and military doctrine affect each other? How does the growing demand among military forces for emerging technologies impact their connection with the civilian sector? What are the conditions that promote, or alternatively hinder, the spin-on of 4IR technologies? Finally, how do 4IR technologies impact regional stability?

Relying on official IDF documents, analyses, and reports by IDF officers, official bids, reports of Israeli governmental bodies and universities, as well as the existing literature, I provide an initial comprehensive analysis of the forces, channels, and conditions underlying 4IR technology spin-ons and their assimilation in Israel's armed forces. In doing so, the study makes several contributions. It expands the empirical and conceptual knowledge on the military assimilation of 4IR technologies, describes the interaction between military doctrine and technology using current evidence, enriches the evolving discussion on the stabilizing effect of emerging technologies, and demonstrates how 4IR technologies blur the traditional boundaries associated with the military realm.

The paper is organized as follows. Beginning with a contextual presentation of the evolution of Israel's military doctrine since the late 1990s, it then examines the IDF's increasing demand for 4IR technologies. Next, the attention shifts to the supply side, exploring Israel's hi-tech sector and its connection with the defence establishment, followed by a detailed examination of Israel's spin-on channels, enablers, and challenges. Then, based on Israel's experience in the military utilization of 4IR technologies, I suggest some preliminary insights concerning their implications for regional strategic stability. The concluding section presents my main findings.

The context: Israel's changing military doctrine

The IDF's interest in 4IR technologies is the continuation of a longstanding legacy. Since its early years, the IDF has emphasized material technological superiority over its quantitatively superior rivals as the key to Israel's survival.[10] As part of this guiding principle, Israel established the capability to develop and produce arms in-house, the underlying rationale of which was ultimately consolidated by the late 1980s: Israel's military superiority would rely on domestic state-of-the-art technologies installed mostly on imported platforms, thereby substantially upgrading their capabilities. Concurrently, the role of technology in the Israeli military's build up and deployment steadily expanded. Its reliance on technological solutions has resulted in a wide array of techno-military innovations.[11] The development and assimilation of world-class tactical missiles, radar, observation satellites, precise guided ammunition, fire control systems, and heads-up display (HUD) systems, to name but a few striking examples, illustrates this point.[12]

The emphasis on technology in Israel's strategic thinking has only intensified over the years, as its security forces have faced an ever more complex environment in terms of both military challenges and political and social conditions. On one hand, the country faces increasingly unconventional and asymmetrical challenges, such as the launching of missiles and rockets at its home front, its enemies' attempts to develop nuclear military capabilities, terror and guerrilla attacks, and various cyber threats. On the other hand, the public expects the government to provide it with a safe environment. However, it is unwilling to accept long wars and the cost associated with the long-term occupation of enemy territory, both measured in large numbers of casualties.[13] Attuned to the prevailing theoretical expectations of military innovation, it was these strategic and socio-political developments, rather than technological advances, that since the early twenty-first century have driven the change in Israel's military doctrine.[14] These changes, in turn, have proven feasible, and even capable of expanding, due to the availability of new technologies.

Since the early 2000s these developments have given way to a comprehensive change in the IDF's military doctrine. It was officially presented in 2015 in a first of its kind formal document, entitled 'IDF Strategy' (Hebrew: *Estrategiat Tzahal*), delineating Israel's strategic conditions, military

---

[10]This concept was part of a set of principles and guidelines put together in the early 1950s by Israel's Prime Minister and Minister of Defence, David Ben-Gurion, and served as the IDF's operational concept through the late twentieth century. Israel Tal, *Bitachon leumi: meatim mul rabim* [*National Security: The Few against the Many*] (Tel Aviv: Dvir 1996), 11; Itamar Rabinovich and Itai Brun, *Israel Facing a New Middle East: In Search of National Security Strategy* (Stanford: Hoover Institution Press 2017), 2–3.

[11]Adamsky, *The Culture of Military Innovation*, 113–15. See also Amir Rapaport, 'On the Superpowers' Playing Field', *Israel Defense*, 19 December 2011, https://www.israeldefense.co.il/en/content/super powers%E2%80%99-playing-field.

[12]Yaakov Katz and Amir Bohbot, *The Weapon Wizards: How Israel Became a High-Tech Military Superpower* (New York: St. Martin's Press 2017).

[13]Yagil Levy, 'Social Convertibility and Militarism: Evaluations of the Development of Military-Society Relations in Israel in the Early 2000s', *Journal of Political and Military Sociology* 31/1 (2003), 76–80; Rabinovich and Brun, *Israel Facing a New Middle East*, 25–44; Ariel Levite, *Offense and Defense in Israeli Military Doctrine* (New York: Routledge 2019), ch. 3.

[14]See note 2.

attributes, and course of action.[15] In this document, as well as in analyses by high-ranking officers and military experts, the IDF assumes a strategic situation of enduring enemy efforts to prepare for war or to conduct one.[16] To meet this challenge, the IDF must constantly be engaged in either low-scale warfare aimed at shaping the starting conditions of the next war in Israel's favour, dubbed by the IDF as 'a campaign between wars', or in a full-scale campaign or war. When a war breaks out, most likely against a non-state organization, the tactics of large-scale ground manoeuvres and seizing control of vast enemy territories, as the IDF did through the early 1980s, are regarded as no longer feasible politically. Instead, efforts will be made to penetrate the enemy's territory swiftly in order to destroy critical military capabilities and various strategic infrastructures, and thwart the enemy's capability to hit the Israeli home front. As part of this approach, the IDF emphasizes the massive use of precise, lethal, and often standoff fire.[17] Realizing this goal requires the ability to obtain and analyse accurate, current information about the enemy's forces, means, and infrastructure prior to and during the battle, and transfer it to field units. Other capabilities include precise and intense fire power of various types, the ability to penetrate the enemy's strongholds swiftly, pursue and destroy his forces, and protect the civilian front, including sensitive communication infrastructures and cybernetic space.[18] The elements that play a major role in implementing this strategy are the Air Force, highly trained and equipped special units, intelligence forces, strategic defence and other anti-missile systems, as well as information technology (IT), and cyber and logistics units, all jointly operated through efficient command, control, communication, computer, intelligence, and reconnaissance (C4IR) systems.[19]

Demand: The new military strategy and 4IR technologies

It is against this backdrop that I examine the assimilation of 4IR technologies into the IDF's war preparations and warfare. Public IDF publications, Ministry of Defence (MOD) bids, and press reports

---

[15]The conceptualization of the 2015 document's guidelines was the outcome of a decade-and-a-half-long effort following the realization that the existing operational concept no longer suited the existing political and strategic circumstances. Rabinovich and Brun, *Israel Facing a New Middle East*, 1–5, 109–111. See also Charles D. Freilich, *Zion's Dilemmas: How Israel Makes National Security Policy* (Ithaca: Cornell University Press 2012), 27–60.
[16]Israel Defence Forces (IDF), *Estrategiat Tzahal* [IDF Strategy] (April 2018), Clause 8, <https://www.idf.il/media/34416/strategy.pdf>.
[17]*Ibid*, Clause 10.a; Rabinovich and Brun, *Israel Facing a New Middle East*, 113–15; Charles D. Freilich, *Israeli National Security: A New Strategy for an Era of Change* (New York: Oxford University Press 2018), ch. 7; Raphael D. Marcus, *Israel's long war with Hezbollah: Military innovation and adaptation under fire* (Washington, D.C.: Georgetown University Press 2018), 143, 215–18.
[18]IDF, *Estrategiat Tzahal*, Chapters B, E.
[19]*Ibid.*, Chapter B.

reveal that Israel's defence establishment is profoundly interested in 4IR technologies and is already engaged to varying degrees in the acquisition, development, and deployment of some of them. They include robots, multi-sensor autonomous vehicles for different arms and services, nanotechnology and nanomaterials, sensors and sensing technology, the networking of people and things, artificial intelligence (AI), technological human empowerment, electromagnetic pulse (EMP) weapons, and quantum technology for diverse uses.[20] The deployment of such systems had already begun in the mid-2000s. For instance, in 2006 the IDF began deploying the advanced command and control Digital Ground Army system (DGA). This system provides field and staff commanders with real-time visual and other data on the battlefield, including the location of 'friend and foe' forces, assesses the nature of the threats to friendly forces, recommends attack means, and identifies communication problems among the forces and their automatic repair. The system is upgraded continuously. For example, a recent development whose deployment was scheduled for 2019 is the Shaked Warfare system, comprising a specially adjusted Android smartphone and a digital watch. Among other things, the system allows field commanders and soldiers to navigate and direct the battle using a digital blue-red map of the enemy and of friendly forces, provides alerts and updates regarding enemy forces and terrain conditions, recommends the vehicles to be used and detects whether the target can be reached on foot, and allows flagging and tracking a target by smartphone.[21]

The deployment of these systems is not an isolated event but part of a trend. There are various indications that in the 2010s, having realized their revolutionary impact, the IDF has assigned a greater role to the combination of sensors, large databases, AI, the internet-of-things (IoT), advanced energy preservation means, and other related technologies. In 2017 the commander of a large IT development unit in the IDF's C4IR and Cyber Defence Directorate ('Lotem') said that the IDF is a 'multi-sensor machine in every one of its dimensions – from computing systems with excellent network learning capabilities to the battle tank – and the challenge is to get the

---

[20]Technion R&D Foundation Ltd., 'IMOD DDR&D: Call for a Proposal for Research for the Defense Establishment', <https://www.trdf.co.il/heb/kolkoreinfo.php?id=4332>; 'Technologia besde hakrav ha'atidi' [Technology in the future battlefield], *Ma'arachot* 477 (April 2018), 48–53; Hertzi Halevy, A. and Y. (full names unavailable), 'Elionut modi'init beidan technologi' [Intelligence superiority in a digital era], *Ma'arachot* 477 (April 2018), 26–31; 'Hauniversita haivrit tivne madgim leumi letikshoret quantit' [The Hebrew University will build a national demonstrator for quantic communication], *TechTime*, 12 June 2017,<https://techtime.co.il/2017/06/12/quantum-communications/>.
[21]'IDF Technological Revolution Reaches Warrior on Field', *iHLS*, 28 December 2017, <https://i-hls.com/archives/80503>. See also Elad Rotbaum, 'Hatsayad Hamshudrag' [The upgraded DGA], *Bamahane*, 19 September 2017.

maximum benefit of this information'.[22] His high rank – Brigadier-General – reflects the importance that the IDF assigns to this field.

Still, the deployment and assimilation of such revolutionary technologies involve a variety of considerable challenges. Given that covering all of the major challenges exceeds the scope of this paper, I touch on a few typical ones at both ends of the continuum – the individual and the organizational – that pertain to the IDF's distinctive features. On the individual level, the challenges that pertain to soldiers and commanders naturally include the latter's scepticism about new technologies and reluctance to rely on decision-making support systems (AI), as well as combat soldiers and commanders' lack of professional skills to operate sophisticated digital equipment. Additional concerns are that over-reliance on such equipment erodes their basic military skills and the IDF's core values, such as the 'follow me' ethos (commanders lead their units personally in the battlefield) and 'the man in the tank will win' (the superiority of human beings over technology).[23] One example of these concerns was the fierce criticism of field commanders who allegedly commanded their units from the rear in the 2006 Lebanon War by using advanced intelligence and communication systems.[24] Ever since, any introduction of sophisticated equipment to combat units is followed by warnings that they should not replace basic capabilities but only support them.[25]

On the macro level, despite its routine engagement in fighting wars, the IDF is nevertheless a 'large, conservative, and hierarchical organization, which engages in an operational reality ... and therefore ... doesn't tend to take risks'.[26] As such, it struggles to find the right balance between equipping itself with the very latest means while concurrently ensuring that these technologies are safe and reliable. According to a senior officer, with some exceptions the IDF does 'not follow any new trend ... We try identifying technologies that are not too new but are still in the first third of their life cycle'.[27] But in a rapidly changing environment the armed forces realize that they do not have the luxury of being so selective. In fact, the IDF strategy document states that rapid

---

[22]Na'ama Zaltzman, 'Mefakedet yehidat lotem: "anachnu lokhim et hameida vemvi'im oto lesde hakrav"' [Lotem unit commander: 'We take the information and bring it to the battlefield'], *Bamahane*, 28 November 2017.

[23]Tali Caspi-Shabbat and Or Glik, 'Mahapechat hameida baolam hamivtsai harav-zroi betzahal' [The information revolution in the IDF's multi-arm operational world], *Bein Haktavim* 18 (2018), 38–47; Yossi Hatoni, 'Kli haneshek haba shel tzahal: bina mlachutit' [The IDF's new weapon: artificial intelligence], *Anashim Ve'mahshevim*, 24 October 2017, <https://www.pc.co.il/news/251638/>.

[24]Amir Rapaport, *The IDF and the Lessons of the Second Lebanon War*, Mideast Security and Policy Studies No. 85 (Ramat Gan: The Begin-Sadat Center for Strategic Studies, Bar-Ilan University 2010), 49.

[25]For example, Yoav Zeitoun, 'Hamishkefet hadigitalit hachadasha shel tsahal' [The IDF's new digital binoculars], *YNET*, 25 June 2019, <https://www.ynet.co.il/articles/0,7340,L-5533205,00.html>.

[26]Caspi-Shabbat and Glik, 'Mahapechat hameida', 32.

[27]'Haetgar hagadol hu mitzuy hayeda' [Datamining is the big challenge], *Israel Defense*, 15 May 2013.

technological challenges and the rapid exhaustion of military-use technologies is a major, challenging feature of Israel's strategic environment.[28]

These challenges do not, of course, stop 4IR technologies from being increasingly deployed across the IDF's arms and services. This deployment, in turn, raises one of the most crucial questions concerning the assimilation of 4IR technologies in the armed forces: their source of supply. Certainly, the defence establishment, the IDF included, has R&D units of its own, which have successfully undertaken various 4IR-related developments.[29] However, as 4IR-related R&D is increasingly expanding into new scientific fields involving advanced basic research, and its progress is constantly accelerating, neither the IDF nor the defence industries have the ability to undertake related developments entirely in-house and to close the gaps.[30] Acknowledging this reality, they search for collaborations with academia and the hi-tech sector, while struggling to achieve the precise balance between in-house development and reliance on external sources.[31] Elaborating on this issue, a former commander of a military R&D unit said: 'What's important is our relative advantage. We keep asking ourselves where the line is between what we purchase from civilian sources and what we should develop by ourselves'.[32]

Supply: The development of military-related 4IR technologies in Israel

The Israeli hi-tech sector has been closely related to the defence establishment since its early days. It was founded largely by veterans of military technology units and kept absorbing their veterans in the years to come.[33] In the 1970s, it received a significant boost with the formation of the Israeli Industry Centre for R&D (MATIMOP, transformed in 2016 into the Israel Innovation Authority). The purpose of this Israeli government body, envisioned and founded by a former commander of the IDF's division for

---

[28]IDF, *Estrategiat Tzahal*, Clause 8.A.5.
[29]For instance, 'The Future of Artificial Intelligence in the IDF', *Israel Defense*, 2 July 2017.
[30]In this paper, the term 'defence industries' refers to state-owned, private or public companies that develop and produce weapons, ammunition, and/or other equipment for purely military use. Companies that develop dual-use products or supply non-military products to military and other security organizations are not included in this category. As of 2019, there were three major defence industry corporations in Israel: IAI, Rafael and Elbit Systems.
[31]'Government Industries Are Not Investing in Research', *Israel Defense*, 16 February 2012; 'Technologia besde hakrav ha'atidi' [Technology in future battlefield], *Ma'arachot* 477 (April 2018), 53; 'Ha'etgar hagadol hu mitzuy hayeda'.
[32]'Ha'etgar hagadol hu mitzuy hayeda'.
[33]For the contribution of the veterans of IDF technology units to the development of Israel's hi-tech sector, see Dan Breznitz, 'The Military as a Public Space: The Role of the IDF in the Israeli Software Innovation System', *MIT Working Paper* IPC-02-004 (April 2002); Benson Honig, Miri Lerner, and Yoel Raban, 'Social Capital and the Linkages of High-Tech Companies to the Military Defense System: Is There a Signalling Mechanism?' *Small Business Economics* 27/4-5 (2006), 420–21.

weaponry and military equipment development, was to advance industrial R&D in Israel.[34] The hi-tech sector's link to the military has remained close ever since and seems to serve both sides well. Thanks to the IDF's positive professional image, engaging in military-related projects or becoming an MOD supplier often promotes a company's reputation. A 2006 study found a positive correlation between the selling of technologies to the IDF and a start-up's ability to obtain investments.[35] As of 2018, there were approximately 700 such companies.[36]

As of the late 2010s, Israel's vibrant and innovative hi-tech sector had some 5,000 start-up companies, with 600 new ones being established yearly – the largest number in the world relative to the size of the country's population.[37] As such, this sector enjoys relatively large investments and excellent support conditions. Israel's R&D investments in 2017 accounted for 4.2% of the GDP – the second largest in the world[38] – and it enjoys close collaboration with the global economy and hi-tech scene. In 2016, 87% of the revenue of Israel's elite technology companies was from exports. In the following year, foreign investments constituted 77% of the total investments in the hi-tech sector. In the last several decades, over 350 multinational corporations (MNCs) including Intel, Apple, Google, Microsoft, Facebook, IBM, Toshiba, Huawei, Samsung, Ford, GM, HP, and Philips established R&D centres in Israel.[39] The international connection expands the availability of 4IR technologies to the military by keeping Israeli hi-tech companies close to recent technological developments. In addition, collaborating with Israeli companies rather than the defence sector directly is politically easier for European companies, particularly when dual-use or other military-related technology is involved.[40]

The development of 4IR technologies is attracting growing attention and resources in Israel's hi-tech sector, academia, and government bodies. As of 2018, about 230 start-ups in Israel were focused on 4IR-related technologies, including AI, robotics, IoT, big data, energy, operation optimization,

---

[34]Itzhak Yaakov, *Adon klum baribua* [*The Memoires of Mr. Zero Squared*] (Tel Aviv: Yedioth Ahronoth 2011), 274–75.
[35]Honig et al., 'Social Capital', 429.
[36]Gay Faglin, *Merutz hachidush: Technologiot mishariot vetzvai'yot bee'mtzaei lehima – nekudat ha'izun hamatima* [*The Innovation Race: Commercial and Military Technologies in Military Systems – the Right Balance*] (Haifa: Chaikin Chair in Geostrategy 2018), 35.
[37]Other sources claim that as of 2018, over 8,300 hi-tech companies were active in Israel, the great majority of them start-up companies. IVC Research Centre, 'Israeli High-Tech Companies that Ceased Operations', December 2018, <https://www.ivc-online.com/Portals/0/RC/Media/Ceased%20Operation%20-%20report%20FINAL%20241218.pdf?timestamp=1545809432251>.
[38]UNESCO Institute for Statistics, *Startup Ranking*, <http://uis.unesco.org/apps/visualisations/research-and-development-spending/>; Israel Innovation Authority, <https://innovationisrael.org.il/en/>.
[39]Israel Central Bureau of Statistics, 'Revenue, exports and sales of R&D', <https://old.cbs.gov.il/hodaot2019n/12_19_258t5.pdf >; John Ben-Zaken, 'Mehkar IVC: 77% mehashkaot bahi-tech halsraeli – zarot' [IVC research: about 77% of the investments in the Israeli hi-tech are foreign], *Anashim Ve'Machshevim*, 26 November 2018; Israel Innovation Authority, 'Innovation in Israel', <https://innovationisrael.org.il/en/contentpage/innovation-israel>.
[40]Tzila Hershko, 'Haroman mithadesh?' [Is the love affair starting over?], *Ma'arachot* 456 (2014), 37.

autonomous vehicles and drones, and nanotech. The field that attracts the most interest is AI.[41] The strong interest in these areas is the outcome of considerable business incentives, but also of government and academic initiatives and investments. In the late 2000s and early 2010s, Israel made an effort to become a leading global player in the area of cyber security. Building on existing capabilities and demands in this field, it established several academic research programs and centres, and promoted collaborations between academia and industry.

A similar process seems to be happening in the quantum computing field. In 2014, the Technion (Israel's leading institute of technology) and Israel's Council for Higher Education passed a resolution assigning high priority to quantum computing as an area of high national priority.[42] The resolution was echoed by a call from the Israeli Hi-tech Association, which identified quantum computing, together with digital healthcare and robotics, as a field of considerable potential that should be further developed through governmental investments.[43] Then, in May 2018 Prime Minister Benjamin Netanyahu announced that Israel was about to develop the quantum field as part of a national science and technology program for national security.[44] Subsequently, as of 2018, about 800 researchers have engaged in quantum computing, and related research centres have been established in five out of Israel's eight research universities.[45]

The spin-on process: The symbiosis between technology spinoffs and spin-ons

Civilian research and development activity is relevant to the defence establishment only as long as channels and supporting conditions for the transfer of know-how between the sectors exist. Indeed, such conditions are excellent in Israel due to the central place that defence issues occupy in the country, and the firm connections between the military and the rest of Israeli life. This

---

[41] Gil Press, '230 Industry 4.0 Startups In Israel Playing A Leading Role In Data-Driven Digitized Production', *Forbes*, 5 August 2019; Agmon David Porat, 'Infographica: mapat hevrot hastartup betchum ta'asiya 4.0 [Infographic: map of startup companies in the area of industry 4.0], *Ta'asia 4.0*, 13 June 2018, <http://www.smart-factory.co.il/%D7%90%D7%99%D7%A0%D7%A4%D7%95% D7%92%D7%A8%D7%A4%D7%99%D7%A7%D7%94-%D7%9E%D7%A4%D7%AA-%D7%97%D7% 91%D7%A8%D7%95%D7%AA-%D7%94%D7%A1%D7%98%D7%90%D7%A8%D7%98-%D7%90% D7%A4-%D7%91%D7%AA%D7%97%D7%95%D7%9D-%D7%AA%D7%A2%D7%A9%D7%99%D7% 99%D7%94-4-0.html>.

[42] Tal Shahaf, 'Israeli Gov't Allocates NIS 300 m for Quantum Computing', *Globes*, 2 July 2008, <https://en.globes.co.il/en/article-government-allocates-nis-300 m-for-quantum-computing-1001244244>.

[43] Nati Yefet, 'Hevrot hi-tech alulot la'avor lehul shelo meshikulim technologiyim' [Hi-tech companies may move out of the country for non-technological reasons], *Globes*, 12 May 2018, <https://www.globes.co.il/news/article.aspx?did=1001235492>.

[44] Shahaf, 'Israeli Gov't Allocates'.

[45] *Ibid.*; Avi Blizovsky, 'Hatochnit haleumit lehishuv quanti hiunit lekach shelsrael tishaer bahazit' [The national program for quantum computing is crucial for Israel's position at the front], *Hayadan*, 5 June 2018, <https://www.hayadan.org.il/nadav-katz-on-quantum-computing-0606183>.

situation has resulted in the extensive growth of spin-offs and spin-ons. In an attempt to describe Israel's 4IR technology spin-on process, this section examines the channels, enablers, and challenges that underlie it. To that end, it examines four major spin-on channels, followed by analyses of the factors that enable spin-ons and the challenges they face.

Spin-on channels

Israel's main spin-on channels include the personal connections of hi-tech leaders and employees with IDF units, the Ministry of Defence's Directorate of Defence Research and Development (DDR&D), the Israel Innovation Authority, and various collaboration frameworks between the defence establishment and academia. The first channel on this list (personal connections) is largely informal and consists of IDF veterans who moved to the hi-tech sector while staying in contact with the military units in which they had served. The DDR&D is the MOD's body in charge of technological development for the IDF, which, as part of its routine work, harnesses business and academia to military R&D. The third channel – the Israel Innovation Authority – is a governmental body as well, though a civilian one. Intended to promote Israel's hi-tech sector and technological innovations in general, it also introduces civilian companies to defence-related projects. The last item on the list refers to various frameworks – inside and outside academia – that allow the flow of scientific knowledge from the universities to the defence sector.

Personal service and relationships with the IDF

Constituting around 60% of Israel's hi-tech entrepreneurs, top executives, and employees, veterans of the IDF's technology and combat units are a crucial link between hi-tech companies and R&D bodies in the defence establishment.[46] This relationship is particularly true for veterans of the IDF's technology units, many of whom first acquired the basis of their professional expertise during their compulsory military service. After their special skills are identified in a pre-recruitment screening process, such soldiers undergo intensive training programs, which occasionally include academic studies. At a relatively young age they become involved in large scale, technologically advanced and complex development projects.[47] Their military service in these units, as well their personal connections with their contemporary and former soldiers and commanders, provide them with ideas for new technologies and products, as well as a clear understanding

---

[46]Ori Swed and John S. Butler, 'Military Capital in the Israeli Hi-tech Industry', *Armed Forces & Society* 41/1 (2015), 127.
[47]*Ibid.*, 133; Breznitz, 'The Military', 16–22.

of the IDF's technological needs. It also gives them multiple opportunities to present their products to the IDF and the defence establishment, while concurrently making them natural candidates when the defence establishment looks for certain technologies or products, or searches for R&D contractors or partners. Thus, these veterans serve as an important link in the symbiotic relationship between spinoffs and spin-ons. They move into the civilian sector as entrepreneurs, executives or employees, developing new products based on their military experience. Then, these products find their way to the IDF and other defence organizations after being adapted to military use. This spin-on process happens both top-down and bottom-up. Sometimes it is the IDF that approaches these companies, asking them to develop certain technological solutions. In other cases, it is the companies that suggest new products to the defence establishment.

In addition, the personal connection constitutes a long-term spin-on channel thanks to the experts' reserve service, through which they keep participating in military R&D projects while preserving and expanding their personal network. Furthermore, reserve service includes teaching in the IDF's professional courses. Given their strong identification with their mission, they often share valuable professional know-how by writing reference books and training materials. Indeed, some of them admitted they would never reveal such professional secrets in civilian circles. In addition, given their personal acquaintances, hi-tech leaders are occasionally asked to advise or serve as mentors in the IDF's technology projects. For instance, as part of a start-up accelerator-like project in the Air Force in 2018, the teams received professional guidance from hi-tech industry experts.[48]

The Ministry of Defence's Directorate of Defence Research and Development (DDR&D)

Subordinate to the MOD, DDR&D (*MAFA'T*) serves as a staff body for both the MOD and the IDF, and is responsible for drawing up the defence establishment's R&D policy. In practice, DDR&D is the link between the planning bodies and the R&D's management in the MOD and the IDF, and between the IDF, defence industries, and other companies and non-profit entities that engage in defence-related R&D. As part of their work, the DDR&D is involved in acquiring development projects for the IDF from various types of entities, including academia, hi-tech companies, and even collaboration with other countries (e.g., the Iron Dome anti-rocket and short-range missile system).

DDR&D's objectives, structure, and mode of operation allow a great deal of room for the participation of universities, research institutes, and hi-tech

---

[48]Breznitz, 'The Military', 28–34; Nophar Blit, 'IAF Startup Accelerator', *Israeli Air Force*, 1 November 2018, <http://www.iaf.org.il/4478-50651-en/IAF.aspx>.

companies in Israel's defence R&D. An example is the efforts made by the DDR&D's optronics department to promote relevant innovative development in start-up and small companies.[49] Once they achieve such capabilities, they become a source of spin-on processes.

Of utmost importance to 4IR technology spin-ons is the DDR&D's responsibility to locate, develop, and promote advanced technologies that address Israel's current and future security challenges. To this end the DDR&D operates a scientific research organization – the division for technological research and infrastructure – that works closely with Israel's academic institutes to assess the military potential of new S&T developments such as quantic technologies, nanotechnology, new materials, autonomous systems, and energetic materials. Using common practices such as tenders, research grants, and contacting specific experts, it assembles academic experts in different disciplines and from different institutes for various multi-year research projects.[50]

The Israel innovation authority

The reincarnation of the above-mentioned MATIMOP, the Innovation Authority is a governmental agency that is responsible for planning and executing the country's innovation policy. As part of this mission, it promotes cutting-edge technology projects, supports entrepreneurs and start-up companies in developing their innovative technological concepts, promotes the technological innovation of mature companies, and supports academic groups seeking to transfer their ideas to the market. It also supports joint projects of Israeli and foreign companies. The authority's main tools are programs that provide financial support, access to government-owned trial sites and facilities, and the opportunity to participate in national R&D programs.[51]

Focusing on civilian activities, the Innovation Authority nevertheless constitutes an important technology spin-on channel. Using its incentive programs for innovation with government entities, it supports R&D in defence-related areas. A typical case is a program encouraging R&D in the field of space technologies, operated jointly with the Israel Space Agency.[52] As many advanced capabilities in the field of space can have a military use,[53] the military relevance of the program is self-evident. Likewise, the authority

---

[49]Ministry of Defence, 'Mehkar ve'pituach tzva'i' [Military R&D], <http://www.mod.gov.il/Defence-and-Security/Pages/research_and_development.aspx>.
[50]Ministry of Defence, 'Technological Research and Infrastructure Unit', <http://www.mod.gov.il/Defence-and-Security/Pages/science_research.aspx>.
[51]Israel Innovation Authority, *Endless Possibilities to Promote Innovation* (2018), <https://innovationisrael.org.il/en/sites/default/files/Booklet_2018.pdf>.
[52]*Ibid.*, 20–21.
[53]Duncan Blake, 'Military Strategic Use of Outer Space', in H. Nasu, R. McLaughlin (eds), *New Technologies and the Law of Armed Conflict* (Hague: T.M.C. Asser Press 2014), 97–114; Barry D. Watts, *The Military Use of Space: A Diagnostic Assessment* (Washington, DC: Center for Strategic and Budgetary Assessments 2001).

runs two programs in the area of cyber, operated respectively with the National Cyber Directorate at the Prime Minister's Office and the MOD, supporting the development of innovative solutions for the defence and commercial markets.[54] In addition, the Innovation Authority has programs to transform academic knowledge into applied knowledge that will be implemented in industry, and to develop generic ground breaking knowledge through the collaboration of researchers from academia and industry. This framework provides substantial support for programs associated with 4IR and military-related technologies.

Defence-academia collaboration frameworks

The IDF and the MOD have relied on and collaborated with Israeli universities and academic staff since their early years.[55] For example, both bodies have utilized scientists to identify new scientific fields and state-of-the-art technologies with military potential, which allow the IDF to maintain its qualitative edge. They also use scientists and academic facilities to develop specific know-how or means. To that end, they use various extra-academia platforms such as the DDR&D's financed projects and military reserve service. In addition, the universities serve as a spin-on channel by initiating and operating some platforms of their own.

One such case is the Technology and Social Forecast Unit at Tel Aviv University. Established to follow recent scientific developments and predict future technological developments with national defence implications, the MOD's R&D division created the Technology Forecast Centre at the university in the early 1970s.[56] The centre, known today as the Technology and Social Forecast Unit, still operates. Its current defence-related research programs demonstrate how it introduces and assimilates 4IR technologies into national defence thinking. Included here are projects such as terror threats related to new technologies, new nano-biotechnology-related materials, acoustic concealment, and advanced composite materials.[57]

Spin-on conditions

Taken together, these and other spin-on channels in the country rely on the relations between the civilian realm and the military in Israel's society and economy, the local entrepreneurial capacity, and the MOD's acknowledgement of its growing dependency on civilian R&D. These channels help expand the

---

[54]Israel Innovation Authority, *Endless Possibilities to Promote Innovation*, 29.
[55]Uzi Eilam, *Keshet Eilam: Hatechnologia hamitkademet* [*Eilam's Arc: How Israel Became a Military Technology Powerhouse*] (Tel Aviv: Yedioth Ahronoth 2011), 151.
[56]*Ibid.*, 163.
[57]Tel Aviv University, The Social and Technological Forecasting Unit, <https://education.tau.ac.il/ictaf/odot>.

supply of 4IR-related civilian companies and technologies. They also help companies, scientists, and governmental defence bodies mutually locate opportunities for incorporating new technologies in defence projects and facilitate the participation of civilian companies in defence projects. Indeed, compared with the US and perhaps other countries too, responding to the MOD's tenders or becoming an MOD supplier involves a relatively simple bureaucratic process and reasonable costs.[58] In many cases defence R&D tenders and MOD bids are circulated openly through the websites of the MOD's DDR&D and other relevant bodies, and proposals can be submitted online as well.[59] Moreover, the MOD even allows start-up and hi-tech companies that are only partially owned by Israelis to participate in its projects under the condition that the foreign partners do not receive any access to classified information, as defined by the MOD.[60]

However, spin-on processes in Israel also have some drawbacks. In order to promote the involvement of civilian companies in defence projects, the defence establishment must take steps to secure classified information, particularly when sensitive technologies are involved. The financial costs involved in these measures can make the companies question the project's attractiveness. For examples, the companies may be restricted when it comes to selling products or know-how developed with the MOD's support. According to the MOD's regulations, any know-how developed or obtained with its support 'will remain under the sole ownership of the ministry [of defence] and the supplier will not be allowed to use it for any other purpose than this order'. Similarly, the supplier is not allowed to produce or supply the product or any of its parts to anyone but the MOD, unless the ministry approves it specifically.[61] Therefore, it is no surprise that such conditions discourage companies from taking part in MOD-financed R&D projects because they significantly reduce their prospects of making profits from the product. Replying to a question about whether his company was involved in an R&D project for the MOD, an executive at an Israeli hi-tech company that developed 4IR-related vision technologies said, 'No way. That would force the company to get MOD's approval for every sale'.[62]

---

[58] An interview with Shaul Chorev, former head of the special measures division in the MOD and the Israel Atomic Energy Commission (IAEC). Haifa, 10 January 2019.
[59] Ministry of Defence Online, <https://www.online.mod.gov.il/Online2016/pages/General/Info/start.aspx>.
[60] Ministry of Defence, 'Tofes hatzhara: Hevra ba'alat shutafim zarim' [Declaration form: a company with foreign partners], <https://www.online.mod.gov.il/Online2016/documents/general/rishum_sapak/hazhara.pdf>.
[61] Ministry of Defence, 'Nispach 93: tna'im klaliyim lehazmanat misrad habitachon' [Annex 93: General terms of the Ministry of Defence's order], Items 4. Ministry's Knowhow (a), 9, <https://www.online.mod.gov.il/Online2016/Documents/General/Nispahim/nisB09301.pdf>.
[62] Interview with a hi-tech company's employee. Tel Aviv 7 December 2018.

A related hindrance is the high costs of obtaining the requisite security classification when supplying classified systems to the MOD. Acquiring such a classification requires the company to take various costly steps, such as installing security measures and implementing special procedures, which occasionally exceed the means of small companies. In addition, just as becoming an MOD supplier sometimes increases the likelihood of start-up companies receiving investments, in other cases it can have a negative effect. Investors assume that it will negatively impact the start-up's sales in the civilian market. In such cases start-ups might be wary about such a relationship from the outset.[63] That said, considering the importance of the defence sector for Israel's hi-tech sector, we can also assume that few companies will choose to avoid connections with it. Furthermore, in certain cases companies can overcome some of these administrative and legal obstacles by supplying their products to the MOD through a registered MOD supplier, thus avoiding some of the financial and reputational costs that the status of 'MOD supplier' can bring with it.[64]

4IR technologies in the service of the IDF: Implications for regional stability

4IR technologies provide the military with longer, more accurate, and more lethal strike capabilities in all five dimensions of warfare (ground, air, sea, space, cyber), on various fronts (the frontline, the home front, the enemy's rear, and remote enemies) and by various means. For instance, AI capabilities combined with cybersecurity allow defence forces to analyse large-scale communication traffic, identify suspicious activities, and trace them closely. The combination of remote sensing, location tracing, and precision-guided munitions, all of which require 4IR technologies, allow the armed forces to acquire the precise location of targets and hit enemies operating in populated areas with only limited collateral damage. Advanced cyber capabilities combined with reconnaissance capabilities and precision-guided munitions allow countries to penetrate the enemy's communication and information systems, obtain information about its force deployment and arms production facilities, and launch pre-emptive attacks.[65]

---

[63]Faglin, *Merutz hachidush*, 70–77.
[64]*Ibid.*, 70.
[65]These are just a few examples of the impact of 4IR technologies on military affairs. For a broader review, see Peter Layton, 'Mobilising Defence in the "fourth industrial revolution"', *The Interpreter*, 27 March 2019, <https://www.lowyinstitute.org/the-interpreter/mobilising-defence-fourth-industrial-revolution>; Nah Liang Tuang, *The Fourth Industrial Revolution's Impact on Smaller Militaries: Boon or Bane?* RSIS Working Paper no. 318 (Singapore: S. Rajaratnam School of International Studies 2018); Nien *et al.*, 'At the Leading Edge'.

However, the availability of military means not only allows countries to carry out such military operations. It may also encourage them to use force.[66] For countries located in conflict-intensive regions, the validity of this claim seems particularly strong. Accordingly, one can expect that the assimilation of 4IR technologies into the IDF's capabilities will increase Israel's use of force – both defensively and offensively. Indeed, during the 2010s, Israel executed hundreds of military operations and attacks, the majority of which were much smaller than a full-scale campaign. Included were over 200 aerial attacks against high quality and occasionally long-distance targets – mostly in Syria but apparently also in Iraq. The operations involved cyber-attacks, border defence actions, including the tracing and destruction of tunnels, and the interception of missiles and rockets aimed at the state's home front.[67] From an operational viewpoint, some of these actions were responsive in nature – for instance, intercepting missiles and rockets, while others – such as the destruction of weapons transports in Syria – were initiated by Israel.

Thus, attempting to preliminarily assess the broad implications of the IDF's assimilation of 4IR technologies, it might be fairly safe to argue that these technologies provide the state with more opportunities to use military force.[68] However, the implications for local and regional stability are not straightforward. Recent studies on the strategic effect of emerging technologies show that they may strengthen stability in some ways, while undermining it in others.[69] One reason for this outcome is that, as with military innovation, strategic stability depends on a broader set of variables than technology alone.[70] As Benjamin Fordham put it, 'Even if policy choice is, in part, a function of capabilities, capabilities are also a function of policy choice. Decision makers build military (and other) capabilities based on the ... international conditions they expect to face'.[71] Indeed, during the period examined in this paper (the late 2000s-2010s) Israel's environment became greatly destabilized following the Arab

---

[66]Barry Buzan and Eric Herring, *The Arms Dynamic in World Politics* (Boulder: Lynne Rienner 1998), 201–3; Benjamin O. Fordham, 'A Very Sharp Sword: The Influence of Military Capabilities on American Decisions to Use Force', *Journal of Conflict Resolution*, 48/5 (2004), 632–56.
[67]Krishnadev Calamur, 'The Battle between Israel and Iran Is Spreading', *The Atlantic*, 10 May 2018, <https://www.theatlantic.com/international/archive/2018/05/israel-strikes-iran/560111/>; Carla E. Humud, Kenneth Katzman, and Jim Zanotti, 'Iran and Israel: Tension over Syria', *In Focus*, Congressional Research Service, 5 June 2019.
[68]Chin, 'Technology, War and the State', 771.
[69]Todd S. Sechser, Neil Narang, and Caitlin Talmadge, 'Emerging Technologies and Strategic Stability in Peacetime, Crisis, and War', *Journal of Strategic Studies* 42/6 (2019), 732.
[70]Ronald F. Lehman, 'Future Technology and Strategic Stability', in Elbridge A. Colby and Michael S. Gerson (eds.), *Strategic stability: Contending interpretations* (Carlisle: U.S. Army War College Press 2013)147 ,.
[71]Fordham, 'A Very Sharp Sword', 636.

Spring, thus providing Israel with multiple motivations to exercise force.[72]

Indeed, the occurrence of frequent limited, accurate, and deniable military and cyberattacks can bring about various strategic outcomes in a volatile region such as the Middle East. On one hand, and in accordance with certain balance-of-power-theories, frequent limited incidents of this type clarify the balance of power, help countries signal their red lines and intentions, strengthen deterrence, and allow parties to release tensions.[73] Moreover, they may provide Israel with new regional collaborations. Its developing relationship with the Persian Gulf monarchies is such a case. Interested in Israel's new technological and military capabilities – many of them associated with 4IR technologies – and sharing its concern over Iran, these states have been willing to compromise on some of their political principles in return for technological and strategic cooperation.[74] Thus, Israel has provided these countries with 4IR technologies by allowing (or even encouraging) the direct sales of relevant capabilities by Israeli companies.[75] Such actions further blur the boundaries between the civilian realm and the military, and those between economics and strategy. Given that these countries, particularly Saudi Arabia, have significant regional influence, such a dynamic can improve Israel's overall regional position. Taken together, these developments may delay the eruption of the next large-scale round of violence.

On the other hand, Israel's increasing use of force – even on a limited scale and conducted with deniability in mind – increases fear and suspicion, prompts the attacked players to seek vengeance, draws other players into the conflict, and inflames hatred among the involved populations.[76] Certainly, it inflames tensions and creates crises that might escalate and spin out of control.

Conclusion

Revolutionary as they are, 4IR technologies have not been the driving force behind Israel's changing military doctrine. Rather, it was the strategic and

---

[72] Rabinovich and Brun, *Israel Facing a New Middle East*, 95–102, 111–12; Freilich, *Israeli National Security*, 49–58.

[73] For example, see Alexander L. George, *Forceful Persuasion: Coercive Diplomacy as an Alternative to War* (Washington, D.C.: United States Institute of Peace 1992), 5–7; Thomas C. Schelling, *Arms and influence* (New Heaven; Yale University Press, 2008), 2–11.

[74] Clive Jones and Yoel Guzansky, 'Israel's Relations with The Gulf States: Toward the Emergence of a Tacit Security Regime?' *Contemporary Security Policy* 38/3 (2017), 398–419.

[75] David D. Kirkpatrick and Azam Ahmed, 'Hacking a Prince, an Emir and a Journalist to Impress a Client', *New Yok Times*, 31 August 2018, <https://www.nytimes.com/2018/08/31/world/middleeast/hacking-united-arab-emirates-nso-group.html>.

[76] For example, 'Unhappy with Israeli Strikes in Syria, Russia Outs Israel's Other Operations', *The Arab Weekly*, 22 November 2019, <https://thearabweekly.com/unhappy-israeli-strikes-syria-russia-outs-israels-other-operations>.

socio-political developments in Israel and its surroundings. But once Israel's military leadership assumed that such a change was needed, 4IR technologies became one of the major forces that shaped it, to the extent that the IDF maintained officially that future R&D would contextualize its mid-term force-build-up program.[77] At present, they are distributed across all arms, services, and hierarchical levels of the IDF.

The impact of these technologies on the country's possibilities and strategic position seems significant, even ground breaking, in some areas. Nevertheless, the ultimate strategic impact is still unclear. On one hand, allowing, or even pushing, countries to make more frequent and precise use of force may clarify the actual balance-of-power, allow players to let off steam, and make way for new regional collaborations. On the other hand, tensions may be heightened, creating crises that spiral out of control.

This is not the only dilemma that the deployment of 4IR technologies in the IDF involves. Another issue that I discussed in detail concerns the sources of supply for 4IR technologies. As this paper shows, the close relations between Israel's defence and hi-tech sectors will become tighter, and technology spin-ons will strengthen. This in itself is not a barrier to the IDF's development because the basic features of Israel's society, economy, and civilian-military relations furnish its academic and hi-tech sectors with the capacity and inclination to collaborate with the defence establishment. The structure of the Israeli hi-tech sector and the MOD's regulations even allow local firms to include foreign companies in related projects when necessary. However, becoming an MOD vendor also has some drawbacks. It puts companies in a commercial quandary, restricting their ability to sell the same products to different clients and requiring them to undergo a costly process to obtain security clearance. Still, considering the close relations between the defence sector and Israel's hi-tech industry, and the former's preponderance on the hi-tech sector's client list, few companies are likely to forfeit the defence sector option.

Taking these intermediate conclusions one step further, I maintain that including 4IR technologies in military capabilities may blur the traditional boundaries associated with the military realm. First, by allowing the state to conduct frequent, small scale, and somewhat untraceable military attacks and other operations (including cyberattacks) during ceasefire periods, they blur the boundary between war and non-war situations. Second, by providing the ability to attack the enemy's population centres, civilian infrastructure, and even companies – and the motivation for doing so, they blur the line between the frontlines and the home front. Third, by turning civilian companies and academic institutions into military suppliers, and even assigning them a role in the state's strategic relations with other players, they blur the boundary between military and civilian players inside the country as well as the common

---

[77]IDF, *Estrategiat Tzahal*, Chapter D.

definition of the defence industry. Finally, by assigning a greater role in warfare to emerging technologies, including cyberattacks, attacks by UAVs and the like, they blur the traditional distinction between combat and non-combat units.

Disclosure statement

No potential conflict of interest was reported by the author(s).

ORCID

Yoram Evron http://orcid.org/0000-0002-1933-4858

Bibliography

Adamsky, Dmitry, *The Culture of Military Innovation: The Impact of Cultural Factors on the Revolution in Military Affairs in Russia, the US, and Israel* (Stanford Stanford University Press 2010).
Blake, Duncan, 'Military Strategic Use of Outer Space', in H. Nasu and R. McLaughlin (eds.) *New Technologies and the Law of Armed Conflict* (Hague: T.M.C. Asser Press 2014), 97–114.
Breznitz, Dan, 'The Military as a Public Space: The Role of the IDF in the Israeli Software Innovation System', *MIT Working Paper* IPC-02-004 (April 2002).
Brzoska, Michael, 'Trends in Global Military and Civilian Research and Development (R&D) and Their Changing Interface', *Proceedings of the International Seminar on Defence Finance and Economics* 19 (2006).
Buzan, Barry and Eric Herring, *The Arms Dynamic in World Politics* (Boulder Lynne Rienner 1998).
Caspi-Shabbat, Tali and Or Glik, 'Mahapechat hameida baolam hamivtsai harav-zroi betzahal [The Information Revolution in the IDF's Multi-arm Operational World]', *Bein Haktavim* 18 (2018), 38–47.
Cheung, Tai Ming, Thomas G. Mahnken, and Andrew L. Ross, 'Frameworks for Analyzing Chinese Defense and Military Innovation', in Tai Ming Cheung (ed.) *Forging China's Military Might: A New Framework for Assessing Innovation* (Baltimore: Johns Hopkins University Press 2014), 15–46.
Chin, Warren, 'Technology, War and the State: Past, Present and Future', *International Affairs* 95/4 (2019), 765–83. doi:10.1093/ia/iiz106

Eilam, Uzi, *Keshet Eilam: hatechnologia hamitkademet* [Eilam's Arc: How Israel Became a Military Technology Powerhouse] (Tel Aviv Yedioth Ahronoth 2011).

Faglin, Gay, *'Merutz hachidush: Technologiot mishariot vetzvaiyot beemtzaei lehima – nekudat haizun hamatima* [The Innovation Race': Commercial and Military Technologies in Military Systems – The Right Balance] (Haifa Chaikin Chair in Geostrategy 2018).

Fordham, Benjamin O., 'A Very Sharp Sword: The Influence of Military Capabilities on American Decisions to Use Force', *Journal of Conflict Resolution* 48/5 (2004), 632–56. doi:10.1177/0022002704267935

Freilich, Charles D., *Zion's Dilemmas: How Israel Makes National Security Policy* (Ithaca Cornell University Press 2012).

Freilich, Charles D., *Israeli National Security: A New Strategy for an Era of Change* (New York Oxford University Press 2018).

George, Alexander L., *Forceful Persuasion: Coercive Diplomacy as an Alternative to War* (Washington, D.C. United States Institute of Peace 1992).

Halevy, Hertzi A., Y. (full names unavailable), 'Elionut modi'init beidan technologi [Intelligence Superiority in a Digital Era]', *Ma'arachot* 477 (April 2018), 26–31.

Hershko, Tzila, "Haroman mithadesh?' [Is the Love Affair Starting Over?]', *Ma'arachot* 456 (2014), 34–37.

Holley, I. B., *Technology and Military Doctrine: Essays on a Challenging Relationship* (Maxwell Air University Press 2004).

Honig, Benson, Miri Lerner, and Yoel Raban, 'Social Capital and the Linkages of High-Tech Companies to the Military Defense System: Is There a Signalling Mechanism?', *Small Business Economics* 27/4–5 (2006), 419–37. doi:10.1007/s11187-005-5644-y

Jones, Clive and Yoel Guzansky, 'Israel's Relations with the Gulf States: Toward the Emergence of a Tacit Security Regime?', *Contemporary Security Policy* 38/3 (2017), 398–419. doi:10.1080/13523260.2017.1292375

Katz, Yaakov and Amir Bohbot, *The Weapon Wizards: How Israel Became a High-Tech Military Superpower* (New York: St. Martin's Press 2017).

Krepinevich, Andrew, 'Cavalry to Computer: The Pattern of Military Revolutions', *The National Interest* 37 (1994), 30–42.

Lehman, Ronald F., 'Future Technology and Strategic Stability', in Elbridge A. Colby and Michael S. Gerson (eds.) *Strategic Stability: Contending Interpretations* (Carlisle: U.S. Army War College Press 2013), 147–99.

Levite, Ariel, *Offense and Defense in Israeli Military Doctrine* (New York Routledge 2019).

Levy, Yagil, 'Social Convertibility and Militarism: Evaluations of the Development of Military-Society Relations in Israel in the Early 2000s', *Journal of Political and Military Sociology* 31/1 (2003), 71–96.

Marcus, Raphael D., *Israel's Long War with Hezbollah: Military Innovation and Adaptation under Fire* (Washington, D.C. Georgetown University Press 2018).

Nah, Liang Tuang, *The Fourth Industrial Revolution's Impact on Smaller Militaries: Boon or Bane?* RSIS Working Paper no. 318 (Singapore: S. Rajaratnam School of International Studies 2018).

Nien, Clement Wee, Yong Tay Cheng Chuan, and Ho Jin Peng, 'At the Leading Edge: The RSAF and the Fourth Industrial Revolution', *Pointer: Journal of the Singapore Armed Forces* 44/2 (2018), 1–11.

Posen, Barry R., *The Sources of Military Doctrine: France, Britain, and Germany between the World Wars* (Ithaca Cornell University Press 1984).

Rabinovich, Itamar and Itai Brun, *Israel Facing a New Middle East: In Search of National Security Strategy* (Stanford Hoover Institution Press 2017).
Raska, Michael, 'Strategic Competition for Emerging Military Technologies: Comparative Paths and Patterns', *Prism* 8/3 (2019), 64–81.
Sandler, Ronald L. (ed.), *Ethics and Emerging Technologies* (New York: Palgrave Macmillan 2014)
Schelling, Thomas C., *Arms and Influence* (New Heaven Yale University Press 2008).
Schulzke, Marcus, 'Drone Proliferation and the Challenge of Regulating Dual-Use Technologies', *International Studies Review* 21/3 (2019), 497–517. doi:10.1093/isr/viy047
Schwab, Klaus, *The Fourth Industrial Revolution* (New York Crown Business 2017).
Sechser, Todd S., Neil Narang, and Caitlin Talmadge, 'Emerging Technologies and Strategic Stability in Peacetime, Crisis, and War', *Journal of Strategic Studies* 42/6 (2019), 727–35. doi:10.1080/01402390.2019.1626725
Sevini, Filippo *et al.*, 'Emerging Dual-Use Technologies and Global Supply Chain Compliance', IAEA Symposium on International Safeguards, Vienna, 2018.
Swed, Ori and John S. Butler, 'Military Capital in the Israeli Hi-tech Industry', *Armed Forces & Society* 41/1 (2015), 123–41. doi:10.1177/0095327X13499562
Tal, Israel, *Bitachon leumi: meatim mul rabim* [National Security: The Few against the Many] (Tel Aviv Dvir 1996).
Volpe, Tristan A., 'Dual-use Distinguishability: How 3D-printing Shapes the Security Dilemma for Nuclear Programs', *Journal of Strategic Studies* 42/6 (2019), 814–40. doi:10.1080/01402390.2019.1627210
Watts, Barry D., *The Military Use of Space: A Diagnostic Assessment* (Washington, DC Center for Strategic and Budgetary Assessments 2001).
Yaakov, Itzhak, *Adon klum baribua* [The Memoires of Mr. Zero Squared] (Tel Aviv Yedioth Ahronoth 2011).

Small states and autonomous systems: the Scandinavian case

Magnus Petersson

ABSTRACT
Small states are often described as weak, and unlikely to achieve their goals when confronted by great powers. However, technologies of the 4th Industrial Revolution, especially autonomous weapon systems combined with artificial intelligence, may enable small states to enhance their security. Therefore, it should be rational for small states to develop strategies based on advances in technology. This article explores three small Scandinavian states – Denmark, Norway, and Sweden – in a comparative perspective of their capability and will to incorporate lethal autonomous weapon systems in their defence forces. Surprisingly, they reflect ambiguous adoption strategies and trajectories.

Introduction

Technological innovation often leads to sweeping changes in society, including the armed forces. It changes the way armed forces are used strategically, how they are created, and how they operate. Countries that are technologically advanced and resourceful, such as the United States, systematically pursue technological innovation, while adjusting their strategies and composition of armed forces, which pressures their allies to follow their lead. Military change, caused by technological change is, therefore, a common phenomenon and well researched.[1] When such major changes occur rapidly, it is often called defence transformation. The ongoing diffusion of emerging technologies of the 4th Industrial Revolution (4IR) is leading to the next wave of disruptive defence transformation.

In the US military, the 4IR has manifested itself in the Third Offset strategy; launched in 2014 by then US Secretary of Defence Chuck Hagel and followed up by his successor Ashton Carter. While the strategy no longer exists formally, its ideas and prerequisites certainly do. Reflecting the First and Second Offsets,

---

[1]See, for example, Theo Farrell and Terry Terriff (eds), *The Sources of Military Change: Culture, Politics, Technology* (Boulder, CO: Lynne Rienner, 2002).

the Third Offset aims to sustain US military superiority within politically feasible budget targets through technological innovation. In the First Offset, nuclear weapons were supposed to compensate or *offset* the US and NATO conventional deficits in Europe vis-a-vis the Soviet and Warsaw Pact's large conventional armies. In the Second Offset, aerospace technology created the necessary conditions for conventional (and nuclear) precision strikes deep into the Soviet territory, delivered far away from the actual battlefield. In the Third Offset, robotic technologies, automation and artificial intelligence (AI), and 4IR-related systems and platforms aim to prolong the margins of US military advantages relative to China and other adversaries such as Iran and Russia.[2]

The historical trajectory of the 1st Industrial Revolution relied on water and steam power, the 2nd on electric power, and the 3rd on electronics and information technology. Now, the 4IR is synonymous with a global digital revolution. The 4IR has the potential to raise global income levels and improve the quality of life for populations around the world, but it also has significant ramifications on international security and the future of warfare. When new technologies, such as autonomous weapon systems and AI, become cheaper and easier to use, even small states will be capable of causing mass harm.[3]

In short, the idea behind an offset strategy is to create asymmetric advantages over adversaries in a cost-effective way. The expression 'Gentlemen, we have run out of money; now we have to think' is attributed to Winston Churchill.[4] In other words, an offset strategy should be a preferred strategy for everyone. However, is that the case?

This article argues that select small states would benefit by applying such a strategy. Small states are not entirely powerless, but in the scholarly literature, they are often viewed as 'objects' rather than 'subjects' in the international system. They are described as weak, and unlikely to achieve their goals, especially when confronted by great powers. It should be therefore rational for small states, particularly those that do not have powerful allies, to develop offset strategies and increase military power to compensate for a general lack of power (relative to great powers) in the international system. As Tom Long argues, 'because small states, by definition, lack more traditional forms of power, they must specialise in how they employ their resources and relationships'.[5]

---

[2]Paul McLeary, 'The Pentagon's Third Offset may be dead, but no one knows what comes next', *Foreign Policy*, 18 December 2017; Damon Coletta, 'Navigating the Third Offset Strategy', *Parameters*, Vol. 47, No. 4 (Winter 2017–18), 47–62; Bryan Clark, Dan Patt and Harrison Schramm, *Mosaic Warfare: Exploiting Artificial Intelligence and Autonomous Systems to Implement Decision-Centric Operations* (Washington, DC: Center for Strategic and Budgetary Assessments, 2020).
[3]Klaus Schwab, 'The Fourth Industrial Revolution: What It Means and How to Respond', *Foreign Affairs*, 12 December 2015.
[4]Lawrence P. Farrell, 'Gentlemen, we have run out of money; now we have to think', National Defense, 11 January 2011, https://www.nationaldefensemagazine.org/articles/2011/11/1/2011november-gentlemen-we-have-run-out-of-money-now-we-have-to-think, date accessed 8 August 2019.
[5]Tom Long, 'Small States, Great Power? Gaining Influence Through Intrinsic, Derivative, and Collective Power', *International Studies Review* 19/2 (2017), 187.

By adopting and adapting 4IR technologies, small states have the potential to strengthen their security and freedom of action, in an environment where great power rivalry and the right of the mighty, rather than institutions and respect for international law, sets the agenda. As T. X. Hammes has argued, small states in Europe could use existing and emerging technologies to deter Russia, without increasing their defence budgets, for example, by pursuing Additive Manufacturing (AM), often called three-dimensional (3D) manufacturing, drones and task-specific artificial intelligence (AI). By applying 3D manufacturing, small states could produce thousands of inexpensive drones in a day, that – combined with small warheads and cell-phone target identification – could be used both to defend an invasion. The task-specific AI could be used to identify targets and attack them, while the drones can be spread out and distributed to reserve officers and home guard personnel in the entire country, and thus be almost impossible for the invader to detect and destroy.[6]

However, to what degree are select small states using technologies of the 4IR to increase their military strength? This article explores how three small Scandinavian states – Denmark, Norway and Sweden – have approached emerging 4IR-related military technologies, especially autonomous weapon systems and AI. In doing so, the article asks three essential questions. To what degree have they developed strategies to operationalise these new technologies? What are the strategic implications in terms of alliance dynamics and strategic stability? What are the operational implications of emerging technologies for military organisations?

The article relies primarily on open sources from the three Scandinavian countries, such as Parliamentary debates and publicly available government documents. In addition, secondary sources, such as press articles, policy reports, and scholarly literature, have been used to project their strategic context and analysis. Since the topic is relatively new, there is limited scholarly research on this topic in the Scandinavian countries. Most research has centred on how the great powers – especially China, the US and Russia – are using novel technologies in their strategic and military futures.

The article proceeds as follows. First, it begins with a conceptual overview of defence transformation, 4IR technological concepts and autonomous weapon systems. Then, it projects the evolving strategic context of the select Scandinavian small states followed by an assessment of the three countries' approaches to emerging technologies in their defence strategies and political debates. Finally, the paper draws conclusions and policy recommendations.

---

[6]T. X. Hammes, 'The Melians' Revenge: How Small, Frontline, European States Can Employ Emerging Technology to Defend Against Russia', *Issue Brief*, June 2019 (Washington, DC: Atlantic Council, 2019).

Defence transformation and autonomous weapon systems

Defence transformation can occur when technology changes quickly. There is no generally agreed-upon definition of defence transformation, but as Elinor Sloan argues, 'they range from narrow views on how technology has impacted warfare, to broader ideas on the need to bring together technological, doctrinal, and organisational change'.[7] Theo Farrell and Terry Terriff, for example, argue that transformation includes changes in doctrinal thinking, organisational forms, and operational approaches.[8]

When the US military pursued defence transformation in the 1990s and early 2000s, its direction and character have shaped military modernisation of all of its allies and partners, not least small states.[9] It is therefore likely that the implications of the 4IR, and its diffusion in the US Armed Forces, will spill over to its allies and partners, in terms of increased use of robotics, automation and AI in select weapon systems. This article focuses specifically on autonomous weapon systems – or Lethal Autonomous Weapon Systems (LAWS) – a generic term for robotics, automation, and AI in international strategic studies debates.

Autonomy, in this context, is often defined as 'the ability of a machine to perform an intended task without human intervention using the interaction of its sensors and computer programming with the environment'.[10] At present, there are few autonomous weapon systems in use such as the Harpy loitering weapon system, developed by Israel. Harpy is a weapon system capable of finding and attacking radar installations in a specific pre-programmed area autonomously. It is, thus, not aimed at a predefined target but rather a target area.[11]

The development of autonomous weapon systems such as Harpy is significant, not least for their potential to increase military effectiveness, but also for raising politically sensitive questions on their use. These weapons can conduct operations that pose risks for other types of manned or remote weapon systems, such as suppression of enemy air defences (SEAD). As shown below, the tension between political sensitivity and military efficiency is highly visible in Scandinavian cases.

To begin with, however, a few crucial points on autonomy in weapon systems are in order. As pointed out by Vincent Boulanin and Maaike

---

[7]Elinor Sloan, *Military Transformation and Modern Warfare: A Reference Handbook* (Westport, CT: Praeger, 2008).
[8]Theo Farrell and Terry Terriff, 'Military transformation in NATO', in Terry Terriff, Frans Osinga and Theo Farrell, *A Transformation Gap? American Innovations and European Military Change* (Stanford, CA: Stanford University Press, 2010), 3.
[9]Olof Kronvall & Magnus Petersson, 'Doctrine and Defence Transformation in Norway and Sweden', *Journal of Strategic Studies*, 39/2, 280–296.
[10]Vincent Boulanin and Maaike Verbruggen, *Mapping the Development of Autonomy in Weapon Systems* (Stockholm: SIPRI, 2017), vii.
[11]Boulanin & Maaike Verbruggen, *Mapping the Development of Autonomy in Weapon Systems*, 51–53.

Verbruggen, the question of autonomous weapon systems is quite complex. Since 'autonomous weapon systems' barely exist at the moment, it is more pertinent to talk about 'autonomy in weapon systems' or, more precisely, the *degree* of autonomy in weapon systems. The fact is that semi-autonomous weapon systems have existed since World War II (for example guided munitions, mines and torpedoes), and have been used widely by modern defence forces for a long time.[12]

Therefore, Boulanin and Verbruggen use three categories to classify the degree of autonomy in weapon systems: 'semi-autonomous', 'human-supervised autonomous', and 'fully autonomous'. What differs between the three categories is the interaction between the human and the machine. In the first case, the human is 'in-the-loop', i.e. weapon systems that 'require human input'. In the second case, the human is 'on-the-loop', i.e. the weapon systems that can 'operate independently but are under the oversight of a human'. In the third case, the human is 'out-of-the-loop', i.e. weapon systems that operate 'completely on their own'.[13]

Gary Schaub and Jens Wenzel Kristoffersen explored the case of Denmark and autonomous weapon systems by using the three categories of Boulanin and Verbruggen. In particular, they use the concept of 'weapon systems with autonomous functions' instead of 'autonomous weapon systems', to point out the nuances of such weapon systems. This is a useful framework, as it covers the entire range of systems with the human in, on, or out of the loop. The concept also enables the distinction between automatic, automated and autonomous weapon systems. Systems with automatic functions are simple systems of the stimulus-response type, such as landmines. Systems with automated functions are more complex and can respond in different ways depending on how they are programmed, but they are still – in contrast to autonomous systems – predictable if the way they are programmed is known.[14]

In addition, the term 'sliding autonomy' can be used to characterise several weapon systems, i.e. the ability to go back and forth between semi-autonomy and full autonomy depending on the operational and political context, for example, the Aegis Combat System that can conduct both defensive and offensive missions. In a fully automatic mode, it can conduct self-defence against incoming threats.[15]

Many experts argue that the complexity of autonomous weapon systems makes it difficult to discuss it in a nuanced way in public; the focus tends to be on autonomous systems – 'killer robots' or LAWS – that barely exist, rather

---

[12]Boulanin & Verbruggen, *Mapping the Development of Autonomy in Weapon Systems*, 5–6.
[13]Boulanin & Verbruggen, *Mapping the Development of Autonomy in Weapon Systems*, 5–6.
[14]Gary Schaub, Jr. & Jens Wenzel Kristoffersen, *In, on, or out of the loop: Denmark and autonomous weapon systems* (Copenhagen: Centre for Military studies, 2017).
[15]Boulanin & Verbruggen, *Mapping the Development of Autonomy in Weapon Systems*, 6, 40.

than on semi-autonomous and human supervised autonomous systems, that are common in modern defence forces. As Alexander Harang puts it: 'It is a premature debate, going on far over the head of ordinary people. The combination of tech-talk and difficult ethical dilemmas makes it too complicated for politicians to grasp'.[16]

From a military perspective, the operational advantages of autonomy in weapon systems are apparent. They enable greater speed, agility, accuracy, persistence, reach, coordination and mass (swarming technology), than manned weapon systems. In addition, they can be cost-effective in terms of education, training, personnel, and procurement.[17]

However, as previously mentioned, such systems are also politically sensitive, especially from the varying legal, normative, and ethical vistas. The prevalent argument is that these weapon systems must be used in accordance with international law and operated under 'human control' or, more specifically, 'meaningful human control'. Schaub and Kristoffersen argue that 'meaningful human control' is fulfilled 'only if the technology is designed in such a way to permit a typical user to understand its operation'. Only then, can they 'make informed, conscious, and meaningful decisions about the use of the weapon system'.[18]

Such arguments are particularly common in democracies, where human rights, proportionality, and transparency are deeply embedded in the political system and culture. NATO's Secretary-General, Jens Stoltenberg, for example, argued that: 'We cannot end up in a situation where we do not have human control over the weapon systems.'[19]

There are also concerns among experts and policymakers in the West that authoritarian regimes, such as China, Iran, and Russia have a different view, and therefore can develop and use autonomous weapon systems faster, and more efficiently, than democracies, which could give them political, economic and military advantages. Several experts have also warned that non-state rebel groups or terrorists can ignore the legal and normative aspects of using such systems, in an uncontrolled and inhuman way.[20]

In this context, this paper explores the Scandinavian countries – Denmark, Norway, and Sweden – and their views on autonomous weapon systems, including AI, through the lens of their evolving strategic and security conceptions.

---

[16]Harang quoted in Michael Mayer, *Dronerevolusjon* (Oslo: Kolofon, 2019), 235.
[17]Boulanin & Verbruggen, *Mapping the Development of Autonomy in Weapon Systems*, 61–63.
[18]Schaub & Kristoffersen, *In, on, or out of the loop*, 22.
[19]Stoltenberg quoted in Johan Falnes, 'Krigsrobotarna inntar NATO', *VG*, 24 February 2019.
[20]Boulanin & Verbruggen, *Mapping the Development of Autonomy in Weapon Systems*, 73–77.

The Scandinavian case

The Nordic countries, and especially the Scandinavian ones (Denmark, Norway and Sweden), are often compared, mainly because of their similar political and socio-economic background as welfare states.[21] Regarding defence and security, however, they are different. Denmark is the only country that is a member of both the EU and NATO; Norway is a NATO but not an EU member, and Sweden is an EU but not a NATO member.[22] For this study, however, they seem ideal for a comparison: Denmark and Norway, as NATO members with security guarantees from the US, could be expected to be less dependent on emerging technologies, especially autonomous weapon systems, than non-aligned Sweden.

While Sweden has a close and frequent military cooperation with the US and NATO, it is neither allied bilaterally with the US, nor a member of the NATO alliance and thus it is more dependent on its capabilities and military strength. Historically, Wilhem Agrell and others have shown that non-aligned Sweden has developed its weapon systems in order to mitigate strategic dependencies on other states. The most prominent example is the Swedish nuclear weapons program, which ran from the late 1940s to the late 1960s before it was shut down.[23]

The ties that bind Scandinavian countries, however, are in the shared experience of defence transformation during 1990 and 2010. A central component in that process was a mental and practical shift in emphasis from 'stationary' territorial defence at home towards 'expeditionary' operations abroad. In less than 15 years, the forces of these countries transformed *from* being large, threat- and conscripts-based, focused on territorial defence, *towards* being small, capabilities-based, semi-professional, focused on expeditionary operations.[24] It is fair to argue that the transformation took the Scandinavian countries into the second offset era, and the quantitative consequences were significant. The reduction of the Scandinavian army brigades shown in Table 1 below, can illustrate these enormous changes in force structure. The situation is similar, but not as far-reaching, regarding their navies and air forces.

Since the Ukraine Crisis in 2014, the pendulum has largely swung back from an expeditionary focus to territorial defence. However, the problem is that these small states still have the same small force structures, which makes

---

[21] See, for example, Norbert Götz, 'Norden: Structures That Do Not Make a Region', *European Review of History*, 10/2 (2003), 323–341.
[22] Magnus Petersson, 'Denmark and Norway', in Hugo Meijer and Marco Wyss (eds) *The Handbook of European Defence Policies and Armed Forces* (Oxford: Oxford University Press).
[23] Wilhelm Agrell, *Svenska förintelsevapen: Utvecklingen av kemiska och nukleära stridsmedel 1928–1970* (Lund: Historiska media, 2002).
[24] Magnus Petersson, 'Defense Transformation and Legitimacy in Scandinavia after the Cold War: Theoretical and Practical implications', *Armed Forces & Society*, 37/4 (2011), 701–724.

Table 1. The reduced number of army brigades in Scandinavia, 1990–2010.

Land/Year	Sweden	Norway	Denmark
1990	29 brigades	13 brigades	11 brigades
2000	6 brigades	6 brigades	6 brigades
2010	2 brigades	1 brigade	2 brigades
Total decrease (%)	**93%**	**92%**	**82%**

Source: Magnus Petersson, 'En skandinavisk transformasjonsbølge', in Tormod Heier (ed), *Nytt landskap – Nytt forsvar: Norsk militærmakt 1990–2010* (Oslo: Abstrakt, 2011), 117.

the three countries dependent on external military support in case of Russian military aggression. Their defence forces are too small, vulnerable, and cannot sustain long-term military operations in multiple directions simultaneously.

In addition, both Norway and Sweden have a very long coastal region and large territories (both countries have a territory larger than Germany), which is difficult to defend with a few units. Norway, in particular, has almost all its economic resources (gas and oil) offshore, close to Russia's important Northern Fleet. To handle this problem, one could think that both countries should be interested in novel or emerging technologies, especially autonomous weapon systems, to compensate for the lack of manpower. As Michael Mayer argues:

> Autonomous systems that increase firepower without requiring additional personnel seem ideal for the Norwegian Armed Forces. With large geographical areas to monitor and possibly defend, Norway has a challenge that fits perfectly with a robotised solution that does not require a costly standing force in the north.[25]

Furthermore, as Hammes points out, President Donald Trump's 'America First' policy has made the European NATO allies and partners uncertain about what action the US will take in case of a Russian invasion.[26] Relying on relatively inexpensive, military efficient autonomous weapon systems, such as swarms of drones that could deter Russia from attacking could be an essential supplement to conventional weapons systems and insurance against a reluctant US administration.

However, as will be demonstrated below, the three Scandinavian countries have been relatively lukewarm to such systems, and there is a lack of will to seriously, and systematically discuss the issue among politicians. In principle, small states with scarce resources have more to gain from applying an offset strategy using technology from the 4IR, than a resourceful, military-powerful great power. In the case of Scandinavia, with numerically weak defence forces and a more aggressive Russia, that should be even more obvious. However, public debates about the Third Offset, especially autonomous weapon systems, including AI, is underdeveloped. Political representatives are often entrenched in legal approaches to the issue, while the military establishment

---

[25]Michael Mayer, *Dronerevolusjon* (Oslo: Kolofon, 2019), 237–238.
[26]Hammes, 3.

does not have strong voices arguing for the necessity to integrate emerging technologies. Instead, select 4IR technologies gradually diffuse into their defence forces, without much noise.

Denmark

In general, the issue of autonomous weapon systems has not been widely discussed in Denmark. However, there has been a sporadic discussion about LAWS. Researchers and select experts have argued for more regulation of such weapon systems, regardless of whether Denmark will acquire autonomous weapons or not. Moreover, Denmark should take an active role in creating such regulations, both within institutions – such as the UN – and by showing moral leadership. For example, Johannes Lang, Robin May Schott and Rens van Munster argue that it is in the tradition of the Nordic countries to engage in the issue, as in other similar issues: 'the Nordic countries have "punched above their weight", showing leadership on issues of equality, human rights, development, women's rights, peace, humanitarianism and the environment'.[27]

Generally, the impression is that the debate on autonomous weapon systems, including AI, is premature, albeit some voices are pushing for a more systematic debate. Anders Theis Bollmann, for example, calls for greater nuance and a clarification of the central concepts in the debate in order to lift it from the present, counterproductive discourse. He also argues that politicians, policymakers, and officers should attain more knowledge in this area to be able to make better decisions and therefore, the Danish Defence Forces should increase research and education within the field.[28]

The concept of 'meaningful human control' of autonomous weapon systems has also been debated, but the focus of the Danish government has been on its regulation in accordance with international law, rather than a general ban of LAWS.[29] For example, in an interview, former defence minister Claus Hjort Frederiksen (Liberal), argues that robots should be used in accordance with international law, and that it also should be developed specific sets of rules for that kind of weapons. According to Frederiksen, Denmark will push for such rules.[30]

However, as Schaub and Kristoffersen have shown, Denmark already has weapons that could be characterised as semi-autonomous. For example, the

---

[27] Johannes Lang, Robin May Schott and Rens van Munster, *Four reasons why Denmark should speak up about lethal autonomous weapons* (Copenhagen: DIIS, 2018).
[28] Bollmann, 'Kunstig intelligens, autonome systemer og militærteknologisk acceleration – muligheter og udfordringer i et dansk perspektiv'.
[29] Schaub & Kristoffersen, *In, on, or out of the loop*, 20, and Dag Mygind, 'Forbud moddræberrobotter trækker ud', *Prosa*, 2 November 2018, https://www.prosa.dk/artikel/forbud-mod-draeberrobotter-traekker-ud/(date accessed, 23 August 2019).
[30] Thomas Larsen, 'Claus Hjort: Brug for globale regler mod dræberrobotter', *Berlinske*, 20 January 2019.

Danish Navy's Harpoon Block II anti-ship missile operates autonomously after launch, and the Evolved Sea Sparrow air defence missile operates semi-autonomously after launch. The Danish Air Force also possesses similar air-to-air and air-to-ground missiles. Schaub and Kristoffersen argue that the implications of such weapons systems, perhaps, have not been subjected to significant reflection', especially regarding the man-machine command relationship.[31]

In short, the deployment of semi-autonomous weapon systems such as torpedoes – and autonomous systems such as naval mines – is a reality that has not been much discussed. According to Schaub and Kristoffersen, Denmark has no policy toward weapon systems with autonomous functions, and only a few statements of policy have been made public. They argue that this should change – Denmark should develop a general policy regarding weapon systems with autonomous functions 'before an unforeseen event makes the situation acute'.[32]

In Denmark, there are also initiatives to increase public-private cooperation in the development of emerging technologies. For example, the Danish Acquisition and Logistics Organisation, FMI, supports projects of relevance for the Danish Armed Forces, and at the same time develops new knowledge that can be utilised by the Danish industry.[33]

To sum up the Danish case, there are few traces of developed strategies to operationalise new technologies, at least not in public. Furthermore, strategic implications in terms of alliance dynamics and strategic stability are unclear, and the operational implications of emerging technologies for military organisations are also unclear. Denmark already uses semi-autonomous weapon systems, but there has been almost no discussion about it. When mentioned, autonomous weapon systems and AI are often described as useful, but harmless, tools to improve command and control, intelligence and surveillance.[34]

Norway

In Norway, debates on autonomous weapon systems, including AI, have been more prevalent than in Denmark, both in the scholarly literature and in the media.[35] In the media, the Norwegian government has been criticised for

---

[31] Schaub & Kristoffersen, *In, on, or out of the loop*, 17.
[32] Schaub & Kristoffersen, *In, on, or out of the loop*, 23.
[33] Anders Theis Bollmann, 'Kunstig intelligens, autonome systemer og militærteknologisk acceleration – muligheter og udfordringer i et dansk perspektiv', *krigsvidenskap.dk*, 15 June 2018, https://www.krigsvidenskab.dk/kunstig-intelligens-autonome-systemer-og-militaerteknologisk-acceleration-muligheder-og-udfordringer (date accessed, 23 August 2019).
[34] Forsvarsministeriet, 'Dansk droneindustri mødtes med Forsvaret', 20 February 2019, http://www.fmi.dk/nyheder/Pages/dansk-droneindustri-modtes-med-forsvaret.aspx, date accessed, 26 April 2020.
[35] Erik Reichborn-Kjennerud, *Meningsfull, menneskelig, kontroll?* (Oslo: NUPI, 2020).

being passive on the issue, and for only wanting to regulate novel weapons systems, rather than banning them. Some have argued that the hesitation in banning these systems can be attributed to the protection of Norway's defence industry, and for the political cohesion and interoperability needs with NATO, since the US, and other important allies, are using such systems.[36]

Officers and defence researchers have also encouraged the Norwegian government to be more active when it comes to regulating autonomous weapon systems. Colonel Gjert Lage Dyndal argues that Norway, as a small state, has a particular interest in international regulation of such weapons.[37] Moreover, in an edited volume, *Når dronene våkner* [When the drones awake], several experts – including Dyndal – call for more debate in Norway about this issue.[38]

In June 2019, around 700 Norwegian academics made a public call against autonomous weapons. They argued Norway to encourage and support negotiations on a 'legally binding instrument against the development and use of lethal autonomous weapon systems'. Under-Secretary of Foreign Affairs, Audun Lysbakken, commented that Norway is for the regulation of such weapons and that international law covers all weapons systems.[39]

The Norwegian government's policy is therefore similar to the Danish, i.e. the focus is on regulations and international law, rather than banning such weapon systems. In June 2018, Foreign Minister Ine Eriksen Søreide (Conservative), said in the Parliament that human control and humanitarian law must be secured in the development of autonomous systems. She also said that weapon systems that cannot be used in accordance with humanitarian law, 'must be considered prohibited', and that Norway will take part in future discussions on the development and regulation of these weapons 'to make sure that fundamental principles regarding human control and the rule of humanitarian law are the bottom line'.[40]

The Norwegian Armed Forces do not have a long-term strategy concerning autonomous weapon systems.[41] However, in an interview in October 2018 in Norway's most influential newspaper, *Aftenposten*, the Chief of Defence, General Haakon Bruun-Hanssen, argued that the

---

[36]John Olav Egeland, 'Nå kommer de selvstyrte drapsrobotene', *Dagbladet*, 10 July 2019.
[37]Dyndal quoted in Lene Grimstad, 'Norge er en sinke i arbeidet med å regulere autonome våpen', *Ny tid*, 2 February 2019.
[38]See, for example, Tor Arne S. Berntsen, Gjert Lage Dyndal and Sigrid R. Johansen (eds), *Når dronene våkner: Autonome våpensystemer og robotisering av krig* (Oslo: Cappelen Damm Akademisk, 2016).
[39]Sigrid Moe, 'Norske teknologer med opprop mot autonome våpen', *E24*, 23 June 2019, http://min.e24.no/norske-teknologer-med-opprop-mot-autonome-vapen/a/EWKyr3, date accessed, 24 August 2019.
[40]Ine Eriksen Søreide, 'Svar på spørsmål om hel- og halvautonome våpensystemer', *Skriftlig spørsmål nr. 1900, 2017–2018* (Oslo: The Ministry of Foreign Affairs, 2018). Translation from Norwegian by the author. All translations from Danish, Norwegian, and Swedish in this article is made by the author.
[41]Torunn Aardal, 'Forestill deg en verden med autonome Kalashnikover i hendene på terrorister', *Minerva*, 19 June 2019, https://www.minervanett.no/forestill-deg-en-verden-med-autonome-kalashnikover-i-hendene-pa-terrorister/192044, date accesed, 24 August 2019.

Norwegian Armed Forces should allocate more resources on drones and autonomous systems. Bruun-Hanssen also alluded to the discussion about human control and made a clear difference between offensive and defensive autonomous weapon systems. He acknowledged that Norway already possesses autonomous defence systems, for example, on their frigates.[42] In other official documents, the Chief of Defence also has declared the ambition to procure autonomous demining systems and discussed autonomous drone systems for maritime surveillance.[43]

In other words, the Norwegian government and military leadership are cautious, and the debate is polarised.[44] At the same time, however, Norway has a tradition of supporting its defence industry and develops weapon systems together with private defence companies. For example, the PD-100 Black Hornet drone has been developed by Prox Dynamics together with the Norwegian Defence Research Establishment (FFI). The FFI is also developing Hugin, an unmanned submarine system in cooperation with Kongsberg Defence.[45] The FFI is also developing Unmanned Surface Vehicles (USV), Frigg and Odin, that together with Hugin, could conduct minesweeping autonomously based on AI technology.[46] In the latest defence plan, the government has acknowledged that autonomous systems in the future could be utilised for surveillance, intelligence gathering, and transport.[47]

To sum up the Norwegian case, there are many similarities with the Danish case: minimal advancement of strategies to operationalise new technologies, while the strategic implications in terms of alliance dynamics and strategic stability are equally unclear. In public, defence-related discussion about autonomous systems is visible mostly in defensive, uncontroversial contexts, such as intelligence, surveillance and minesweeping.

One can expect, however, that the low-profile stance of the government and the military is at least partly caused by solidarity with the NATO alliance and the US. The US and other NATO members are using weapon systems with different degrees of autonomy, and Norway – as well as Denmark – are dependent on such systems; the Norwegian Armed Forces, as well as the Danish Armed Forces, already use semi-autonomous weapon systems.

---

[42] Sveinung Bentzrød, 'Ville neppe klart oss hvis vi ikke lar en maskin overta', *Aftenposten*, 16 October 2018.
[43] Michael Mayer, *Dronerevolusjon* (Oslo: Kolofon, 2019), 226.
[44] Michael Mayer, *Dronerevolusjon* (Oslo: Kolofon, 2019), 235, 238.
[45] Michael Mayer, *Dronerevolusjon* (Oslo: Kolofon, 2019), 224–225, 233.
[46] FFI, 'Autonom minerydding: Hvordan kan ubemannade farkostergjøre det tryggere å fjærne miner?', https://www.ffi.no/forskning/prosjekter/autonom-minerydding, date accessed, 26 April 2020.
[47] Det kongelige forsvarsdepartement, Prop. 62 S (2019–2020), Proposisjon til Stortinget (forslag til stortingsvedtak), Vilje til beredskap – evne til forsvar, Langtidsplant il forsvarssektoren (Oslo: Forsvarsdepartementet, 2020).

Sweden

In Sweden, the debate on autonomous systems has been evolving along similar lines, i.e. insufficient and polarised. As in Norway, several academics and experts have called for a ban of LAWS in Swedish mass media.[48] Although the most common argument in the debate is that LAWS should be banned, there are also more pragmatic arguments about accepting them, trying to regulate them, and minimising the risks for escalation through better communication and transparency. For example, in an editorial in *Expressen*, one of Sweden's leading national daily newspapers, Linda Nordlund argues that the weapon systems are so powerful that it is not realistic to believe that China, Russia, and the US, would abstain from developing such systems. Therefore, she argues, they must be accepted just as we accepted nuclear weapon systems and increase diplomatic efforts to minimise the risks associated with these systems.[49]

As in Denmark and Norway, the Swedish debate seems premature, with few experts arguing for a broader debate on emerging technologies and strategies for handling different degrees of autonomy in weapon systems. Martin Hagström at the Swedish Defence Research Agency (FOI), for example, points at the fact that the debate becomes confusing when legal, technological, and military operational perspectives are mixed. In his view, experts within the different fields of knowledge find it challenging to communicate with each other and that they sometimes utilise the confusion for their interests. He calls for a more structured debate from multiple perspectives, including security policy, philosophy, and ethics.[50]

The Swedish government has, similar to the Danish and Norwegian governments, held a low profile, and responded in quite general terms when confronted with the issue. In 2017, MP Stig Henriksson (Left Party) directed a formal question to the Swedish Foreign Minister, Margot Wallström (Social Democrat), in the Parliament. He asked how the government viewed the issue of LAWS more in general, and if Sweden intended to take part in the development of such weapon systems actively.[51] Wallström acknowledged that the issue was 'complex', but that the government's point of departure was that international law covered 'all forms of weapons in armed conflicts'. She also argued that 'LAWS is a technology that is not in use', and that it was clear to her that 'a human being, ultimately, must take responsibility for decisions

---

[48]See, for example, Anders Sandberg et al, 'Förbjud dödliga autonoma vapensystem', *Dagens samhälle*, 11 Apri, 2018, https://www.dagenssamhalle.se/debatt/forbjud-dodliga-autonoma-vapensystem-21566, date accessed 13 August 2019.
[49]Linda Nordlund, 'Vi kan inte förbjuda "mördarrobotarna"', *Expressen*, 15 April 2019.
[50]Martin Hagström, 'Mördarrobotar eller vapen som kan fatta etiska beslut – om vapenteknik och automation', Mänsklig säkerhet, 13 June 2016, http://manskligsakerhet.se/2016/06/13/mordarrobotar-eller-vapen-som-kan-fatta-etiska-beslut-om-vapenteknik-och-automation, date accessed 12 August 2019.
[51]Stig Henriksson, 'Autonoma vapensystem', *Interpellation 2017/18:20* av Stig Henriksson (V) (Stockholm: Swedish Parliament, 2017).

concerning life and death'. However, the concept of 'meaningful human control' was still unclear for her, and she called for clarification of the concept.[52]

In the same debate, Swedish Defence Minister, Peter Hultqvist (Social Democrat), reiterated Wallström's arguments that international law covered the use of all kinds of weapons, and he also, in general terms, commented on the issue of Swedish participation in the development of autonomous systems. He pointed out that different degrees of autonomy in weapons systems have existed for a long time, and that Sweden since 1974 has had a rigid system for controlling the development of new weapons that might be used by the Swedish Armed Forces, and that a general ban was not on the table.[53]

Interestingly, the Swedish Green Party, in government with the Social Democrats since 2014, is for banning LAWS. They argue that such weapon systems threaten international peace and security, that they are incompatible with international law, and that the development of such systems – just as the case with nuclear weapons – will lead to an arms race.[54] In 2018, several MP's of the party suggested a ban in the Swedish Parliament, but it was voted down.[55] How the government handles the issue internally is not publicly known.

Nevertheless, there are also experts arguing that emerging technologies can increase Swedish fighting power in a cost-effective way.[56] For example, Swedish Chief of Defence, General Micael Bydén, has argued that the novel technologies, unmanned systems, and artificial intelligence must be utilised for military purposes.[57] However, as in the case of Denmark and Norway, there is no evidence of strategies to utilise new technologies. Neither are there specific procurement plans for autonomous weapon systems. According to Carl-Martin Larsson at the Swedish Defence Material Administration (FMV), the agency that supports the Swedish Armed Forces with equipment and logistics, the agency does not have a mission to procure autonomous weapon systems for the Swedish Armed Forces, only to learn more about them.[58]

---

[52] Margot Wallström, 'Anf 1' and 'Anf. 3', *Interpellation 2017/18:20* (Stockholm: Swedish Parliament, 2017).
[53] Peter Hultqvist, 'Anf. 8 , 'Anf. 10', 'Anf. 12', *Interpellation 2017/18:20* (Stockholm: Swedish Parliament, 2017).
[54] Bodil Valero, Max Andersson, Linnea Engström & Jakop Dalunde, 'Sverige måste stoppa framtida mördarrobotar', *Expressen*, 22 June 2018.
[55] Rasmus Ling, 'Förbud mot autonoma vapensystem', *Motion 2018/19:2747* av Rasmus Ling m.fl. (MP) (Stockholm: Swedish Parliament, 2018).
[56] Johan Eklund and Gunnar Eliasson, 'Radikal upprustning kan bli självfinansierad', *Svenska dagbladet*, 23 May 2018.
[57] Micael Bydén, 'Ett stärkt militärt försvar', Speech at Rikskonferensen folk och försvar, 15 January 2018 https://www.forsvarsmakten.se/siteassets/3-organisation-forband/overbefalhavaren/tal-och-debattartiklar/nuvarande-obs-tal-och-debattartiklar/180115_ob_salen.pdf, date accessed 3 February 2019.
[58] Christian Catomeris, Alex Bolevin & Mikael Klintevall, 'Militär kapprustning inom AI – FN:s generalsekreterare vill se förbud, *SVT Nyheter*, 7 April 2019, https://www.svt.se/nyheter/utrikes/militar-kapprustning-inom-ai-fn-s-generalsekreterare-vill-se-forbud, date accessed 12 August 2019.

At the same time, Sweden is, since a long time, in possession of semi-autonomous weapon systems, for example, missiles. The radar-guided 'Robot 15' produced by SAAB has been used since 1985 by the Swedish Navy, and later also the Swedish Air Force and Army.[59] Furthermore, the traditionally strong private Swedish defence industry is at the forefront of developing semi-autonomous and autonomous defence systems, especially unmanned vehicles (UAV's, UGV's, and UUV's).[60] Sweden has also decided to buy the semi-autonomous Patriot air and missile defence system from the US.[61]

To sum up the Swedish case, there are many similarities to Denmark and Norway. There are no advanced strategies to operationalise new technologies, while the strategic implications in terms of alliance dynamics and strategic stability are unclear. The operational implications of emerging technologies for military organisations are also unclear.

Conclusion and the way ahead

The varying political and military debates in Scandinavia about autonomous weapon systems, including AI systems, are not very prominent, lacking conceptual clarity and structure, but there are some features worth mentioning. First, political representatives seem to reflect a cautious, legal approach to the issue, and they seldom mention the operational advantages that autonomous systems can provide – i.e. making logistical flows more predictable, helping with automatic terrain recognition for intelligence, and surveillance purposes. Second, defence experts and the military are quite cautious with statements, but they do seem to agree that the 4IR technologic development could be used to increase military efficiency and reduce costs (alternatively gain more military power at the same cost). Meanwhile, however, the armed forces are gradually integrating semi-autonomous systems in their force structures.

The ambiguous character of this debate is not surprising. The tension between legality and military efficiency has been one of the most fundamental debates in military ethics and international law for decades. The Scandinavian countries are champions of international and humanitarian law, arms control and disarmament. Their narratives also include a general scepticism towards the use of military force to achieve political ends, which makes it difficult for defence experts and the military leadership to argue for autonomous systems, even though it would be rational from a strategic and economic perspective.

---

[59] Försvarsmakten, 'Robotsystem 15, https://www.forsvarsmakten.se/sv/information-och-fakta/materiel-och-teknik/vapen/robotsystem-15/, date accesses 5 August 2019.
[60] Mats Olofsson (ed), *Det digitaliserade försvaret: Teknikutvecklingens påverkan på försvarsförmågan* (Stockholm: Kungl Krigsvetenskapsakademien, 2017).
[61] Jen Judson, 'Sweden locked in to buy Patriot missile defense system', *DefenseNews*, 10 August 2018, https://www.defensenews.com/digital-show-dailies/smd/2018/08/10/sweden-locked-in-to-buy-patriot-missile-defense-system/, date accessed 26 April 2020.

None of the countries has developed strategies to operationalise novel 4IR-related weapons technologies. They follow the debate, and to some extent are also starting to initiate research and development of autonomous weapon systems, but they do hesitate in formulating strategies – at least publicly. The strategic implications of autonomous weapon systems in terms of alliance dynamics and strategic stability are also unclear. Their hesitant stance, however, can also be attributed to the need to show solidarity with NATO – for Denmark and Norway as members, and Sweden as NATO partner. The operational implications of the new and emerging technologies for military organisations of the three countries are also unclear.

Given the expectations that small states such as Denmark, Norway, and Sweden should be eager to develop and procure autonomous systems, the picture painted in the article is somewhat surprising. However, as the article shows, many experts argue for broader, and more nuanced, debates about these issues, before reality hits and these weapon systems are suddenly used on a large scale.

Michael Mayer argues that Norway should pursue a three-fold approach to these issues: continue with research and development of autonomous systems, integrate autonomous systems in strategies, doctrines, and operational concepts for territorial defence, and increase the political pressure to achieve a robust set of rules for autonomous systems.[62] These recommendations could serve as a baseline approach for all three Scandinavian countries, as well as for small states in general.

Acknowledgements

The author wants to thank Stefan Borg, Michael Mayer, Mats Olofsson, Michael Raska, Katarzyna Zysk, and the anonymous reviewers for excellent comments on earlier versions of this article.

Disclosure statement

No potential conflicts of interest.

---

[62]Michael Mayer, *Dronerevolusjon* (Oslo: Kolofon, 2019), 246.

Bibliography

Aardal, Torunn, 'Forestill deg en verden med autonome kalashnikover i hendene på terrorister', *Minerva*, 19 Jun. 2019, https://www.minervanett.no/forestill-deg-en-verden-med-autonome-kalashnikover-i-hendene-pa-terrorister/192044, date accesed 24 August, 2019

Agrell, Wilhelm, *Svenska förintelsevapen: Utvecklingen av kemiska och nukleära stridsmedel 1928-1970* (Lund: Historiska media 2002).

Bentzrød, Sveinung, 'Ville neppe klart oss hvis vi ikke lar en maskin overta', *Aftenposten*, 16 Oct. 2018.

Berntsen, Tor, S. Arne, Gjert Lage Dyndal, and Sigrid R. Johansen (eds), *Når droner våkner: Autonome våpensystemer og robotisering av krig* (Oslo: Cappelen Damm Akademisk 2016).

Bollmann, Anders Theis, 'Kunstig intelligens, autonome systemer og militærteknologisk acceleration - muligheter og udfordringer i et dansk perspektiv', *krigsvidenskap.dk*, 15 Jun. 2018, https://www.krigsvidenskab.dk/kunstig-intelligens-autonome-systemer-og-militaerteknologisk-acceleration-muligheder-og-udfordringer (date accessed, 23 August, 2019).

Boulanin, Vincent and Maaike Verbruggen, *Mapping the Development of Autonomy in Weapon Systems* (Stockholm: SIPRI 2017).

Bydén, Micael, 'Ett stärkt militärt försvar', Speech at Rikskonferensen folk och försvar, 15 Jan. 2018 https://www.forsvarsmakten.se/siteassets/3-organisation-forband/overbefalhavaren/tal-och-debattartiklar/nuvarande-obs-tal-och-debattartiklar/180115_ob_salen.pdf, date accessed 3 February, 2019.

Catomeris, Christian, Alex Bolevin, and Mikael Klintevall, 'Militär kapprustning inom AI - FN: sgeneralsekreterare vill se förbud', *SVT Nyheter*, 7 Apr. 2019, https://www.svt.se/nyheter/utrikes/militar-kapprustning-inom-ai-fn-s-generalsekreterare-vill-se-forbud, date accessed 12 August, 2019.

Clark, Bryan, Dan Patt, and Harrison Schramm, *Mosaic Warfare: Exploiting Artificial Intelligence and Autonomous Systems to Implement Decision-Centric Operations* (Washington, DC: Center for Strategic and Budgetary Assessments 2020).

Coletta, Damon, 'Navigating the Third Offset Strategy', *Parameters* 47/4/Winter (2017-18), 47–62.

Det kongelige forsvarsdepartement, Prop. 62 S (2019-2020), *Proposisjon til Stortinget (forslag til stortingsvedtak), Vilje til beredskap - evne til forsvar, Langtidsplant il forsvarssektoren* (Oslo: Forsvarsdepartementet 2020).

Egeland, John Olav, 'Nå kommer de selvstyrte drapsrobotene', *Dagbladet*, 10 Jul. 2019.

Eklund, Johan and Gunnar Eliasson, 'Radikal upprustning kan bli självfinansierad', *Svenska dagbladet*, 23 May 2018.

Falnes, Johan, 'Krigsrobotarna inntar NATO', *VG*, 24 Feb. 2019.

Farrell, Theo and Terry Terriff (eds), *The Sources of Military Change: Culture, Politics, Technology* (Boulder, CO: Lynne Rienner 2002).

Farrell, Theo and Terry Terriff, 'Military Transformation in NATO', in Terry Terriff, Frans Osinga, and Theo Farrell (eds.), *A Transformation Gap? American Innovations and European Military Change*, 1–13. (Stanford, CA: Stanford University Press 2010).

Forsvarsministeriet, 'Dansk droneindustri mødtes med Forsvaret', 20 Feb. 2019, http://www.fmi.dk/nyheder/Pages/dansk-droneindustri-modtes-med-forsvaret.aspx, accessed 26 Apr. 2020.

Götz, Norbert, 'Norden: Structures that Do Not Make a Region', *European Review of History* 10/2 (2003), 323–41. doi:10.1080/1350748032000140822

Grimstad, Lene, 'Norge er en sinke i arbeidet med å regulere autonome våpen', *Ny tid*, 2 Feb. 2019.

Hagström, Martin, 'Mördarrobotar eller vapen som kan fatta etiska beslut - om vapenteknik och automation', Mänsklig säkerhet, 13 Jun. 2016, http://manskligsakerhet.se/2016/06/13/mordarrobotar-eller-vapen-som-kan-fatta-etiska-beslut-om-vapenteknik-och-automation, date accessed 12 August, 2019.

Hammes, T. X., 'The Melians' Revenge: How Small, Frontline, European States Can Employ Emerging Technology to Defend against Russia', *Issue Brief*, June (Washington, DC: Atlantic Council, 2019).

Henriksson, Stig, 'Autonoma vapensystem', *Interpellation 2017/18:20* av Stig Henriksson (V) (Stockholm: Swedish Parliament, 2017).

Hultqvist, Peter, 'Anf. 8', *Interpellation 2017/18:20* (Stockholm: Swedish Parliament, 2017).

Hultqvist, Peter, 'Anf. 8', *Interpellation 2017/18:20* (Stockholm: Swedish Parliament, 2017).

Hultqvist, Peter, 'Anf. 8', *Interpellation 2017/18:20* (Stockholm: Swedish Parliament, 2017).

Kronvall, Olof and Magnus Petersson, 'Doctrine and Defence Transformation in Norway and Sweden', *Journal of Strategic Studies* 39/2, 280–96.

Lang, Johannes, Robin May Schott, and Rens van Munster, *Four Reasons Why Denmark Should Speak up about Lethal Autonomous Weapons* (Copenhagen: DIIS 2018).

Larsen, Thomas, 'Claus Hjort: Brug for globale regler mod dræberrobotter', *Berlinske*, 20 Jan. 2019.

Ling, Rasmus, 'Förbud mot autonoma vapensystem', *Motion 2018/19:2747* av Rasmus Ling m.fl. (MP) (Stockholm: Swedish Parliament, 2018).

Long, Tom, 'Small States, Great Power? Gaining Influence through Intrinsic, Derivative, and Collective Power', *International Studies Review* 19/2 (2017), 185–205.

Mayer, Michael, *Dronerevolusjon* (Oslo: Kolofon 2019).

McLeary, Paul, 'The Pentagon's Third Offset May Be Dead, but No One Knows What Comes Next', *Foreign Policy*, 18 Dec. 2017.

Moe, Sigrid, 'Norske teknologer med opprop mot autonome våpen', *E24*, 23 Jun. 2019, http://min.e24.no/norske-teknologer-med-opprop-mot-autonome-vapen/a/EWKyr3, date accessed, 24 August, 2019

Mygind, Dag, 'Forbud moddræberrobotter trækker ud', *Prosa*, 2 Nov. 2018, https://www.prosa.dk/artikel/forbud-mod-draeberrobotter-traekker-ud/ date accessed, 23 August, 2019).

Nordlund, Linda, 'Vi kan inte förbjuda "mördarrobotarna"', *Expressen*, 15 Apr. 2019.

Olofsson, Mats (ed), *Det digitaliserade försvaret: Teknikutvecklingens påverkan på försvarsförmågan* (Stockholm: Kungl Krigsvetenskapsakademien 2017).

Petersson, Magnus, 'Defense Transformation and Legitimacy in Scandinavia after the Cold War: Theoretical and Practical Implications', *Armed Forces & Society* 37/4 (2011), 701–24. doi:10.1177/0095327X10382216

Petersson, Magnus, 'En skandinavisk transformasjonsbølge', in Tormod Heier (ed.), *Nytt landskap - Nytt Forsvar: Norsk militærmakt 1990-2010* (Oslo: Abstrakt 2011), 101–31.

Petersson, Magnus, 'Denmark and Norway', in Hugo Meijer and Marco Wyss (eds.), *The Handbook of European Defence Policies and Armed Forces*, 360–374. (Oxford: Oxford University Press, 2018).

Reichborn-Kjennerud, Erik, *Meningsfull, menneskelig, kontroll?* (Oslo: NUPI 2020).

Sandberg, Anders et al, 'Förbjud dödliga autonoma vapensystem', *Dagens samhälle*, 11 Apr. 2018, https://www.dagenssamhalle.se/debatt/forbjud-dodliga-autonoma-vapensystem-21566, date accessed 13 August 2019.

Schaub, Gary, Jr. and Jens Wenzel Kristoffersen, *In, On, or Out of the Loop: Denmark and Autonomous Weapon Systems* (Copenhagen: Centre for Military studies 2017).

Schwab, Klaus, 'The Fourth Industrial Revolution: What It Means and How to Respond', *Foreign Affairs*, 12 Dec. 2015.

Sloan, Elinor, *Military Transformation and Modern Warfare: A Reference Handbook* (Westport, CT: Praeger 2008).

Søreide, Ine Eriksen, 'Svar på spørsmål om hel- og halvautonome våpensystemer', *Skriftlig spørsmål nr. 1900, 2017-2018* (Oslo: The Ministry of Foreign Affairs, 2018)

Valero, Bodil, Max Andersson, Linnea Engström, and Jakop Dalunde, 'Sverige måste stoppa framtida mördarrobotar', *Expressen*, 22 Jun. 2018.

Wallström, Margot, 'Anf. 1', *Interpellation 2017/18:20* (Stockholm: Swedish Parliament, 2017).

Wallström, Margot, 'Anf. 3', *Interpellation 2017/18:20* (Stockholm: Swedish Parliament, 2017).

Not so disruptive after all: The 4IR, navies and the search for sea control

Ian Bowers and Sarah Kirchberger

ABSTRACT
Fourth Industrial Revolution technologies and their applicability at sea now dominate debates about the future of naval operations. This article examines the extent to which such technologies, including autonomous and unmanned weapon systems and artificial intelligence, will disrupt naval warfare. Using two case studies, the South China Sea and the Baltic Sea, this article finds that in the key operational output of attaining sea control these technologies will not disrupt naval warfare. While they may intensify the competition between the operational attributes of detection, stealth, range and lethality, they will ultimately sustain existing understandings of seapower and its strategic effects.

Introduction

Militaries across the world acknowledge the need to invest in 4IR technologies to sustain a competitive warfighting edge.[1] The US and China are leading the way, but are by no means the only countries seeking to exploit the 4IR.[2] Advances in big data, connectivity, artificial intelligence, computational power, manufacturing, and robotics will translate into innovations in four categories relevant to the sharp-end of naval warfare: sensors, computers and communications, weapons platforms, and weapon

---

[1] See: The State Council of The People's Republic of China, *China's National Defense in the New Era* (Beijing: Foreign Language Press 2019); US Department of Defense, *Summary of the National Defense strategy of the United States: Sharpening the American Military's Competitive Edge* (Washington D.C.: US Department of Defense 2018).

[2] Roger McDermott, 'Russian Military Science Promotes Innovation in Future Warfare', *Eurasia Daily Monitor* 17, no. 27 (2020). https://jamestown.org/program/russian-military-science-promotes-innovation-in-future-warfare/; David Axe, 'The Royal Navy wants Robotic Submarines (Here's Why That Matters)', *The National Interest*, 17 April 2019, https://nationalinterest.org/blog/buzz/royal-navy-wants-robotic-submarines-heres-why-matters-52942; Nathan Gain, 'French Navy Aiming for 1200 Unmanned Systems by 2030', *Naval News*, 29 July 2019, https://www.navalnews.com/naval-news/2019/07/french-navy-aiming-for-1200-unmanned-systems-by-2030/.

systems.[3] This has led to extensive and sometimes hyperbolic commentary on the capacity of these technologies to fundamentally alter the generation, exercise, and strategic effect of seapower.[4] In a counter to this narrative, others argue that the revolutionary effect of these technologies should be assessed with caution, given the multitude of factors that intervene between the drawing board and actual operations.[5]

Undoubtedly, the potential of 4IR technologies is attractive on multiple levels. They could provide navies with cost-effective and possibly game-changing capabilities. However, there has been little analysis of their disruptive effect on naval operations. This article seeks to cut through the noise. Using the concept of disruptive naval innovation, we ask how disruptive innovations emerging from the 4IR will be to the sharp end of naval warfare. The complex interaction between differing technologies, and the need to integrate them into warfighting systems and doctrines, combined with the scope and speed of the 4IR make assessing its potential impact on naval operations and strategy challenging. To address the challenge, this article will focus on two 4IR-enabled inputs to seapower – unmanned systems and maritime domain awareness (MDA) – and one output, sea control. Marrying the two seapower inputs emerging from the 4IR with their potential to change the operationalisation of sea control allows us to engage with the inherent complexity of naval operations.

In viewing disruption through the lens of sea control strategies including the use of sea denial as a way of securing sea control, we argue that 4IR innovations may alter how navies conduct operations. For example, manned-unmanned balances will change, and navies will have a greater ability to detect and prosecute enemy assets resulting in a more intense competition between detection, range and stealth. However, the 4IR will not disrupt how navies seek to attain sea control. Instead, the integration of 4IR technologies with existing capabilities and subsequent adjustments in doctrine will likely lead to sustaining innovations in how navies achieve sea control.

---

[3]Michael O'Hanlon, *Forecasting Change in Military Technology, 2020–2040* (Washington D.C.: Brookings Institution 2018), 4; Peter Layton, *Prototype Warfare, Innovation and the Fourth Industrial Age* (Canberra: Air Power Development Centre 2018), 5–6.

[4]See: Christian Brose, 'The New Revolution in Military Affairs', *Foreign Affairs* (May/June 2019), https://www.foreignaffairs.com/articles/2019-04-16/new-revolution-military-affairs; Tyler Rogoway, 'DARPA's Unmanned Submarine Stalker Could Change Naval Warfare Forever', *JALOPNIK*, 3 April 2015, https://foxtrotalpha.jalopnik.com/darpas-unmanned-submarine-stalker-could-change-naval-wa-1695566032; Kris Osborn, 'The U.S. Navy Is Trying To Build What Could Be The Ultimate Weapon: A Swarm 'Ghost Fleet', *The National Interest*, 1 February 2017, https://nationalinterest.org/blog/the-buzz/the-us-navy-trying-build-what-could-be-the-ultimate-weapon-19285?page=0%2C1; Hiroyuku Akita, 'US Fears of China's AI-Armed Military are Well-Founded', *Nikkei Asian Review*, 10 April 2019, https://asia.nikkei.com/Spotlight/Comment/US-fears-of-China-s-AI-armed-military-are-well-founded.

[5]See: Laura Schousboe, 'The Pitfalls of Writing About Revolutionary Defense Technology', *War on the Rocks*, 15 July 2019, https://warontherocks.com/2019/07/the-pitfalls-of-writing-about-revolutionary-defense-technology/.

In positing this argument, this paper makes an important contribution to the growing literature that critically examines the effects of modern technology and innovation on contemporary and future military operations. Studying how navies will integrate what are often highly classified technologies into existing and future force structures is difficult. Consequently, this article utilises a mix of primary and secondary sources including open source intelligence and government studies to assess the impact of the 4IR on naval warfare.

The article proceeds with a discussion of the 4IR and the use of disruption as a tool for understanding its impact on naval operations. It then focuses on two broad areas where navies will utilise 4IR technologies: First, the article explores the developmental trajectory and expected operational utility of unmanned naval systems, specifically unmanned air vehicles (UAV), unmanned surface vehicles (USV) and unmanned underwater vehicles (UUV). Second, we perform an analysis of how the 4IR will increase the potential of MDA capabilities. Next, we look at the Baltic and the South China Seas, asking how the introduction of these 4IR-enabled capabilities will alter the attainment of sea control in those two theatres. We conclude by assessing whether these technologies are truly disruptive to the concept and exercise of sea control and identify some areas in the field of naval warfare where disruption may occur.

The 4IR and disruption at sea

The characteristics of the 4IR and the technological and doctrinal complexity of naval operations makes assessing how they interact particularly challenging. To meet this challenge, this article uses the concept of disruptive innovation.[6] This was first developed to describe the impact of discontinuous technological innovation in the business sector but has since been adapted for the military realm.[7] To the extent that the 4IR fundamentally alters operations at sea, it may be disruptive. This section first describes why the 4IR is particularly challenging for naval innovators. It then outlines the concept of disruptive naval innovation and explains why sea control is an appropriate operational concept with which to analyse the 4IR.

Navies, innovation, and the 4IR

In the civilian world, the 4IR is creating rapid, society-altering technological advances in diverse but interconnected fields including manufacturing, artificial

---

[6]See: Joseph L. Bower and Clayton M. Christensen, 'Disruptive Technologies: Catching the Wave', *Harvard Business Review* (January-February 1995).
[7]See: Terry Pierce, *Warfighting and Disruptive Technologies: Disguising Innovation* (OXON: Routledge 2004); Peter J. Dombrowski, Eugene Gholz and Andrew L. Ross, 'Military Transformation and the Defense Industry after Next: The Defense Industrial Implication of Network-Centric Warfare', *Naval War College Newport Papers 18* (2003), 14.

intelligence, autonomy, and quantum computing.[8] The breadth and velocity of these developments are what separate the 4IR from previous industrial revolutions.[9] The nature of the 4IR in combination with the realities of naval innovation both challenges traditional naval pathways for the introduction of new technology and makes efforts to analyse such innovation particularly difficult.

Navies have not been historically resistant to change, but typically require time to test new technologies, find effective ways to integrate them into existing force structures and create appropriate operating doctrines. Once technologies are proven to have an impact on operational outcomes, they tend to be introduced quickly to prevent navies from becoming out-of-date. In the era of the 4IR, one of the difficulties for navies is to absorb these technological advances to create useable operational and strategic outputs when the pace and scope of developments may rapidly render new technologies obsolete. The breadth of the 4IR also ensures that it is not one, but rather the dynamic convergence of numerous technologies that will contribute to innovative warfighting outputs at sea.[10]

Although technology arising from the 4IR may provide the foundation for a transformation in naval operations, doctrinal and structural innovation are equally as vital.[11] Past operational transformations have only occurred when navies developed doctrines and operational procedures to use new technologies effectively and integrate them into new or existing systems and force architectures.[12] Moreover, no element of seapower is executed by one technology, rather, it results from the integration of multiple technologies on various platforms into effective systems, operated according to a common doctrine. As one analyst argues, 'the key to identifying important developments for the future is to concentrate on the synthesis of different technologies and how that synthesis can produce fundamental change in mission capabilities.'[13]

Naval disruption

Disruptive innovations come in two related forms: hardware-based and architectural innovations.[14] The former describes breakthroughs in specific technologies

---

[8]Klaus Schwab, 'The Fourth Industrial Revolution: What it Means, How to Respond', *World Economic Forum*, 14 January 2016, https://www.weforum.org/agenda/2016/01/the-fourth-industrial-revolution-what-it-means-and-how-to-respond/.

[9]Klaus Schwab, *The Fourth Industrial Revolution* (London: Penguin Books 2017), 1.

[10]Michael Raska, 'Strategic Competition for Emerging Military Technologies: Comparing Paths and Patterns', *Prism* 8/3 (2019), 66–67; T.X. Hammes, 'Expeditionary Operations in the Fourth Industrial Revolution', *MCU Journal* 9/1 (Spring 2017), 89.

[11]Andrew F. Krepinevich, 'Cavalry to Computer: The Pattern of Military Revolutions', *The National Interest* (1 September 1994).

[12]Tim Benbow, *The Magic Bullet? Understanding the Revolution in Military Affairs* (London: Brassey's 2004), 19.

[13]Karl Lautenschläger, 'Technology and the Evolution of Naval Warfare', *International Security* 8/2 (1983), 50; Geoffrey Till, Seapower: A Guide for the Twenty-First Century 2nd ed., (OXON: Routledge 2009), 136-137.

[14]Tai Ming Cheung, Thomas G. Mahnken and Andrew L. Ross, 'Assessing the State of Understanding of Defense Innovation', *STIC Research Briefs*, Series 10 (2018–1), 3–4.

or in more complex technological systems, such as warships. An example of disruptive hardware innovation is the battleship *HMS Dreadnought*, which through combining superior armour, firepower and speed instantly rendered extant battleships obsolete and forever changed the nature of the capital ship.[15] In contrast, sustaining hardware innovations are incremental improvements in existing technologies and platforms.[16] This could be increased armour, more precise missiles or, in the case of a warship, a new and improved vessel design. For example, the Ford class aircraft carrier has multiple technological innovations which make it superior to the previous Nimitz class of vessels. These innovations may make carrier aviation more efficient and lethal, but do not fundamentally alter its nature.[17] It should be noted than sustaining innovations are more common that disruptive innovations.

Architectural innovations involve changes in doctrine and organisations. In the same vein as hardware innovations, disruptive architectural change fundamentally alters the nature of combat or introduces new metrics by which success can be measured. Sustaining architectural innovations are incremental improvements in doctrines or organisations. Architectural innovations can occur independently of, contiguous with, or after hardware innovations, but more commonly lag behind technological innovation.[18]

This paper argues that in order to assess whether the 4IR will disrupt the exercise of naval power and given the nature of naval innovation as described above, it is necessary to analyse the combination of hardware and architectural innovations. The gradual development of carrier aviation is a perfect example of this kind of innovation. In this case, new discontinuous technology – the aircraft – was introduced and gradually became integrated into naval doctrine and organisational structures. During WWII, carrier aviation became the dominant platform in surface naval warfare. As aircraft carriers and the aircraft aboard them advanced in technology, doctrine was gradually and then rapidly developed to fully exploit their combat potential.[19] By the end of WWII, the aircraft carrier had displaced the battleship as the primary naval surface combatant and provided navies with power projection capabilities that had never previously been considered.

---

[15] See: Eric Grove, 'The Battleship is Dead: Long Live the Battleship. HMS Dreadnought and the Limits of Technological Innovation', *The Mariner's Mirror* 93/4 (2007), 415–427.
[16] Andrew L. Ross, 'On Military Innovation: Toward an Analytical Framework', *STIC Policy Brief no. 1* (2010).
[17] C. Anthony Pfaff, 'The Ethics of Acquiring Disruptive Technologies', *Texas National Security Review*, 3/1 (Winter 2019/2020), 38.
[18] Tai Ming Cheung, Thomas G. Mahnken and Andrew L. Ross, *Assessing the State of Understanding of Defense Innovation*, 4–5.
[19] Haico te Kulve and Wim A. Smit, 'Novel Naval Technologies: Sustaining or Disrupting Naval Doctrine', *Technological Forecasting & Social Change*, 77 (2010), 999–1013, 1006–1007.

What is being disrupted?

To effectively assess the disruptive effects of the 4IR on naval operations, the key question is what is being disrupted. In the case of disruption in the business world, it is markets and value chains and established companies therein.[20] Given the breadth of naval operations and the number of tasks even a single small warship can carry out, it is necessary to narrow the scope of this study to a core aspect of naval operations; in this case, the attainment of sea control. The operational realities behind sea control in contested waters and its relationship with sea denial provide the article with adequate scope to assess the disruptive potential of the 4IR.

Sea control is a central concept in naval operations, and the attainment of sea control is a pre-requisite for the use of the sea for military and non-military purposes during wartime.[21] Normally it does not mean the permanent control of the sea – this is almost impossible, given the size of the operational area and the capacity of even weak adversaries to complicate operations at sea.[22] Nor does it mean that an opponent cannot contest sea control, but rather that a navy has freedom of action within a specific area of operations for a specific period of time.[23] For example, the US Navy, to project power from the sea onto land, requires sea control in both the area of operations and during deployment to that area.

Contrary to common belief, sea denial strategies, aimed at preventing an opponent from using a specific operational area can contribute to the attainment of sea control strategies.[24] Even strong navies may need to pursue sea denial at the outset of a conflict or may seek control in one operational area while denying the enemy the use of the sea in another.[25]

Importantly, sea control in littoral or enclosed seas involves more than just operations at sea, but also includes operations against targets on land. While sea control is a wartime concept, navies must be ready to establish it in short order should war break out.[26] Therefore the attainment of contemporary sea control in contested waters requires navies to operationalise numerous, and networked

---

[20]This theory has proven extremely popular to the point that the theory itself is falsely used to 'describe any situation in which an industry is shaken up and previously successful incumbents stumble'. See: Clayton M. Christensen, Michael E. Raynor and Rory McDonald, 'What is Disruptive Innovation', In Clayton M. Christensen (ed.), *Selected Articles from the World's Foremost Authority on Disruptive Innovation* (Boston: Harvard Business Review Press 2015) 157–158.
[21]Milan Vego, *Modern Strategy and Sea Control* (Oxon: Routledge 2016), 24.
[22]Milan Vego, *Naval Strategy and Operations in Narrow Seas 2nd edition* (Oxon: Frank Cass 2003), 110–111.
[23]Milan Vego, *Naval Strategy and Operations*, 117.
[24]Geoffrey Till, *Seapower: A Guide for the Twenty-First Century*,193–194.
[25]Milan Vego, 'The navy Must Not Neglect "Defensive" Warfighting', *Proceedings*, 145/7/1397 (2019).
[26]Thomas A. Rowden, 'Sea Control First', *Proceedings* 143 1/1367 (2017).

elements simultaneously. These include MDA combined with multi-domain distributed warfare capabilities, and the doctrines to use them efficiently.[27]

The 4IR and operational inputs

This article focuses on two 4IR-enabled inputs that may transform the exercise of sea control: unmanned naval systems and 4IR-enabled MDA. Diverse unmanned naval systems are currently operational, and there are active plans to increase both their numbers and level of sophistication. MDA capabilities are the totality of platforms (manned and unmanned), sensors, processors and connectors that provide information in the maritime domain.[28] In the era of the 4IR, the fidelity and accuracy of MDA will improve particularly in the 'opaque' underwater domain. While unmanned systems are a family of platforms, and 4IR-enabled MDA is an operational input, both require the integration of a multitude of 4IR technologies for their optimal operationalization, and thus are effective case studies.

Unmanned systems in the maritime domain

The potential of unmanned systems to transform warfare at sea has gripped the popular imagination. The concept of scores of unmanned air, surface and subsurface platforms working autonomously in contested maritime zones is attractive to both rich and resource-starved navies.[29] For example, the US Department of Defense believes future autonomous and semi-autonomous unmanned systems will have the capacity, either independently or collectively, to organically detect, track, recognise, target, counter and engage targets at sea, in the air and on land.[30] However, significant technical hurdles exist, and while UAV technology is rapidly diffusing, the entry barriers to USV and UUV remain extremely high.

For unmanned systems to reach such lofty goals, the limitations posed by a maritime operational environment need to be overcome. Increases in distance between the operational area of the platform, operating base and operator present greater challenges at sea. Power requirements, not just for propulsion but also for the effective use of sensors, weapon systems and communications place significant limitations on the capabilities of contemporary classes of unmanned naval systems.[31] The size and type of platform

---

[27] See Robert C. Rubel, 'Talking about Sea Control', *Naval War College Review* 63/4 (2010), 38–47.
[28] See Andrew Metrick and Kathleen H. Hicks, *Contested Seas: Maritime Domain Awareness in Northern Europe* (Washington D.C.: CSIS 2018), 11–12.
[29] CSBA, *Taking Back the Seas: Transforming the U.S. Surface Fleet for Decision-Centric Warfare* (Washington D.C.: CSBA, 2019), 62–65.
[30] See: US DOD, *Unmanned Systems Integrated Roadmap* (Washington D.C.: US DOD 2018).
[31] Jonathan Gates, 'Is the SSBN Deterrent Vulnerable to Autonomous Drones?', *RUSI Journal* 161/6 (December, 2016), 29.

may to some extent alleviate such issues. For example, UUV have higher power requirements compared to USV, and larger platforms can carry more batteries or more sophisticated power systems. Greater sophistication in power systems, however, creates maintenance problems and reduces the ability to remain at sea for extended periods. Indeed, operating any high-technology system at sea without crews to carry out maintenance is problematic. Unmanned systems operating at significant distances from their bases will have to demonstrate a hitherto unseen level of operational durability. Communications and data transfer in a maritime theatre are also problematic. While current technologies can mitigate such problems in USV, in UUV the transmission of large amounts of data or direct communications through water at longer distances is a technological challenge yet to be solved.[32] This currently makes the transfer of real-time intelligence or remote control at distance virtually impossible when submerged.[33]

It is worth considering the high number of sub-tasks that a single autonomous unmanned vehicle must accomplish. For a USV or UUV to navigate autonomously over distance, it must localize, plan routes, avoid collisions, follow routes and station keep in various sea states. In addition, unmanned systems will need the processing power and AI sophistication to deliver mission requirements such as object recognition, detection, tracking, the delivery of kinetic effects or countermeasures, which requires further battery, sensor and processing capacities. Due to these realities, one comprehensive study of AI and naval unmanned systems concluded, 'the capability for autonomous systems to interpret context and make independent decisions, particularly in a dynamic environment, is not realistic in the short term.'[34]

These challenges do not mean that unmanned systems have no utility. Rather, it will take time for the technology to mature. Remote-controlled UAV have already demonstrated their utility in military operations across the world, performing ISR and strike in various conflicts. At sea, navies and governments have slowly begun turning to ship and shore-launched UAV to improve MDA. Proven and commercially available drones have shown to be a low-tech but important force multiplier. For example, the Irish Naval Service deployed off-the-shelf drones to improve their ability to detect vessels in distress when deployed in the Mediterranean.[35]

More advanced drones such as the US-made Scan Eagle have an endurance of over 12 hours, can carry a range of sensors and are deployed by smaller vessels

---

[32] Heiko Borchert, Tim Kraemer and Daniel Mahon, 'Waiting for Disruption! Undersea Autonomy and the Challenging Nature of Naval Innovation', *RSIS Working Paper No. 302*, 2 February 2017, 2.

[33] See: Chiara Lodovisi, Pierpaolo Loreti, Lorenzo Bracciale and Silvello Betti, 'Performance Analysis of Hybrid-Optical-Acoustic AUV Swarms for Marine Monitoring', *Future Internet* 10/65 2018, 4.

[34] Bradley Martin et. al, *Advancing Autonomous Systems: An Analysis of Current and Future Technology for Unmanned Maritime Vehicles* (Santa Monica: RAND Corporation 2019), xi.

[35] Nick Bramhill, 'Drones to Aid Ireland's War on Illegal Fishing and Pollution', *Irish Central*, 12 July 2018, https://www.irishcentral.com/news/irishvoice/drones-ireland-drugs-sea.

where space is scarce. Larger, more expensive medium and high altitude long endurance UAV (MALE, HALE) including the MQ-4 C Triton or Elbit Hermes 900 can be equipped with a variety of sensors including electro optical, IR, radar, SIGINT and ELINT. Beyond ISR, the US Navy now deploys the MQ-8B Fire Scout, a helicopter-style VTOL UAV that not only has ISR capabilities but can also facilitate battlefield communications. The US is also in the advanced testing phase of the MQ-25 Stingray, an unmanned carrier-launched tanker UAV intended to refuel US Navy aircraft in contested theatres.

In contrast to UAV, USV are in a more embryonic stage of development and have significant extant constraints. Proven platforms such as the Israeli-made *Protector* or the Singaporean *Venus* have limited operational capacity with a focus on force-protection, littoral ISR and limited anti-surface warfare (ASuW).[36] While autonomous seakeeping and waypoint-guided navigation are now possible, operational limitations remain.[37] Israel has now suspended its USV program, as power constraints, survivability factors and poor handling at sea reduced their operational utility.[38]

Development patterns for USV suggest that mine warfare (MCM), anti-submarine warfare (ASW) and maritime security are the focus for most navies. However, China and the US are seemingly intent on procuring capabilities that will be able to carry out a wider range of missions at greater distances from their operating base. The US is developing medium and large USV (MUSV/LUSV) that can perform a range of missions, either autonomously or by remote control. These vessels will be able to carry out ISR and close surveillance in contested waters, carry large amounts of weapon systems operating in concert with existing fleets, or provide persistent ASW capabilities, potentially acting as a hub around which smaller UUV could operate. The US concept for its MUSV and LUSV is for relatively cheap platforms with a proven design into which the US Navy can insert increasing levels of autonomy and more advanced mission payloads.[39] China reportedly has similar USV under development. An example is an autonomous system for ASuW, the JARI USV. It is a 20 m, 15-ton, heavily armed, fast platform developed by shipbuilder CSIC. The JARI is armed with a vertical launch system and carries a phased-array radar system and according to news reports has already conducted its first sea trials.[40]

---

[36]'Multi-Purpose USV', *Raphael Advanced Defense Systems*, http://www.rafael.co.il/5670-2676-EN/Marketing.aspx.

[37]'Venus Unmanned Surface Vehicle', *ST Engineering*, https://www.stengg.com/en/electronics/companies-affiliates/st-electronics-large-scale-systems-group/venus-unmanned-surface-vehicle/.

[38]'Israel Scraps Programme for Maritime Patrols with USVS', *Maps and Conflict Database* (27 April 2020), https://maps.southfront.org/israel-scraps-programme-for-maritime-patrols-with-usvs/.

[39]US DOD, 'Navy Justification Book Volume 2 of 5: Research, Development, Test & Evaluation, Navy', *US Department of Defense Fiscal Year 2021 Budget Estimates* (Washington D.C.: Department of Defense, February 2020), 2-1 – 2-8.

[40]Zhen LIU, 'China's new killer robot ship goes through its first sea trial', *South China Morning Post* 17 January 2020, https://scmp.com/news/china/military/article/3046601/chinas-newkiller-robot-ship-goes-through-its-first-sea-trial.

Navies also increasingly deploy small UUV for mine-sweeping/clearance and oceanographic and hydrographic purposes.[41] Advances in technology have increased the number of missions that UUV can carry out, with US systems reportedly now capable of performing ASW and 'far forward' ISR.[42] Large and Extra Large UUV (XLUUV) are currently under development in the United States and other countries. The aim is for longer endurance and a modular payload capability, including offensive and defensive weapons.[43] Reports from the US indicate that the Office of the Secretary of Defense now believes that XLUUV should be a procurement priority given their low cost relative to manned equivalents.[44] This would free up manned systems to perform sophisticated operations, while unmanned variants could perform less complicated assignments.[45]

A British government competition for the development of an XLUUV reveals some of the intended capabilities, including a minimum three-month independent operating capability, a range of up to 3000 nm and the ability to carry payloads of 2 metric tons.[46] Core missions would include intelligence gathering and ASW. The latter would entail identifying, tracking and reporting hostile contacts.[47] Russia is reportedly developing the torpedo-carrying Cephalopod UUV that is designed with ASW as its primary mission.[48]

China is also developing a wide range of UUV, including a torpedo-shaped Semi-Autonomous Robotic Vehicle (SARV) Robotic Vehicle that can be launched from submarines. Other systems under development include dual bodied USV carrying ASW sensor equipment; conventional underwater gliders for measuring a variety of oceanic environmental conditions; and even a 5–10 ton Autonomous Robotic Vehicle (ARV) intended for long endurance missions and hauling larger payloads, likely for ISR, MCM and ASW.[49] In addition, the PLA is developing submarine decoys and XLUUV. In June 2018, the existence of a classified '912 Project' was confirmed. The

---

[41] Massimo Annati, 'Unmanned Naval Systems: Surface/Subsurface Vehicles: New Capabilities and Missions', *Military Technology*, (Special Issue: 2013), 25–26.
[42] Pete Small, 'Navy Unmanned Systems: An Overview', *Undersea Warfare* 67 (Spring 2019), 8.
[43] US DOD, Navy Justification Book Volume 2 of 5: Research, Development, Test & Evaluation, Navy, 2–3.
[44] David B. Larter, 'To Compete with China, an Internal Pentagon Study Looks to Pour Money into Robot Submarines', *Defense News* (1 June 2020). https://www.defensenews.com/naval/2020/06/01/to-compete-with-china-an-internal-pentagon-study-looks-to-pour-money-into-robot-submarines/.
[45] Ibid.
[46] Defence Science and Technology Laboratory, *Competition Document: Developing the Royal Navy's Autonomous Underwater Capability*, 6 June 2019. https://www.gov.uk/government/publications/competition-developing-the-royal-navys-autonomous-underwater-capability/competition-document-developing-the-royal-navys-autonomous-underwater-capability.
[47] Ibid.
[48] Kyle Mizokami, 'Russia Working on New 'Cephalopod Underwater Attack Drone', *Popular Mechanics*, 30 July 2018, https://www.popularmechanics.com/military/navy-ships/a22593766/russia-working-on-new-cephalopod-underwater-attack-drone/.
[49] Jeffrey Lin and P.W. Singer, 'The Great Underwater Wall of Robots: Chinese Exhibit Shows Off Sea Drones', *Popular Science*, 22 June 2016. https://www.popsci.com/great-underwater-wall-robots-chinese-exhibit-shows-off-sea-drones/

goal is to develop 'large, smart and relatively low-cost unmanned submarines' for 'a wide range of missions, from reconnaissance to mine placement to even suicide attacks against enemy vessels,' and to deploy these autonomous submarines during the 2020s.[50]

4IR-enabled maritime domain awareness

MDA is a necessary and critical input for all outputs of seapower. The goal of MDA is to achieve a persistent, resilient and real-time picture of the subsurface, surface and air domains in any designated operational area. Contemporary MDA requires the ability to collect and transmit data from multiple cues, then interpret that data to create an actionable operational picture.

In the surface and aerial domains, contemporary MDA is achieved through a mix of ship-based transmitters (AIS), sea and shore-based radar, ISR and SAR satellites, maritime patrol aircraft, and more recently UAV. Indeed, surface and aerial MDA has undergone consistent sustaining innovation, with new capabilities gradually increasing coverage and fidelity, allowing advanced states such as the US and China to maintain a consistent maritime picture. Even smaller littoral states, through the operation of UAV, can increase the level of MDA within their maritime operation areas. Contemporary MDA remains hostage to external conditions such as weather and in wartime, kinetic and non-kinetic enemy action such as anti-satellite weapons and electronic warfare.

The development of commercial nanosatellite constellations for Earth observation, when combined with other sensor platforms and exploited by AI algorithms for automated sensor data fusing has the potential for an enhanced awareness of global ship movements, particularly in remote areas like the Arctic. One US firm already has a constellation of ca. 150 nanosatellites in orbit that can provide an image per day, at 3.7 m resolution, of the entire Earth's landmass. Commercially available nanosatellites could provide three major innovations in the maritime domain; first, the high number and small size of these systems will allow for greater fidelity and coverage over specific operational areas. Second, the number of satellites may provide greater resilience against anti-satellite weapons, and their relative cost may make replacement easier when compared with traditional satellites.[51] Finally, low cost and commercial availability means that states that previously found space-based capabilities to be too costly now could have access to satellite coverage over their areas of maritime operations. In isolation, however, it is

---

[50]Stephen Chen, 'China military develops robotic submarines to launch a new era of sea power', *South China Morning Post*, 23 July 2018, https://www.scmp.com/news/china/society/article/2156361/china-developing-unmanned-ai-submarines-launch-new-era-sea-power.

[51]Monty Khanna, 'Get ready for the next RMA at sea', *USNI Proceedings* Vol. 146/1 (January 2020).

difficult to argue that 4IR technologies will disrupt surface MDA. Instead, the trajectory of surface MDA with better coverage and wider availability combined with greater but not total persistence suggests such innovation is sustaining.

The potential for disruptive capabilities of the 4IR may be more evident in the subsurface domain. Advances in data exploitation, together with the development of unmanned systems and new sensor arrays form the basis of modern networked forms of ASW that are currently under development in the western countries as well as China.

In a study of networked ASW, scientists from the German Bundeswehr Technical Centre for Ships and Naval Weapons, Naval Technology and Research describe 4IR technology as allowing for vastly enhanced subsurface domain awareness even with low-quality input data. Existing high-fidelity low frequency active sonar systems (LFAS) towed behind vessels can be supplemented by distributed unmanned sensor systems to massively improve subsurface MDA in bounded geographic areas such as chokepoints.[52]

Despite this potential, there is significant debate surrounding the previously unsurmountable stealth of conventional and nuclear submarines, and whether 4IR-enabled MDA could undermine this advantage. Numerous authors argue that the technological limitations of unmanned systems when combined with the capabilities of modern submarines and the operational difficulties imposed by the sea, ensure that the underwater environment will remain opaque and that the submarine will retain its traditional advantages.[53] Others however contend that the trackability of submarines is often under-estimated, and the US during the Cold War likely had the capability to track Soviet submarines using a multitude of high-technology, covert solutions.[54] Additionally, given the technical challenges of linking and operationalising multiple surface, subsurface and air assets, it is difficult to envisage when subsurface 4IR-enabled MDA will be wholly effective.[55] While removing the total opacity of the ocean may be impossible given the size of the operating space and the technological limitations of UUV, contested and confined operational areas such as littoral waters, narrow channels and

---

[52]See: Schulz, Arne, Holger Schmaljohann, Kathrin Wilkens, Ivor Nissen, Christian Kubaczyk and Wolfgang Jans, *Systems and Concepts for Networked ASW*, Paper for Underwater Acoustics Measurements (UAM) 2011 (Kos, Greece, 2011): 1. https://www.researchgate.net/publication/267841249_SYSTEMS_AND_CONCEPTS_FOR_NETWORKED_ASW.

[53]See: Jonathan Gates, *Is the SSBN Deterrent Vulnerable*, 28–35; Norman Friedman, 'Strategic Submarines and Strategic Stability: Looking Towards the 2030s', in Rory Medcalf, Katherine Mansted, Stephan Frühling and James Goldrick (eds.), *The Future of the Undersea Deterrent: A Global Survey* (Canberra: Australian National University 2020), 69–79.

[54]Brendan Rittenhouse Green and Austin Long, 'Conceal or Reveal? Managing Military Capabilities in Peacetime Competition', *International Security* 44/3 (Winter 2019/2020), 48–83.

[55]Sebastian Brixey-Williams, 'Prospects for Game-Changers in Detection Technology', in Rory Medcalf, Katherine Mansted, Stephan Fruhling and James Goldrick (eds.), *The Future of the Undersea Deterrent: A Global Survey* (Canberra: Australian National University 2020), 83.

maritime chokepoints may become increasingly difficult for submarines to transit or operate without detection.

Given the operational possibilities, navies and industry are investing heavily in developing and operationalizing networked sub-surface MDA capabilities. Western navies are pursuing this within the framework of the EU-funded Ocean2020 project, a €35.5 million program by 42 partner consortiums from 15 countries under the lead of the Italian firm Leonardo.[56] In November 2019, a first live demonstration involving nine unmanned systems and six naval units from Italy, Spain, Greece and France took place in the Gulf of Taranto. The test set-up comprised four UAVs, three USVs and two UUVs; six naval vessels, plus 'five satellites for communication and surveillance, four National Maritime Operations Centres (MOC), two ground communication networks, and a prototype of a European Maritime Operations Centre (EU MOC) to build a comprehensive maritime picture.'[57] A similar NATO exercise was held in September 2019: REP (MUS) 19 tested the interoperability between seven nations' unmanned systems in a number of operational tasks including MCM and MDA.[58]

The 4IR and sea control in the Baltic Sea

The peace and wartime threat posed by Russia in the Baltic Sea requires NATO navies and their partners to have the ability to secure sea control in a complex operational environment. The use of 4IR technologies presents significant opportunities to improve their ability to maintain MDA and apply kinetic force. However, beyond MCM there is little evidence of the deployment of such capabilities, as resource-constrained regional navies are struggling to operationalise extant high-end technologies. Nevertheless, given exercise patterns, it is evident that regional NATO navies and their partners will in the future seek to utilise such systems, and of course, the US has the capacity to deploy 4IR systems to the region should the strategic situation demand it.

In peacetime, some argue that Russia poses a hybrid challenge to the region.[59] It has the military capability and political will to launch an

---

[56]Ocean2020 is the largest EU-funded defence project. See *OCEAN2020 Fact Sheet*, (Brussels, EDA, 21 November 2019), https://www.eda.europa.eu/info-hub/publications/publication-details/pub/fact sheet-ocean2020.

[57]EDA, *Largest EU funded defence research project tested in the Mediterranean Sea*, 21 November 2019, https://eda.europa.eu/info-hub/press-centre/latest-news/2019/11/21/largest-eu-funded-defence-research-project-tested-in-the-mediterranean-sea.

[58]Martin Banks, '4 Questions with NATO on its Unmanned Tech Test', *Defense News* 28 October 2019, https://www.defensenews.com/training-sim/2019/10/28/4-questions-with-nato-on-its-unmanned-tech-test/; 'Portugal Hosts Maritime Exercise in Support of NATO's Maritime Unmanned Systems Initiative', *NATO News* 25 September 2019, https://www.nato.int/cps/en/natohq/news_168925.htm?selectedLocale=en.

[59]This article uses the NATO definition of hybrid threats: 'Hybrid threats combine military and non-military as well as covert and overt means, including disinformation, cyber attacks, economic pressure, deployment of irregular armed groups and use of regular forces.' See: 'NATO's Response to Hybrid Threats', *NATO*, (8 August 2019). https://www.nato.int/cps/en/natohq/topics_156338.htm.

aggressive coercive campaign against the Baltic States at a level below the threshold of war.[60] At sea, Murphy and Schaub argue, Russia has a large number of options to exploit economic, geographic and political weaknesses in the Baltic States for specific strategic gains. These options could include targeting vulnerable islands such as Swedish-controlled Gotland and Denmark's Bornholm, regional ports, individual ships, and undersea cables. Russia possesses a potent special forces capacity able to deliver small numbers to strategic areas on land and also maintains other deniable capabilities such as sea mines and cyber and electronic warfare.[61] Technical advances here have resulted in new threats, such as GPS spoofing, jamming, and offensive cyber-attacks against ships and land-based installations including harbours that can be difficult to attribute and counter.[62]

Russian and western naval and air forces since 2014 have consistently performed naval suasion activities including provocative air and naval manoeuvres, exercises and presence operations.[63] While not overt threats in themselves, these activities place pressure on other navies and raise the potential for accidental clashes or escalation.

In the advent of war between Russia and NATO in the Baltics, the Baltic Sea would be a secondary theatre given the likelihood of horizontal escalation and Russia's overwhelming focus on land. Nevertheless, maintaining sea control of the Baltic region is vital for NATO in such a scenario. Given the infrastructural and geographic difficulties of moving reinforcements overland to the Baltic, reinforcement via the sea is an important element in any wartime scenario. Moreover, the sea acts as a route through which to degrade Russian forces deployed in Kaliningrad. Conversely, the sea is also a potential vulnerability for NATO, providing Russia with the ability to launch multiple small-scale attacks on the littoral regions of Baltic states.

The geography of the region increases the operational complexity of maintaining sea control. An archetypal narrow sea, the Baltic theatre creates operational pressures due to compressed detection and engagement times that could have a substantial impact on decision-making.[64] Additionally, the confined operational area ensures that seapower in the Baltic can not only be defined by ships in the water, but the totality of assets that can apply power

---

[60]Martin Murphy, Frank G. Hoffman and Gary Schaub Jr., *Hybrid Maritime Warfare and the Baltic Sea Region* (Copenhagen: Centre for Military Studies 2016), 9.

[61]Martin Murphy, and Gary Schaub Jr. '"Sea of Peace" or Sea of War – Russian Maritime Hybrid Warfare in the Baltic Sea', *Naval War College Review* 71/2, article 9 (2018).

[62]See e.g.: C4ADS, *Above Us Only Stars: Exposing GPS Spoofing in Russia and Syria* (2019); Abaimov and Ingram, *Hacking UK Trident*; Andy Greenberg, 'The Untold Story of NotPetya, the Most Devastating Cyberattack in History,' *Wired*, 22 August 2018, https://www.wired.com/story/notpetya-cyberattack-ukraine-russia-code-crashed-the-world/; Jukka Savolainen, *Hybrid Threats and Vulnerabilities of Modern Critical Infrastructure – Weapons of Mass Disturbance (WMDi)?* (Helsinki: Hybrid CoE 2019).

[63]Franklin D. Kramer and Magnus Nordenman, 'A Maritime Framework for the Baltic Sea Region', *Issue Brief Scowcroft Center for Strategy and Security* (March, 2016), 2–3.

[64]Nils-Ove Jannson, 'The Baltic: A Sea of Contention,' *Naval War College Review* 41/3 (1988), 2.

into the sea and the surrounding littorals. This includes shore-based air and missile capabilities. Variable depths and differing levels of salinity make it a challenging environment for both anti-submarine and submarine operations.[65] Water depth, temperature, salinity, seabed conditions, dense ship traffic, and the character and shape of the coast in 'confined and shallow waters' such as the Baltic have a detrimental effect on the performance of sensors particularly in the underwater domain. Air temperature, wave height, wind speed, humidity, and other meteorological phenomena such as fog also 'affect radar, infrared sensors, and radio communications, while haze and other forms of visual distortion affect the performance of optical devices' in the surface domain.[66]

Of course, Russia's naval challenge is to some extent defined by its weaknesses. Of Russia's four naval fleets, the Baltic Fleet is the smallest, with a modest number of modern vessels when compared with the German, Danish, Swedish and Finnish fleets, all of which possess modern surface capabilities, with two (Germany and Sweden) operating submarines optimised for the variable depths of the Baltic.[67] However, Russia maintains substantial military capabilities in Kaliningrad, including advanced shore-based anti-ship and anti-air assets which could theoretically hold any vessel or aircraft operating in that region hostage to Russian intentions or at least deny an enemy the ability to attain sea control.[68] Nonetheless, legitimate questions exist about the feasibility of this approach as Russia may struggle to both efficiently enact and sustain a sea-denial strategy in a time of peer-conflict.[69]

The strategic situation indicates that 4IR technologies at sea have operational utility in the Baltic theatre. In peacetime, 4IR-enabled MDA would provide NATO navies with a clearer operational picture for monitoring Russian activity. For example, large and medium USV and UUV could be deployed in international waters proximate to Kaliningrad and other Russian ports to maintain constant overwatch of Russian naval movements. This would vastly increase the ability of NATO to attribute any hostile action, thereby reducing one of the core advantages of hybrid warfare. Additionally, the use of unmanned systems for MDA frees up manned platforms to respond quickly to unknown or potentially dangerous intrusions.

---

[65]Heinrich Lange et al., *To the Seas Again: Maritime Defence and Deterrence in the Baltic Region* (Tallinn: ICDS 2019), 6.
[66]Stavros Karlatiras, 'The changing nature of naval conflicts in confined and shallow waters (CSW),' in Joachim Krause and Sebastian Bruns (eds.), *Routledge Handbook of Naval Strategy and Security* (London: Routledge 2016), 168.
[67]See: Anders Puck Nielsen, 'Sømilitær Vurdering af Ruslands Østersøflåde og de Militære Implikationer for Danmark,' *Scandinavian Journal of Military Studies* 2/1 (2019), 148–164.
[68]See: Stephan Frühling and Guilaume Lasconjarius, 'NATO, A2/AD and the Kaliningrad Challenge', *Survival* 58/2 (2016), 95–116.
[69]See: Dalsjö, Robert, Christofer Berglund and Michael Jonsson, *Bursting the Bubble? Russian A2/AD in the Baltic Sea Region: Capabilities, Countermeasures, and Implications* (Stockholm: FOI 2019).

A networked 4IR-MDA system would also allow NATO to maintain awareness and secure sea control of the vital straits leading into the Baltic. Permanent and deployable surface and subsurface systems could protect ports and other vital maritime infrastructure. Maintaining this level of awareness would provide NATO navies with the capacity to prosecute enemy targets should war break out. Moreover, existing unmanned MCM capabilities would assist in ensuring that SLOCs could remain open in the face of increasingly advanced mine warfare systems.

In the event of war, even if NATO secures a comprehensive and persistent level of MDA, the Baltic Sea will be a contested environment until Russian capabilities operating out of Kaliningrad are neutralised. Arguably unmanned systems in all three domains will in the future have the capacity to counter these capabilities. For example, arming large and medium USVs and UUVs with strike capabilities could rapidly destroy or deplete difficult-to-replace Russian offensive and defensive munitions. Such capabilities already exist in the form of long-range stand-off precision weaponry including sea and air-launched cruise missiles. Rather than adding a new string to NATO's already considerable bow, unmanned systems performing this role would act as a force multiplier, complementing existing capabilities.

The 4IR and sea control in the South China Sea

For China, wartime sea control of the SCS is of increasing strategic import due to the location of China's main strategic submarine base on Hainan Island. From China's point of view, the geostrategic importance of the SCS ensues from the PLA Navy's lack of access to the open Pacific from the Chinese coast. The SCS is China's only directly accessible body of water that is not 'confined and shallow' and therefore unsuitable for strategic submarine operations.[70] The SSBN base on Hainan has the potential to serve as the cornerstone of China's envisaged sea-based nuclear deterrent, because it offers Chinese SSBNs a chance to reach deeper waters in the SCS's abyssal plain without having to traverse through any of the highly monitored choke points within the First Island Chain.[71]

The driving force behind China's attempts to establish a full nuclear triad may have been a threat perception that arose from new US military concepts that aim to achieve 'absolute security,' in particular Conventional Prompt

---

[70]See the discussion of water depth levels in Xinhua LIU 刘新华, 中国发展海权战略研究 (A Study on China's Strategy of Development of Sea Power) (Beijing: Renmin chubanshe 2015), 180–83; 310; and Wenmu ZHANG 张文木, 乌克兰事件的世界意义及其对中国的警示 (The Ukraine Crisis: What does it Mean to the World and China), 国际安全研究 (Journal of International Security Studies) 2014, (4): 1–26, http://www.guancha.cn/ZhangWenMu/2014_12_28_304621.shtml.

[71]Mathieu Duchâtel and Eugenia Kazakova, 'Tensions in the South China Sea: the nuclear dimension,' SIPRI Commentary 27 August 2015, https://www.sipri.org/commentary/essay/2015/tensions-south-china-sea-nuclear-dimension.

Global Strike and Ballistic Missile Defence. Discussions in Chinese military circles assume that the combination of these capabilities could endanger the survivability of China's relatively modest and primarily land-based nuclear deterrent.[72] From this vantage point, the realization of a credible seaborne second-strike capability seems to have become an urgent requirement. This explains the perceived need for establishing a layered defence around Hainan. The aim is to secure the SSBN base against attacks from the sea and air, and to avoid having SSBNs trailed when they leave base. A 2017 Chinese-language news article detailed suggestions from Chinese military experts regarding the installations required to safeguard artificially enhanced Paracel and Spratly features that form the outward defensive layer. The list of ISR infrastructures named includes radars; infrared and optical reconnaissance systems in case a radar encounters 'serious electromagnetic interference in a complex electromagnetic environment,' and for detecting stealth targets; electronic reconnaissance and communications monitoring systems for monitoring 'fire control systems of foreign military aircraft and warships in nearby sea areas;' sonar systems to prevent reconnaissance by other countries' submarines at close range; communication systems including satellite ground stations, VHF radios and HF radios, as well as submarine cable systems.[73] The interviewed experts point out that while anti-air warfare is China's most urgent concern, ASW comes second. Strikingly, they mention that all the installations should interlink with naval vessels, thus forming a coherent and resilient MDA system.[74]

Satellite imagery analyses show that many of these installations are already in place. Furthermore, three of the Spratly reefs – Fiery Cross, Subi, and Mischief Reef – feature large berths and sufficient hangar capacity for an entire Liaoning class air wing.[75] With runways between 2.8 and 3.1 km length, they are able to handle the largest types of aircraft, including strategic bombers.[76] When operating in conjunction with an actual aircraft carrier in the vicinity or with other naval vessels and naval and land-based aircraft, this distributed network of outposts can enable China to gain air superiority in the early stages of a conflict.

---

[72] See Lora Saalman, *Prompt Global Strike: China and the Spear* (Honolulu: Daniel K. Inouye Asia-Pacific Center for Security Studies 2014), http://apcss.org/prompt-global-strike-china-and-the-spear/; Ningbo YUWEN 宇文静波 and Liwen TANG 唐立文, '美国"快速全球打击"计划探讨与启示 (Discussion and Inspirations About Prompt Global Strike of the US),' in 装备指挥技术学院学报 (*Journal of the Academy of Equipment Command & Technology*) (Vol. 22 No. 3, June 2011), 58–61.
[73] Yunsheng XU 许云圣, '解放军不再留手, 南海岛礁需哪些防御装备? (What defensive equipment is needed on the South China Sea islands if the PLA leaves?)', 凤凰新闻 *Fenghuang xinwen* (4 March 2017), https://share.iclient.ifeng.com/news/shareNews?forward=1&aid=119549750#backhead.
[74] Ibid.
[75] AMTI, 'Updated: China's Big Three Near Completion,'(AMTI, CSIS, 29 June 2017), https://amti.csis.org/chinas-big-three-near-completion/.
[76] Renny Babiarz, 'China's Nuclear Submarine Force', *Jamestown Foundation China Brief* 17/10 (2017). https://jamestown.org/program/chinas-nuclear-submarine-force.

In the subsurface domain, China is attempting to create a so-called ASW 'great wall'[77] in the SCS. The intention is to detect and deter enemy submarines from entering the security perimeter. Beijing's increased assertiveness towards foreign surveillance aircraft and surface vessels since the opening of the SSBN base are further indicators of its goal to create a submarine sanctuary in the SCS. Furthermore, China has developed ASW helicopter bases on Palm and Duncan Islands in the Paracels that could act as a cornerstone of China's effort to track enemy submarines.[78] Similar installations exist on the smaller, innermost three Spratly features Gavin, Hughes, and Johnson South Reef.[79]

Gaining comprehensive MDA as a precursor for exercising area control would be impossible to achieve without a robust networked cross-domain ISR system. This is enabled by a dedicated space infrastructure that can cover the area from above, including satellites that provide SATNAV, SATCOM, and all-weather remote sensing. Distributed air defence capabilities on the warships and island outposts form an interlinked network able to perform surface warfare and area defence in the outer defensive layer. Finally, a subsurface sensor grid of satellite-linked deep-sea sonobuoys gathers data and operates in conjunction with other anti-submarine assets monitoring environmental conditions and submarine traffic. Chinese shipbuilding conglomerate CSSC publicly displayed a model of this network in 2016. They intend for its passive sensors (some of which are located up to 3,000 meters below the surface) to connect with the wide range of Chinese USV under development.[80]

Space assets form another part of this ambitious MDA project. At least two SCS features host satellite tracking stations,[81] and the deep-sea sensor arrays described by Wang et al. are connected to buoys on the surface that are fitted with satellite uplinks that transmit data to computing centres.[82] In addition to the Chinese global navigational satellite system BeiDou and the remote sensing/ISR satellite constellations Yaogan and Gaofen, China is now developing a dedicated remote sensing satellite constellation to monitor the SCS area specifically. The Hainan constellation will consist of optical, hyperspectral, and synthetic aperture satellites to enable 'non-stop all-weather observations' of the SCS.[83]

---

[77] See Catherine Wong, '"Underwater Great Wall": Chinese firm proposes building network of submarine detectors to boost nation's defence', *South China Morning Post* 19 May 2016, http://www.scmp.com/news/china/diplomacy-defence/article/1947212/underwater-great-wall-chinese-firm-proposes-building.
[78] AMTI, 'UPDATE: China's Continuing Reclamation in the Paracels' (AMTI, CSIS, 9 August 2017), https://amti.csis.org/paracels-beijings-other-buildup/.
[79] Babiarz, 'China's Nuclear Submarine Force'.
[80] Jeffrey Lin and P.W. Singer, 'The Great Underwater Wall of Robots'.
[81] John W. Lewis and Litai Xue, 'China's security agenda transcends the South China Sea', *Bulletin of the Atomic Scientists* 72/4 (2016), 212–221, http://dx.doi.org/10.1080/00963402.2016.1194056.
[82] Wang et al., '海底观测网水下环境实时监控系统设计与实现', 194.
[83] Silu GUO, 'Hainan satellite constellation system provides shield for South China Sea,' *China Military Online*, 3 January 2018, http://eng.chinamil.com.cn/view/2018-01/03/content_7894167.htm.

To achieve real-time data transmission and exploitation, immense computing power and the assistance of AI algorithms are needed. One supercomputing research station that can integrate and analyse complex oceanographic data from multiple sources with 'a dedicated mission of helping China's maritime expansion' is located in Shandong province.[84]

The evidence suggests China is determined to exploit the potential of networked ASW and ISR to obtain vastly enhanced MDA in the subsurface, surface and air domains, likely as a prerequisite for a comprehensive sea control strategy.[85] These capabilities also have utility in contesting the ability to operate in waters adjacent to or in the approaches of the SCS. Enhanced MDA linked to air and ground-launched anti-ship missiles could provide China with a potent capability, forcing opponents to fight for access to deny China the secure use of the SCS.[86]

The successful implementation of an advanced MDA-enabling underwater monitoring system in combination with other surveillance infrastructures, and when paired with the potential of offensive strike and asymmetric capabilities of unmanned systems may enable China to secure sea control in the SCS.

Where is the disruption?

This article has examined 4IR technologies at sea and their future role in the attainment of sea control using the Baltic and the SCS as case studies. In both theatres, 4IR technologies have the potential to enhance sea control and to provide navies with more avenues to exploit such control. However, there is little evidence that they will disrupt what is the operational core of naval operations. Instead, by taking the concept of NCW to another level, 4IR technologies will more likely sustain existing concepts and capabilities. Advances in computing power and machine learning will contribute to vastly enhanced ISR and enable near real-time MDA in the littorals – at least for the great powers that have access to these technologies. However, legitimate questions exist as to the survivability of these systems in peer-to-peer conflict where cyber, electronic and space warfare capabilities will likely disrupt the networks needed to sustain 4IR MDA.

---

[84] Stephen Chen, 'The World's Next Fastest Supercomputer Will Help Boost China's Growing Sea Power', *South China Morning Post*, 23 August 2017, https://www.scmp.com/news/china/society/article/2107796/worlds-next-fastest-supercomputer-will-help-boost-chinas-growing.

[85] For a Chinese technical journal article describing an undersea real-time monitoring network infrastructure under development in the SCS since at least 2016, see Jun WANG 王俊 et al., '海底观测网水下环境实时监控系统设计与实现' (Design and Realization of Underwater Environment Real-time Monitoring System for Ocean Observatory Network), in 浙江大学学报 □工学版□ *Journal of Zhejiang University (Engineering Science)* (Vol. 50, No. 2, Feb. 2016), 193–200. For a newspaper article commenting on this system, see Wong, 'Underwater Great Wall'.

[86] Cf. Eric Heginbotham et al, *The U.S. – China Military Scorecard: Forces, geography, and the evolving balance of power 1996–2017* (Santa Monica: RAND 2015), 170–172.

As described in the case of the SCS, China's search for sea control is closely related to its ability to deny adjacent seas to opposition forces. 4IR-enhanced MDA linked to capabilities such as anti-ship ballistic missiles, air-launched cruise missiles and UAV are changing the offensive-defensive balance, theoretically making the attainment of sea control particularly challenging in waters increasingly distant from shore. Of course, the significant caveat exists that persistent MDA may not be achievable in wartime. If it is achieved, the connection between 4IR MDA and existing strike capabilities resulting in improved sea-denial in support of China's sea control ambitions could be described as disruptive naval innovation, as it fundamentally changes how navies such as the US will operate in contested waters.[87]

In the littorals, 4IR MDA could potentially degrade the stealthy nature of the submarine, posing challenges to both conventional and nuclear submarine operations that have so far been difficult to detect in most realistic scenarios. This development could have a 'game-changing impact' and might threaten the viability of future submarines in some respects.[88] As a result, the subsurface domain in contested areas such as the Baltic and SCS may become less opaque to some, but not necessarily all players. Yet, improved ASW is not disruptive, but rather fits within a common cycle of evasion and detection.

In a situation of heightened threat within the subsurface domain, it is likely that UUVs of various kinds will increasingly proliferate and may to some degree takeover functions so far performed by manned submarines, for example, offensive mining and ISR. 4IR-enabled systems will therefore take over and sustain existing missions, but will not transform the assertion of sea control.

Some argue that the proliferation of 4IR-enabled technologies may alter the balance of power at sea.[89] The research in this article reveals an important pattern regarding the diffusion of 4IR technologies: It is evident the US and China are currently leading in the development race for unmanned systems. Both countries are investing in substantial and broad-sweeping 4IR technologies. Resource-weaker states including NATO allies are further behind. Even as technology diffuses, the existing order of power at sea will therefore be maintained. Moreover, if smaller navies increase investment in unmanned systems, it is likely that both peer and larger competitors will invest in similar capabilities.

---

[87]This dilemma has been well covered in the existing academic and policy literature. Indeed, the U.S. is already developing doctrines to overcome this advanced form of sea denial. See: Stephen Biddle and Ivan Oelrich, 'Future Warfare in the Western Pacific: Chinese Antiaccess/Area Denial, U.S. AirSea Battle, and Command of the Commons in East Asia', *International Security* 41/1 (2016): 7–48.
[88]Stanislov Abaimov and Paul Ingram, *Hacking UK Trident: A Growing Threat* (London: British American Security Information Council 2017), 34.
[89]See: T.X. Hammes, 'Defending Europe: How Converging Technology Strengthens Small Powers', *Scandinavian Journal of Military Studies* 2/1 (2019), 20–29.

Conclusions and a future research agenda

Envisaging how developing technologies will alter the future of combat is a difficult objective made even more problematic by the speed and unpredictability of the 4IR.[90] To capture this complexity, we chose to examine the 4IR by centring on its disruptive potential on the exercise of sea control. We found that in their existing, reported form, 4IR technologies will not disrupt, but sustain existing concepts of sea control. While significant improvements may be seen in the enabling of MDA and the kinetic application of power at sea, these improvements will occur along a trajectory that has already been established in previous waves of military innovation. This does not mean that the 4IR will not disrupt other areas directly or indirectly connected with naval warfare. If persistent wartime MDA can be achieved, the potential of sea-denial strategies both in isolation from and in support of sea control could be described as disruptive, particularly to long-held western concepts of seapower.

How the 4IR affects the generation and operation of seapower in areas such as manning and decision-making is worthy of further research. The case studies included in this paper raise interesting questions that have significant implications for the generation of naval power, the exercise of naval warfare, and stability at sea.

The sharp end of naval warfare is still defined by large offensive power-projection platforms. The degree to which their survivability will be compromised through the introduction of 4IR technologies will decide whether navies will continue to invest in them, or whether functions traditionally performed by manned platforms will become the domain of unmanned systems. This competition will not happen in a vacuum, instead there will be a dynamic contest between new offensive and defensive technologies.[91] The adaptability of existing platforms and operational concepts in such a competitive environment will serve to determine their future.

Strategists should not look to 4IR technologies to create an immediate operational advantage. Rather, a measured approach to the benefits and drawbacks, opportunities and limitations of the 4IR is required. For now, naval fleets will continue to look and operate as they do now, with the 4IR providing incremental, but not disruptive effects to the strategic outputs of naval power.

Disclosure statement

No potential conflict of interest was reported by the author(s).

---

[90]Lawrence Freedman, *The Future of War: A History* (London: Penguin 2017), XVI.
[91]A good example of this dynamic can be found in the race between quantum decryption and encryption. See: Jon R. Lindsay, 'Surviving the Quantum Cryptocalypse', *Strategic Studies Quarterly*, 14/2 (2020), 49–73.

ORCID

Ian Bowers http://orcid.org/0000-0003-4628-6764

Bibliography

Abaimov, Stanislov and Paul Ingram, *Hacking UK Trident: A Growing Threat* (London: British American Security Information Council 2017).
Annati, Massimo, 'Unmanned Naval Systems: Surface/Subsurface Vehicles: New Capabilities and Missions', *Military Technology* 37/8 (2013), 25–26, 24–28.
Benbow, Tim, *The Magic Bullet? Understanding the Revolution in Military Affairs* (London: Brassey's 2004).
Borchert, Heiko, Tim Kraemer, and Daniel Mahon, 'Waiting for Disruption! Undersea Autonomy and the Challenging Nature of Naval Innovation', *RSIS Working Paper No. 302*, 2 Feb. 2017.
Bower, Joseph L. and Clayton M. Christensen, 'Disruptive Technologies: Catching the Wave', *Harvard Business Review* 73/1 (1995), 43–53.
Brixey-Williams, Sebastian, 'Prospects for Game-Changers in Detection Technology', in Rory Medcalf, Katherine Mansted, Stephan Frühling, and James Goldrick (eds.), *The Future of the Undersea Deterrent: A Global Survey* (Canberra: Australian National University 2020), 80–83.
C4ADS, *Above Us Only Stars: Exposing GPS Spoofing in Russia and Syria* (Washington DC: C4ADS 2019).
Cheung, Tai Ming, Thomas G. Mahnken, and Andrew L. Ross, 'Assessing the State of Understanding of Defense Innovation', *STIC Research Briefs* Series 10 (2018), 3–4.
CSBA, *Taking Back the Seas: Transforming the U.S. Surface Fleet for Decision-Centric Warfare* (Washington D.C.: CSBA 2019).
Dalsjö, Robert, Christofer Berglund, and Michael Jonsson, *Bursting the Bubble? Russian A2/AD in the Baltic Sea Region: Capabilities, Countermeasures, and Implications* (Stockholm: FOI 2019).

Dombrowski, Peter J., Eugene Gholz, and Andrew L. Ross, 'Military Transformation and the Defense Industry after Next: The Defense Industrial Implication of Network-Centric Warfare', *Naval War College Newport Papers 18*, 2003.

Freedman, Lawrence, *The Future of War: A History* (London: Penguin 2017).

Friedman, Norman, 'Strategic Submarines and Strategic Stability: Looking Towards the 2030s', in Rory Medcalf, Katherine Mansted, Stephan Frühling, and James Goldrick (eds.), *The Future of the Undersea Deterrent: A Global Survey* (Canberra: Australian National University 2020), 69–79.

Frühling, Stephan and Guillaume Lasconjarias, 'NATO, A2/AD and the Kaliningrad Challenge', *Survival* 58/2 (2016), 95–116. doi:10.1080/00396338.2016.1161906.

Gates, Jonathan, 'Is the SSBN Deterrent Vulnerable to Autonomous Drones?', *The RUSI Journal* 161/6 (December 2016), 28–35. doi:10.1080/03071847.2016.1265834.

Grove, Eric, 'The Battleship Is Dead: Long Live the Battleship. HMS Dreadnought and the Limits of Technological Innovation', *The Mariner's Mirror* 93/4 (2007), 415–27. doi:10.1080/00253359.2007.10657038.

Hammes, T.X., 'Expeditionary Operations in the Fourth Industrial Revolution', *MCU Journal* 8/1 (Spring 2017), 82–107. doi:10.21140/mcuj.2017080105.

Hammes, T. X., ''Defending Europe: How Converging Technology Strengthens Small Powers', *Scandinavian Journal of Military Studies* 2/1 (2019), 20–29. doi:10.31374/sjms.24.

Heginbotham, Eric et al, *The U.S. - China Military Scorecard: Forces, Geography, and the Evolving Balance of Power 1996-2017* (Santa Monica: RAND 2015).

Heinrich, Lange et al., *To the Seas Again: Maritime Defence and Deterrence in the Baltic Region* (Tallinn: ICDS 2019).

Jannson, Nils-Ove, 'The Baltic: A Sea of Contention', *Naval War College Review* 41/3 (1988), 47–61.

Karlatiras, Stavros, 'The Changing Nature of Naval Conflicts in Confined and Shallow Waters (CSW)', in Joachim Krause and Sebastian Bruns (eds.), *Routledge Handbook of Naval Strategy and Security* (London: Routledge 2016), 166–76.

Khanna, Monty, 'Get Ready for the Next RMA at Sea', *USNI Proceedings* 146/1 (January 2020). https://www.usni.org/magazines/proceedings/2020/january/get-ready-next-rma-sea

Kramer, Franklin D. and Magnus Nordenman, 'A Maritime Framework for the Baltic Sea Region', *Issue Brief Scowcroft Center for Strategy and Security* (March 2016).

Kulve, Haico te and Wim A. Smit, 'Novel Naval Technologies: Sustaining or Disrupting Naval Doctrine', *Technological Forecasting & Social Change* 77/7 (2010), 999–1013. doi:10.1016/j.techfore.2010.03.005.

Lautenschläger, Karl, 'Technology and the Evolution of Naval Warfare', *International Security* 8/2 (1983), 3–51. doi:10.2307/2538594.

Layton, Peter, *Prototype Warfare, Innovation and the Fourth Industrial Age* (Canberra: Air Power Development Centre 2018).

Lin, Jeffrey and P.W. Singer, 'The Great Underwater Wall of Robots: Chinese Exhibit Shows off Sea Drones', *Popular Science* (22 June 2016). https://www.popsci.com/great-underwater-wall-robots-chinese-exhibit-shows-off-sea-drones/

Lindsay, Jon R., 'Surviving the Quantum Cryptocalypse', *Strategic Studies Quarterly* 14/2 (2020), 49–73.

Lodovisi, Chiara, Pierpaolo Loreti, Lorenzo Bracciale, and Silvello Betti, 'Performance Analysis of Hybrid-Optical-Acoustic AUV Swarms for Marine Monitoring', *Future Internet* 10/7 (2018), 65. doi:10.3390/fi10070065.

Martin, Bradley et. al, *Advancing Autonomous Systems: An Analysis of Current and Future Technology for Unmanned Maritime Vehicles* (Santa Monica: RAND Corporation 2019).

Metrick, Andrew and Kathleen H. Hicks, *Contested Seas: Maritime Domain Awareness in Northern Europe* (Washington D.C.: CSIS 2018).

Murphy, Martin, Frank G. Hoffman, and Gary Schaub Jr., *Hybrid Maritime Warfare and the Baltic Sea Region* (Copenhagen: Centre for Military Studies 2016), 9.

Murphy, Martin and Gary Schaub Jr., 'Sea of Peace" or Sea of War – Russian Maritime Hybrid Warfare in the Baltic Sea', *Naval War College Review* 71/2, article 9 (2018), 122–148.

Nielsen, Anders Puck, 'Sømilitær Vurdering Af Ruslands Østersøflåde Og De Militære Implikationer for Danmark', *Scandinavian Journal of Military Studies* 2/1 (2019), 148–64. doi:10.31374/sjms.27.

O'Hanlon, Michael, *Forecasting Change in Military Technology, 2020-2040* (Washington D.C.: Brookings Institution 2018).

Pierce, Terry, *Warfighting and Disruptive Technologies: Disguising Innovation* (OXON: Routledge 2004).

Raska, Michael, 'Strategic Competition for Emerging Military Technologies: Comparing Paths and Patterns', *Prism* 8/3 (2019), 64–81.

Rowden, Thomas A. 'Sea Control First', *Proceedings* 143/1/1367, 2017. https://www.usni.org/magazines/proceedings/2017/january/commentary-sea-control-first

Rubel, Robert C., 'Talking about Sea Control', *Naval War College Review* 63/4 (2010), 38–47.

Saalman, Lora, *Prompt Global Strike: China and the Spear* (Honolulu: Daniel K. Inouye Asia-Pacific Center for Security Studies 2014).

Schwab, Klaus, *The Fourth Industrial Revolution* (London: Penguin 2017).

Small, Pete, 'Navy Unmanned Systems: An Overview', *Undersea Warfare* 67 (Spring 2019), 6–9.

Till, Geoffrey, *Seapower: A Guide for the Twenty-First Century* 2nd ed. (OXON: Routledge 2009).

Vego, Milan, *Naval Strategy and Operations in Narrow Seas 2nd Edition* (Oxon: Frank Cass 2003).

Vego, Milan, *Modern Strategy and Sea Control* (Oxon: Routledge 2016).

Vego, Milan, 'The Navy Must Not Neglect 'Defensive' Warfighting', *Proceedings*, 145/7/1397, 2019. https://www.usni.org/magazines/proceedings/2019/july/navy-must-not-neglect-defensive-warfighting

Wang, Jun, 王俊, et al., "海底观测网水下环境实时监控系统设计与实现' [Design and Realization of Underwater Environment Real-time Monitoring System for Ocean Observatory Network]', 浙江大学学报 (工学版) *Journal of Zhejiang University [Engineering Science]* 50/2 (Feb. 2016), 193–200.

Yuwen, Ningbo, 宇文静波 and Liwen Tang 唐立文, '美国"快速全球打击"计划探讨与启示 [Discussion and Inspirations About Prompt Global Strike of the US]', 装备指挥技术学院学报 *[Journal of the Academy of Equipment Command & Technology]* 22/3 (June 2011), 58–61.

Index

Note: Figures are indicated by *italics*. Tables are indicated by **bold**. Endnotes are indicated by the page number followed by "n" and the endnote number e.g., 20n1 refers to endnote 1 on page 20.

Adamsky, Dima 10, 69
additive manufacturing (3D printing) 7, 23, 55, 146
additive technology 95, 98
Aegis Combat System 148
aerospace technology 145
Afghanistan 11, 18, 21
Aftenposten (newspaper) 154
AFWERX accelerators 44, 46–7
Agrell, Wilhem 150
Air Force 32, 51; of Denmark 153; Platform One 45, 52, 57; of Republic of Singapore 23; Russia 176; Sweden 153; of US 43–7
AirLand Battle (ALB) concept 10, 15, 47
Air-Sea Battle (ASB) concept 21–2
Android operating systems 38
anti-access, area-denial threats (A2AD) 54–5
anti-submarine warfare (ASW) 52, 171
Apple 38, 130
architectural innovations 166–7
Army Futures Command (AFC) 23, 47, 48, 49, 50
Army 32; of China 65, 85; Russia 99; Scandinavian 150; of US 17, 35, 47–50
artificial intelligence (AI) 2, 23, 43, 74, 95, 127, 130, 163; application in grey zone operations 3; automation and AI 145; in Chinese military 65–6; -enabled networks 53; -enabled RMA wave 8; -enabled unmanned systems 95; in Russia 110–14; RMA wave 2, 8, 19, 20, 21, 23–4, 25; systems 7; Task Force 50
Australia 10, 19, 23
automated decision-making 95, 98, 108

automated warfare and strategic competition 19–24
automatic target recognition (ATR) 85
Autonomous Robotic Vehicle (ARV) 172
autonomous vehicles 131
autonomous weapon systems 2, 8, 88, 108, 115, 134, 144, 145, 148–9, 151, 153, 156, 170; defence transformation and 147–9; in Denmark 152; in Norway 153–4; in Sweden 157; in US 151
Avangard intercontinental ballistic missile system 110

Baltic Sea 3; 4IR and sea control in 175–8
Ben-Gurion, David 125n10
big data 74, 95, 113, 130, 163; harvesting and exploiting 108
Bitzinger, Richard 16, 18
Block, Harpoon 153
Bollmann, Anders Theis 152
Boulanin, Vincent 147, 148
Bowers, Ian 3
Bruun-Hanssen, Haakon 154, 155
Brynjolfsson, Erik 39
Bydén, Micael 157

C2ISTAR infrastructure 109
Carter, Ashton 144
Cebrowski, Arthur K. 16
Chesbrough, Henry 31
Cheung, Tai Ming 31, 122–3
China 3, 19, 22, 145, 149, 163, 179, 180; AI-enabled RMA wave, implementing 8; artificial intelligence in 65; bureaucratic and organisational

dynamics 68–9; creative insecurity 67–8; 'fifth-generation' of operational regulations 87; intelligentisation, emerging concepts of 78; literature on military innovation and diffusion 66; military learning and conceptual evolution 79–84; new revolution in military affairs 70–6; PLA reforms and initiatives in innovation 76–8; potential challenges in chinese military innovation 86–9; realist learning 67; revolution in military affairs 65; strategic culture 69–70; timeline in Chinese military innovation **72**; unmanned underwater vehicles (UUV) 172; US-China rivalry, implications for 89–90
China Military Science 79
Chinese People's Liberation Army (PLA) 65; academics and strategists 84; Academy of Military Science (AMS) 77; AI/ML projects research and development 84–5; Central Military Commission (CMC) Science and Technology Commission 76; National University of Defence Technology (NUDT) 77; Naval Engineering University 84; reforms and initiatives in innovation 76–8; strategic culture 69–70
Churchill, Winston 145
Chvarkov, Sergei 113
civil-military relations school 41
cloud investments 45, 52, 56
Cold War 1, 15, 22, 174
command, control, communication, computer, intelligence, surveillance, and reconnaissance (C4IR) systems 14, 78, 114, 126
commercial-military gap 35, 37
compact sensor design 6
computational photography 6
computational power 36, 163
computers and communications 163
conceptual adaptation in US military 12–14
connectivity 15, 82, 88, 163
Cooper, Jeffrey 13
Coté, Owen R. 41, 68
Covid-19 pandemic 106
Cronin, Audrey Kurth 31, 40
cultural dynamics 41n46
cultural model 42
cutting-edge technologies 1, 98, 100; in Chinese military 74

cyber-attacks 138, 140, 176
cybernetic space 126

Dapeng, Li 84
data 82–3, 88; analytics 23; and development 44; management 57; in operations 35; storage 54; systems 49; transmission 44
deep-sea sensor arrays 186
defence-academia collaboration frameworks 135
defence industries 23, 129n30, 133
Defence Innovation Initiative (DII) 22
defence transformation 144, 18–19, 150; and autonomous weapon systems 147–9; and digitised warfare 15–17
Defense Digital Service 55
Dengyun, Zuo 82
Denmark 3, 146, 149; autonomous weapon systems 152, 156; military applications of 4IR 3; semi-autonomous weapon systems 153
DevSecOps model 39, 45, 49, 55
Deyi, Li 77
Digital Air Force 43, 44
Digital Ground Army system (DGA) 127
digitised warfare and defence transformation 15–17
directed energy 7, 98, 99
disruptive innovations 19, 164, 166–7
Dombrowski, Peter 19
Dominant Battlespace Knowledge (DBK) 14
Dongheng, Chen 81
drones 23, 82, 85, 102, 112, 131, 146, 151, 155, 170
Dyndal, Gjert Lage 154

effects-based operations (EBO) 17
electromagnetic pulse (EMP) weapons 127
electronic warfare 23, 54, 100, 114, 173, 176; and military-technical revolution (MTR) 10–11
energy 7, 95, 106, 127, 130
Era technopolis model 99–100, 105
European Union (EU) 150
Evron, Yoram 3
Expressen (newspaper) 156

FaceN algorithm 101
FalconView 36–7
Farrell, Theo 97, 147
Federal Acquisition Regulations 37–8, 50

Fedor robot 98
fire control systems 125, 179
first offset strategy, of US military 145
Fordham, Benjamin 138
Fourth Industrial Revolution technologies (4IR) 1, 2, 7, 22, 23, 96, 130, 144, 145; artificial intelligence (AI) 95; automated decision-making 95; in Baltic Sea 175–8; big data 95; disruptive effects of 165, 168–9, 181–2; human-machine hybrid intelligence 95; and innovation 165–6; in Israel Defence Forces (IDF) 122; and maritime domain awareness 173–5, 178; naval disruption 167–8; and navies 165–6; and operational inputs 169; quantum computing 95; Russian defence innovation model 97; and sea control 163; in South China Sea 178–181; strategic context and battlefield advantages of 106–114; unmanned systems in maritime domain 169–173
France 10, 23, 103, 110, 175
Fravel, M. Taylor 68
Frederiksen, Claus Hjort 152
Future Combat System (FSC); concept 19; programme 48
future warfare 7, 8, 11, 22, 23, 69, 71, 80, 81, 83, 94, 111, 112, 116
futuropolises 97

Gareev, Makhmut Akhmetovich 10, 11
Gates, Robert 18, 21
Germany 103, 151, 177
Geurts, James F. 51
Gilday, Michael 53
Gilli, Andrea 33
Gilli, Mauro 33
global digital revolution 145
Goldman, Emily O. 67
Google 38, 130
Gorbachev 10
Gray, Colin 7, 8
Greece 175
Gref, German 111
Griffin, Stuart 42
Grissom, Andrew 38n35
ground-based robotic systems 112
Ground-Based Strategic Deterrent (GBSD) 45
Guanrong, Yun 83
Gulf War (1991) 13, 40
Guozhi, Liu 76–7
Guriyev, Sergey 105

Hagel, Chuck 144
Hagström, Martin 156
Hammes, T. X. 146, 151
Harang, Alexander 149
hardware-based and architectural innovations 166–7
Harpy loitering weapon system 147
heads-up display (HUD) systems 125
Henriksson, Stig 156
high-end military technologies, in US military services 32
high-power lasers 7
Horowitz, Michael C. 37, 43, 69
Hultqvist, Peter 157
human-machine hybrid intelligence 95, 108
hybrid warfare and modernisation-plus 17–19
hypersonic(s) 95, 109; and AI 108; boost glide vehicles 107, 110; glide vehicles 85; missile systems 96, 110; technology in Russia 108–10
hyperspectral imagery 6

Ilnitskii, Andrei 104
iLoc Development team 52
information technologies RMA (IT-RMA) 8, 20, 101, 113; information warfare and technophilia 14–15
information technology, in Chinese military 65–6, 145
informatised warfare 65, 70, 72, 81
innopolises 97
innovation: closed model of 31, 33–6; open model of 41, 36–40
innovative combat systems 112
intelligence support system 109
intelligence, surveillance, and reconnaissance (ISR) systems 14, 170, 171, 172, 179, 180, 181, 182
intelligent robotics 77, 95, 98, 108
intelligentisation 74–5, 77, 83, 88; concept of 78
intelligentised warfare 21, 65, 72, 87
International Monetary Fund (IMF) 105, 111
Internet of Things (IoT) 81, 127, 130
iOS operating systems 38
Iran 139, 145, 149
Iraq 18, 21, 138
Israel 3, 10, 19, 23, 147, 171; elite technology companies 130; 4IR technologies in IDF service 137–9; Harpy loitering weapon system 147; hi-tech sector's link to military 130;

military-related 4IR technologies 3, 124–6, 129–131; new military strategy and 4IR technologies 126–9; R&D investments 130; spin-on process 131–7; vibrant and innovative hi-tech sector 130
Israel Defence Forces (IDF) 19, 122, 124–6, 137; personal service and relationships with 132–3
Israel Innovation Authority 132, 134–5
Israel Space Agency 134
Italy 175

Jie, Song 82
Jinping, Xi 70, 71, 74, 75, 77, 89
Joint All-Domain Command and Control (JADC2) 44, 58
Julin, Dong 81

Kalashnikov 100
Kania, Elsa 3
Kirchberger, Sarah 3
Kollars, Nina 36
Krause, Keith 1
Kristoffersen, Jens Wenzel 148, 152, 153

Lake, Daniel 44
Lang, Johannes 152
Larsson, Carl-Martin 157
'leapfrog development' 75
Lebanon War 128
Lee Sedol 71
Lethal Autonomous Weapon Systems (LAWS) 116, 147, 154
Lindsay, Jon 36
LinkedIn 115
liquid breathing technology 98
Long, Tom 145
Lysbakken, Audun 154

MacGregor Knox 13
Mahnken, Thomas G. 42, 39–40, 67
Makarov, Nikolai 102
manufacturing 163, 165
Marine Corps, US 32, 54–6, 58
maritime domain awareness (MDA) 173; capabilities 169; 4IR-enabled MDA 169; unmanned systems and 164
Marshall, Andrew 12
Mattis, James 17
Mayer, Michael 151, 159
McAfee, Andrew 39
McCain, John 35
media: in Norway 153; in Sweden 156
Medvedev, Dmitrii 98

Middle East 139
military innovation 17, 20, 40, 41, 42; challenges in China 86–9; definition of 38n35; and diffusion 66–70
military intelligentisation, concept of 78, 80, 85
military-related technologies 1, 135
military-technical revolution (MTR) 10, 94
mine warfare (MCM) 171, 175, 178
Minghai, Li 83
Ministry of Defence's Directorate of Defence Research and Development (DDR&D) 133–4
Moscow 94, 101, 104
multi-sensor autonomous vehicles 127
Murray, Williamson 13

nanotechnology 23, 99, 100, 131, 134; and nanomaterials 127
National Innovation Institute of Defence Technology (NIIDT) 78
NATO 19, 107, 114, 150, 154, 155, 175, 177, 178; Follow-on Forces Attack (FOFA) 10
naval disruption and 4IR 167–8
navy 172, 175, 177; and 4IR technology 165–6; unmanned systems in 51; US 50–4
Neller, Robert B. 54, 56
Netanyahu, Benjamin 131
Network-Centric Warfare (NCW) 17, 24
networking of people and things 127
new military intelligentisation revolution 79–80
9/11 terrorist attacks 15–16
Nordic countries 150, 152
Nordlund, Linda 156
Norway 146, 149, 151, 153–5; autonomous drone systems 155; military applications of 4IR 3; semi-autonomous weapon systems 155
Norwegian Defence Research Establishment (FFI) 155
NTechLab 101
nuclear weapons 22, 107, 145, 150, 156, 157

Ogarkov, Nikolai V. 11
operation optimization 130
optoelectronic devices 7
Osipov, Gennadii 111
Other Transaction Authorities (OTAs) 37, 47
Owens, William 14, 15

Persian Gulf 139
Petersson, Magnus 3
photonics technologies 7
platform ecosystem 38
Popov, Pavel 100
Posen, Barry 42, 68
pre-4IR technologies 115
precise guided ammunition 125
Programme budgeting 36
Putin, Vladimir 94, 97, 111

quantum computing 40, 82, 95, 98, 116, 131, 166; and quantum cryptography 7
quantum technology 127

radar 10, 125, 147, 171, 173, 179
Raska, Michael 2
Resende-Santos, João 67
Revolution in Military Affairs (RMA) 6; automated warfare and strategic competition 19–24; in China 65, 70–6; concept 12; conceptual adaptation in US military 12–14; digitised warfare and defence transformation 15–17; electronic warfare and military-technical revolution (MTR) 10–11; hybrid warfare and modernisation-plus 17–19; information warfare and IT-RMA technophilia 14–15; six waves of 9
Richardson, John 52–3
robotics 7, 77, 84, 86, 95, 98, 108, 130, 145, 147, 163
robots 98, 114, 127, 148, 152
Rogozin, Dmitrii 93
Roper, Will 44–5, 46
Rosen, Stephen Peter 41, 68, 94
Ross, Andrew 19
Rumsfeld, Donald 16, 18
Run, Kessel 46, 50
Russia 3, 19, 22, 93, 145, 149, 151, 172, 176; AI-enabled technologies 113; artificial intelligence (AI) 110–14; 4IR defence innovation model 96, 97; hypersonic technology 108–10; limitations 102–6; and NATO 176; strategies 97–102, 106–8; top-down innovation model 95

satellites, observation of 103, 125, 173, 175, 180
Scandinavian countries 3, 146, 150–2; army brigades in **151**; defence transformation and autonomous weapon systems 147–9; Denmark 152–3; Norway 153–5; Sweden 156–8
Schaub, Gary, Jr 148, 152, 153, 176
Schott, Robin May 152
The Science of (Military) Strategy 79
science, technology, engineering and mathematics (STEM) 97
sea control 183; in Baltic Sea 175–8; disruptive effects of 168–9; and 4IR technology 163; and innovation 165–6; MDA system 173–5, 178; naval disruption 167–8; and navies 165–6; and operational inputs 169; and strategic effects 3, 164; in South China Sea 178–181; unmanned systems in maritime domain 169–173
second offset strategy, of US military 22, 145, 150
Semi-Autonomous Robotic Vehicle (SARV) 172
sensors 6, 163, 170, 174, 180; advanced technologies 6; and sensing technology 127
Serdyukov, Anatolii 102
Shaked Warfare system 127
Shoigu, Sergei 103, 109
Singapore 10, 23
Skolkovo Innovation Centre 98, 101
sliding autonomy 148
Sloan, Elinor 147
SOFWERX 51
Søreide, Ine Eriksen 154
South China Sea (SCS) 165, 178–181
South Korea 10, 23
Soviet strategic thinking 94
Soviet Union 11, 69, 98, 100
Spain 175
spin-on process 131–5; conditions 135–7; Defence-academia collaboration frameworks 135; Israel innovation authority 134–5; Ministry of Defence's Directorate of Defence Research and Development (DDR&D) 133–4; personal service and relationships with IDF 132–3; symbiosis between technology spinoffs and spin-ons 131–2; technology 32, 123
Stanley-Lockman, Zoe 3
state-of-the-art materials 7, 45, 125, 135
Stoltenberg, Jens 149
Sukhoi 100
sunk infrastructural costs 39
supercomputing, advanced 2
suppression of enemy air defences (SEAD) 147

Sweden 146, 149, 151, 156–8, 177; autonomous systems 156; military applications of 4IR 3
Swedish Defence Research Agency (FOI) 156
Syria 114, 138
'system of systems' 14, 15, 49, 78, 82, 84

target: detection 7; recognition 7
task-specific artificial intelligence (AI) 146
Technion 131
technological: human empowerment 127; optimism 40; innovations 10, 20, 35, 144
technology 1, 90; additive 95, 98; aerospace 145; hypersonic(s) 95, 109; liquid breathing 98; quantum 127; spinoffs and spin-ons, symbiosis between 131–2
techno-military innovations 125
technopolises 97
Telegram 115
Terriff, Terry 97, 147
third offset (3O) strategy 22, 33, 71, 144–5, 151; of US military 145
three-dimensional (3D) manufacturing 146
Tianliang, Xiao 79
Transformation Planning Guidance (TPG) 16
Trump, Donald 151

Ukraine 114; crisis 150
United Kingdom (UK) 10, 23
United States (US) military services 3, 7, 21, 33, 103, 111, 150, 163, 172; AI-enabled RMA wave, implementing 8; air force 32, 43–7; AirLand Battle (ALB) 10; army 32, 47–50; and China rivalry, implications for 89–90; closed model of innovation 33–6; first offset strategy 145; innovation in 30, 40–3; marine corps 32, 54–6; navy 32, 50–4;

open innovation, championing 43; open model of innovation 36–40; second offset strategy 145; third offset strategy 145
unmanned aerial vehicles 17, 99, 112–13
unmanned air vehicles 165
unmanned boats 112
unmanned ground combat vehicle (UGV) 98, 158
unmanned surface vehicles (USV) 155, 165
unmanned systems 7, 11, 77, 53, 169–170, 178, 182, 183; autonomous systems 98; and maritime domain awareness (MDA) 164, 169–173; naval systems 165, 169
unmanned underwater vehicles (UUV) 112, 158, 165, 178, 182; Large and Extra Large UUV (XLUUV) 172

Valerii Gerasimov 103
van Munster, Rens 152
Verbruggen, Maaike 147–8
VKontakte 115

Wallström, Margot 156, 157
Waltz, Kenneth 67
waterfall-acquisition process 39
weapon systems 24, 95, 99, 108, 146, 154, 158, 163–4, 171; autonomy in 147–8
Wirtz, James 52, 53
Work, Robert 22, 116
World Bank 105, 111
world-class tactical missiles 125

Yom Kippur War (1973) 10
Yonghua, Wang 80
You, He 82

Zhanjun, Zhang 79
Zhong, Liu 85
Zysk, Katarzyna 3